Mountain Passages

Mountain
Passages

Jeremy
Bernstein

University of
Nebraska Press

Lincoln and London

The contents of this book have previously appeared elsewhere in somewhat different form.

The New York Times first published chapter 1 (May 28, 1978) and chapter 3 (March 7, 1971). © 1978 and © 1971 by the New York Times Company. Reprinted by permission.

The following chapters were first published in The New Yorker: chapter 2 (January 31, 1977); chapter 4 (April 15, 1974); chapter 5 (October 30, 1971); chapter 6 (March 26, 1966); chapter 7 (September 26, 1977).

Chapters 8 and 9 were first published as a four-part series in Mountain Gazette, 1974.

Library of Congress Cataloging in Publication Data

Bernstein, Jeremy, 1929–
    Mountain passages.

    1. Mountaineering—Addresses, essays, lectures.   2. Skiing—Addresses, essays, lectures.   3. Mountains—Recreational use—Addresses, essays, lectures. I.   Title.
GV200.B5   796.5'22   78–15996
ISBN 0–8032–0983–5

Manufactured in the United States of America

Contents

Illustrations

Maps

Mountain Passages

1   A Life in the Mountains

There is no mountainous region on earth that provides a wider and more varied theater for climbing than the French Alps in the region near Chamonix. Mountain climbing and the mountain aesthetic were invented in Chamonix, and guides who have made hundreds of different climbs in the Chamonix Valley have told me that they have barely scratched the surface of what is available there. The publicity brochures about Chamonix advertise that it is the world capital of alpinism, and they are right. In a real sense, "climbing" and "the Chamonix Valley" are practically synonymous.

I am neither a very distinguished climber, nor a very conventional one. I was first introduced to the high mountains, entirely by chance, in 1937, when I was eight—I have an ancient photograph that shows me clinging to a small rock and looking very worried. (I have a number of more recent photographs showing me clinging to *large* rocks with about the same expression.) Since then I have done some climbing in the western United States and elsewhere, but my climbing activities have largely been confined to the French Alps around Chamonix. I had the good fortune to stumble into Chamonix, and to meet the French alpine guide Claude Jaccoux, at a time when I could take advantage of it and at a time when I was in a position to write about it. Everything that has happened to me since in the way of mountaineering and travel has followed from this happy accident.

In September of 1959 I arrived in Paris with a two-year fellowship to do physics, only to learn that the academic year did not begin until November. I had a small car and decided to explore the country; knowing little about it in advance, I wandered into the Chamonix Valley. I was overwhelmed by the beauty of the place, but it certainly did not occur to me to climb anything; one

1

look at the Aiguilles—needles—of Chamonix convinced me that they were not meant for the rational man. I recall taking a ride, with an elderly stranger, above the Vallée Blanche in a small gondola suspended from wires. As we swayed over the sickening void his seraphic smile never varied, and when, finally, I asked him about it, he told me that he had a literal and unwavering belief in the afterlife.

It is very unlikely that I would have returned to Chamonix except for two further twists of chance. The French physicists with whom I had been working in Paris had set up a summer school on the island of Corsica and, for its second summer, I was invited to join the faculty. I made friends with many of the French physicists, and especially with a young Parisian named Georges Bonnevay. He looked extremely frail and sported a long, narrow beard; I was surprised to learn that Bonnevay was a first-class Chamonix climber and that, moreover, most of my young colleagues at the school also climbed regularly in Chamonix. (Largely because of this, there is now at Les Houches, in the Chamonix Valley, one of the most distinguished physics summer schools in the world.) It seemed to me that the sheer lunacy of the climbing enterprise appealed to Georges's rather wild sense of humor. In fact, after he was married, the father of a young child and the expectant father of a second, he gave up high climbing. In the summer of 1963 he was persuaded to go out one more time, and on the north face of the Aiguille de Bionnassay, a beautiful peak near Les Houches, he was killed in a fall. It was just in the summer of 1963 that I began my own climbing in Chamonix.

From 1961 to 1966, I spent every summer at the gigantic nuclear laboratory CERN (Conseil Europeén pour la Recherche Nucléaire) in Geneva, from which, on a clear day, one has a perfect view of Mont Blanc. On weekends I began going to Chamonix, which is about fifty miles by road from Geneva. In the beginning I had no intention of climbing anything. I was now past thirty—an age after which even many youthful climbing fanatics begin to calm down—and was, at least for a while, content to wander around the hiking trails in, or slightly above, the valley.

After two summers I simply ran out of trails and, if I were to continue to come to Chamonix, I had to learn to climb. I presented myself to Nicolau Barthélémy, who was then the chef des guides of the Compagnie des Guides de Chamonix. I tried to convince Barthélémy that, as a climber, I was a near cipher. Perhaps I secretly hoped that if I painted a bleak enough picture, he would simply send me away and I could honestly say that I had tried without actually having to put foot to rock. But in 150 years the Chamonix guides have transported such an unlikely cargo of people into the mountains that my case was routine. That very afternoon I was presented to my first guide, Henri Dufour. We drove a short way out of town to the practice cliffs— Les Gaillands—which have been serving in that capacity for about half a century. The cliffs are about three hundred feet high, which is not a lot by Chamonix standards, but they looked to me like the Empire State Building and about as vertical. Dufour assured me that abject fear—which is what I was feeling—was a perfectly normal survival instinct, and shot up the rocks like a cat. He had tied me to the other end of his climbing rope, and once he had settled into a comfortable belay stance he instructed me to come up using my feet and using my hands only for balance. I did as I was told and soon found myself several feet off the ground. When I reached Dufour, he took off again, and now I found myself even farther off the ground.

Henri Dufour

JEREMY BERNSTEIN

If I had an elderly aunt who wanted to learn technical climbing I would encourage her to begin with Dufour. He is about my age, short and agile, with the alert and amused face of certain hunting dogs. He is a master of what the French would call finding *trucs*—gimmicks—to make things as easy as possible. Some years ago, Dufour and I climbed the Couzy route on the Aiguille de l'M (named for its M-shaped twin peaks). The *Guide Vallot*—the four-volume climbing guide to the mountains around Chamonix—says of the Couzy, "TD"—meaning "very difficult"—and "very sustained with several passages of V and V superior" (rock climbs are classified from I to VI, with VI being the hardest). Somewhere near the top, my morale began to sag. Since I talk a lot while climbing, there is no doubt that Dufour sensed it. He slithered up a particularly horrible looking thin crack and vanished from view. I was left alone in my morbidity when, from above, I heard Dufour engaging in what appeared to be a lively conversation. He was saying things like, "Ah, madam, you have certainly found a lovely spot for a picnic. No, I don't think I *would* like one of your sandwiches since my wife is expecting me for lunch." "My God," I thought, "we are home free!" I shot up the crack in no time, only to find myself alone with Dufour and confronted by a short, blank wall which led to the summit.

In the summer of 1963, after I had managed to climb one of the practice cliffs, Dufour suggested that we next tackle the normal route of the Aiguille de l'M—a standard beginner's climb that is a perfect introduction to Chamonix climbing. First, it features a struggle with a couple of hundred fully equipped climbers and guides, at five in the morning, to get a place on the first *téléphérique* (aerial tramway) up to the Plan des Aiguilles, some 2,500 feet above Chamonix. From the upper station there is a comfortable path that leads to a small glacier that in turn leads to a steep couloir, or gorge, which debouches at the Col de la Buche, about a two-hour climb above the station. At this point Dufour suggested that we have some lunch while I took in the scenery. Looking over one side of the col, I saw a drop of what looked like miles. In front of us was another blank rock wall. I would have called it a day, but Dufour took off up the rocks.

Finally we reached the summit and, it seemed, years later arrived back on the path below. I felt a wonderful sense of fatigue, relief, and satisfaction. I had forgotten how scared I had been and was even vaguely thinking about my next climb.

We did a few more easy classics that summer and when I returned the next year I learned that Dufour had ruptured an Achilles' tendon while skiing and would be out of action for the season. I went back to the Guide Bureau and Nicolau Barthélémy and entered the lottery that has matched climbers and guides almost since the founding of the company. One submits his proposed climb to the guide bureau, and that evening, when the guides assemble, the list of proposed climbs is read out, sounding something like a fish auction: "I have two for the 'M' normal, six for the Mont Blanc (two guides), one Grépon Mer de Glace . . . ." All of the guides are on a roll, and each night the roll call begins where it left off the previous night; the first guide has the right to choose any of the climbs that have been requested. An established guide, during the season, will usually have a fixed clientele, and may never have to find clients through the *tour de rôle*. As it happened, I appeared in late June when the season had hardly started and, by chance, I drew Claude Jaccoux.

Dufour and Jaccoux, who are good friends, represent different colors in the social spectrum of Chamonix. Dufour is a *Chamoniard*—a native of the valley. As such he speaks with the somewhat flat accent of the Savoie and in the special patois of the mountains—the word *sarpé*, which is patois for "serpent," for example, is used by the guides to describe weak clients who cling to the rocks like lizards. Dufour lives with his wife and child and his parents in a sprawling house in the center of town. Chamoniards have the reputation of being rather *enfermé*—insulated. Dufour is one of the friendliest people imaginable, but it would never occur to me to drop in and visit him at home. Between Dufour and his clients—especially those of his generation or older—there is a certain reserve, a formal respect, which is, no doubt, a remnant from the days when the clients, mainly English, were very much the *monchus*—the "misters"—and the guides were expected to keep their place. When the nineteenth-

century British heiress Isabella Straton married her guide, Jean Charlet, he took his *wife's* name. Dufour is a superb professional, and his life is in, and of, the Chamonix Valley.

Jaccoux, on the other hand, is an outsider, even though he was born in Sallanches, just a few kilometers from Chamonix. When Roger Frison-Roche, a Paris-born Chamonix guide and well-known journalist and novelist, compiled a list of Chamonix guides "foreign" to the valley, Jaccoux was on it. So were Lionel Terray, born in Lyons, and Gaston Rébuffat, perhaps the most famous of the guides still active, who was born in Marseilles. It took a special dispensation from the company to get these men admitted, one of the requirements of admission being that either the guide or his wife be valley-born. A dispensation is given only when an individual is of such merit as a climber that he would be of special value to the company. (Some of the young, nonnative guides, resenting the exclusivity of the company, have formed their own company, Les Guides Independant du Mont Blanc.) Jaccoux's parents were both *lycée* professors, and Jaccoux had actually grown up in Paris, where, eventually, he went to the Sorbonne to study French literature. He did not begin climbing until he was eighteen—very late for a guide; the Chamonix guides usually begin climbing in their mountains when they are still practically babies.

When I first went climbing with Jaccoux in 1964, we tackled a fairly difficult practice rock climb in the Aiguilles Rouge, and afterwards Jaccoux asked me to join him and his now ex-wife, Michèle, for dinner. (Some years later Jaccoux told me that he had gone home and told Michèle that he had met a very funny American who spoke argot.) The Jaccoux—both Jaccoux and Michèle, and now Jaccoux and his second wife, Colette—have always had a rather Bohemian ménage. I can rarely remember a meal at which there were less than ten peple, with some of them coming and going all the time. If the meal is at night, someone pops up every half hour or so to go outside and look at the stars. If they are visible, the weather will usually be good the next day, which means that anyone climbing will have to be up long before sunrise. During that summer we did a number of climbs; I began to learn about the life of a guide and, through Jaccoux, I

Claude Jaccoux

PHOTOGRAPH © 1978 GIANFRANCO GORGONI/CONTACT

met most of the great French guides and many of the best climbers in Europe.

As climbers, Jaccoux and Dufour have contrasting styles. Dufour is not especially powerful and relies on perfect technique and acrobatic elegance. Jaccoux, at about six feet, is both taller and heavier than most guides. He is extremely strong and, like most guides, has especially strong hands and fingers. Maneuvers with the rope can involve a lot of hand strength since the rope is often under high tension when one is trying to manipulate it. There are nonetheless limitations to what sheer physical strength can accomplish in climbing. For example, belaying—protecting a climber who is held on a rope—makes use of friction and mechanical advantage, and a guide like Dufour, who is not extremely powerful but knows just how to use pitons as pulleys and the drag of rock outcroppings, and how to react if someone begins to fall, can provide very safe and solid belays. Belays from above are, by far, the safest. When I have fallen I have always been belayed from above, which is why I have never fallen very far.

The riskiest belays are those involving traverses. Here the rope is stretched out horizontally and, unless there is a piton or a rock somewhere in the middle, a climber who falls will go quite a long way. The main disadvantage of this—apart from the fact that one can hit the rock pretty hard—is that one can land in a place from which it is very difficult to extricate oneself. It is almost impossible for one person to pull another up over an overhang. The friction on the rope is too great at the point where it makes contact with the rock or snow.

My closest call involved an overhang. Jaccoux and I, along with another client and another guide and his wife, also an excellent climber, set out to do one of the difficult routes on the South Face of the Aiguille du Midi. This one is called the Cosmic Spur, not for metaphysical reasons, but because there is an old cosmic ray laboratory at the base of the ridge. The key passage on the route is an overhang that is ascended by planting an *étrier*—a small rope ladder—near the top of it. To get to the rope ladder requires some delicate negotiating of a couple of passages of V. Jaccoux had led, and had planted his ladder. Above the

The Cosmic Spur, Chamonix GASTON REBUFFAT

ladder was a carabiner—a snap link—through which two ropes were now running. One was attached to me and the second to his other client. I was next and inched my way up to where the ladder was. These ladders swing in midair, and when one puts a foot on them, they move—not the world's most pleasant sensation, a couple of hundred feet above a glacier. I managed to get out on the ladder and to the top of it. The next task was to take the ropes out of the carabiner, since they were blocking all further progress. But there were two ropes each under rather high tension and blocking the gate of the carabiner which I simply could not open. I was in no danger of falling since Jaccoux had me from above, but I swung back and forth on the ladder for something like (I was told later) forty-five minutes, by the end of which (I was told) I was speaking nothing but English—a sure sign of trouble. Occasionally I would lean back and look at the glacier below, which seemed seductively tranquil. Finally, in a moment of desperation, I grabbed the ropes and the gate and somehow got everything detached. I was so exhausted that I fell backwards, swinging the ladder into the rock so that my feet were on the rock. This was what Jaccoux had been waiting for, and the minute my foot hit the rock he pulled me up. I remember saying to him that I hoped that this was the hardest passage on the climb. He answered that for me it was since we were going back down. I then rappelled over the overhang while the climbers waiting below pulled me in like a fish. Later I asked Jaccoux what he would have done if I had not been able to detach myself. He said that he would have thought of something.

No climbing, not even guided climbing, is risk free. Over the years, I have worked out roughly the odds of getting hurt or killed. The climbing season in Chamonix lasts about sixty days—all of July and August except during bad weather, and a few days in June and September. On these sixty perfect climbing days there are some two thousand climbers in the Mont Blanc massif, on both the French and Italian sides as well as the Swiss. In recent years there have occurred between sixty and seventy-five climbing *deaths* per season, and at least twice as many accidents that were serious enough to require the intervention of the mountain rescue services available in the massif. Hence, there is about one death per two thousand climbing days in the massif. A very serious amateur climber might put in some thirty climbing days a season, which gives some idea of the fatal risk. The Chamonix guides have only about one fatal accident a *year*. Many of these accidents occur during the spring skiing season, and many others occur when the guides are climbing on their own either on expeditions or simply for the fun of it. Almost never are the clients seriously injured, and it has been years since I can remember a fatal accident involving a client of a Chamonix guide. There are many reasons for this, but the main one, I think, is the experience—the *métier*—that guides bring to their work. In the typical accident, the climbers were in the wrong place at the wrong time. There are rigorous timetables that must be respected in alpine climbing. A glacier or snow couloir that is quite safe in the early morning, for example, can become a death trap by noon, when the sun has begun to melt the snow and ice. Climbs that look simple when one studies them in the guide book are extremely dangerous under the wrong conditions.

I recall one example, among many, which illustrates how the guide's *métier* works. A few years ago Jaccoux and I decided to climb the Aiguille des Pélerins, which, by the normal route, is an easy Chamonix climb. One goes up a steepish glacier to a rock couloir, which ends on a ridge leading to a small pointed summit. We were sitting on this summit when Jaccoux spotted four or five climbers all roped together—a large number of people on a single rope—beginning to climb the ridge. After a brief glance Jaccoux said, "Let's get the hell out of here!" This struck me, at the time, as a curious idea, since it was a perfect day and we had hardly begun to take in the view. But one of the rules of the game is that the guide, who has the legal responsibility for his clients, calls the shots. So down the ridge we went and at high speed. We passed the other group coming up and it was obvious that they were beginners and were having a tough time of it. We arrived at the long rock couloir and, still at top speed, went down it. Once on the glacier below I assumed that we would stop for a rest, a drink, and a chocolate bar. But no—off we went still at high velocity. About an hour had passed since we had left the summit. Just as we were getting to the bottom of the glacier an explosion of rocks came down the couloir and some of them, about the size of footballs, bounded down the glacier, stopping a few feet above where we were. When it was over, I asked Jaccoux where the rocks had come from and why. It turned out that when he had first spotted these climbers he realized that they were very weak. He knew that once they started down they were going to begin kicking loose rocks over the side and that these would inevitably be channeled into the couloir, where they would disengage more loose rocks and produce a small avalanche. By moving very fast he had gotten us to a place where we would be safe. It was a lesson in climbing safety that I have never forgotten.

Since I have known him, Jaccoux has had three serious accidents while guiding clients. In none of these accidents has the client been injured. They are, however, an illustration of the

risks that the guides assume almost daily during the season. In one of them he was hit by a rock coming down a couloir. He told me that he spotted the falling rock almost as soon as it had begun to slide. He began moving from one side of the couloir to the other and, each time he moved, the rock above him also moved. He simply could not get out of its way and finally it hit him and he lost several teeth. In another of these accidents he was doing a classic climb in the Aiguilles. This climb, each move of it, had been done hundreds of times. He had started up a standard pitch, using all of the canonical holds, when, for no apparent reason, the rock simply gave way. This can, and does, happen in Chamonix even though the climbing rock is, as a rule, very solid and stable granite. Sometimes it simply fractures. He fell onto the ledge where he had left his client, and severely cut his scalp. He treated himself by applying large quantities of snow on the cut to bind it temporarily. Although he had lost a good deal of blood Jaccoux was able to get everyone down off the Aiguille safely. In the third accident he sprained an ankle; by coincidence this had been observed from a helicopter being used to make a film on mountain rescues. In minutes Jaccoux and his client were transported back to Chamonix, and a few days later he was climbing again. He told me that he once had the occasion to discuss these accidents with Armand Charlet, the late Chamonix guide who was regarded as the greatest alpine guide of the period between the world wars. Charlet had told him that he had had some forty serious accidents in his long career, so that Jaccoux was practically unscathed.

Considering the risks, Chamonix guides do not earn that much per climb. Guiding in France is a federally regulated profession. The guides are trained, in Chamonix, at the École National de Ski et Alpinisme, and the standards are very high. It takes several years for someone to earn a full guide's diploma, and of the 150 or so men who try to qualify for entrance in the school each year about thirty are accepted, and many fewer go all the way to the end. The prices are also regulated. These have been increasing each year and it now costs something like sixty dollars a day for an average guided climb. This means that in a good season a guide might earn three or four thousand dollars.

Gaston Rébuffat atop the Gendarme of the Pic du Roc, Chamonix
GASTON RÉBUFFAT

No guide can live by guiding alone, and all of them have second or even third callings. Jaccoux teaches skiing in the winter, and Colette has a boutique, at La Plagne, where Jaccoux does his skiing. They now lead a comfortable but hardly extravagant life, and the security is nil. We all know many climbers who have been injured or have lost their lives while climbing. But we also all know climbers and guides in their sixties and seventies in wonderful health and in the highest good spirits—a *lot* of them. Now that Jaccoux is approaching middle age I have asked him how he feels about being a guide. I know that, because of his high intelligence and personality, he has been asked to do all sorts of administrative jobs connected with climbing and skiing, so that he could do something else any time he wanted to. He tells me that he is as enthusiastic about it as he ever was. The only question is physical. He still has his skill and confidence in the mountains, but he no longer has the stamina he had twenty years ago, when he did extreme climbing days at a time.

Like every other beautiful spot in the world, the French Alps have attracted many more tourists in recent years than were around when I was first introduced to climbing in Chamonix in 1963. Many of these new travelers are young Americans. There are Americans in Nepal, and probably more on the slopes of Mount Kilimanjaro than Hemingway would have dreamed. The Mont Blanc massif is overrun with climbers now, and although most of them by far are Europeans, a great many Americans have come to make the classic climbs of Chamonix. One of the best of these young American climbers was Gary Hemming, whose story is told in this book. With them the Americans brought the inventive and intricately fashioned mountaineering equipment that has been designed and made in the United States in recent years. It was in Chamonix, very far from the Sierra, that I first encountered Yvon Chouinard's Realized Ultimate Reality Piton, which in turn led me to write the essay about Chouinard with which this book opens.

It was the explosion of affluent adventurers that made possible Jaccoux's third occupation. We had trekked in Nepal together, and in 1969, on a lark, Jaccoux and Michèle and I decided to travel overland from Chamonix to Pakistan, as recounted in the second half of this book. Jaccoux found that he liked the life and began organizing tours to odd corners of the world for adventurous travelers. His work as a Chamonix guide has given him experience not only in climbing rocks but also in leading novices to places where they are not sure they are capable of going. On one of these tours I went with Jaccoux to climb Mount Kilimanjaro (I didn't, I am sorry to report, quite get to the top).

Alpine guiding offers enormous freedom and flexibility, and by picking his climbs, Jaccoux can keep guiding for years, decades if he wants to. Sometimes, as a sort of joke, we plan our retirement; on the beach in the south of France, with various families. There will be music and plenty of books, lots of wine and sunshine, and the snow-covered mountains of Chamonix will seem very far away.

2   Chouinard, Ascending

Devotees of mountain climbing say that Yvon Chouinard, a thirty-nine-year-old climber who lives in Ventura,
California, cannot get his hands on a piece of mountaineering
equipment without instantly trying to think of ways to improve
it. Chouinard has been climbing as often as possible, wherever
possible, since he was sixteen years old, and today he is
regarded as one of the greatest active mountain climbers in the
world. He has done what is known among mountaineers as
extreme climbing—often first ascents—in Canada, the United
States, and Mexico, and as far south as Patagonia. He has made
fifteen climbing trips to Britain and the Continent. He has
climbed in New Zealand, on Mount Kenya (where some of the
guides used the metal climbing loops known as carabiners for
earrings), and in the Himalayas of Pakistan. A list of Chouinard's first ascents would be almost endless, but one of the most
notable was made in October of 1964 with Thomas Frost, Royal
Robbins, and Chuck Pratt, all well-known California climbers.
This was the ascent of the North America Wall of El Capitan, in
Yosemite National Park—an area so called because in the middle
of the wall is a large section of black diorite whose shape is
roughly like that of the North American continent. The climbers
spent ten days on the wall, with nine hanging bivouacs—nine
nights in hammocks suspended horizontally from the rock face,
and with only down jackets for warmth. Harder climbs have
subsequently been made in Yosemite, but when Chouinard and
his friends climbed the North America Wall it was regarded as
the hardest rock climb ever done anywhere in the world. The
four men managed to haul two hundred pounds of food and
sixty quarts of water along with them up a rock face that is three
thousand feet high and absolutely vertical.

Quite apart from his extraordinary record as a climber, Choui-- nard has the reputation of being a virtuoso in the design of equipment. Alone or in collaboration with Frost, who was his business partner from 1966 until 1975 and then retired, Choui- nard has systematically redesigned almost every piece of equip- ment used in climbing. His company, the Great Pacific Iron Works, in Ventura, has become one of the largest manufacturers of climbing equipment in the world, and this year Chouinard expects more than two million dollars in gross sales of climbing gear—both hardware (nuts, ropes, ice axes, crampons, car- abiners, pitons of all sorts) and software (climbing pants, shirts, sweaters, packs).

The improvements that Chouinard and Frost have made in the design of climbing tools over the years have always had their start in some difficulty that the two men encountered in adapting existing equipment to their own climbing. The number and variety of their innovations are as dazzling as the list of their climbs; among their designs are the Chouinard-Frost ice axe and the RURP (Realized Ultimate Reality Piton). The design of the ice axe grew out of an attempt by Chouinard in 1968 to learn the French technique of ice climbing. Essential to ice climbing are crampons—downward-pointing metal claws to be strapped to the soles of climbing boots. In 1908, a British climber named Oscar Eckenstein developed a ten-point design that became widely accepted, and in 1931 an Italian guide and blacksmith named Laurent Grivel modified this design by adding to it two prongs pointing forward from the toe. The change enabled the climber to mount steep ice with front-pointing—driving the two forward prongs into the ice with hard kicks and climbing the ice as one would climb stairs. This technique, which came to be known as the German method, is especially suitable for the eastern Alps, where the climber encounters what is known as water ice. Water ice is frozen water that has been running—a frozen stream or a waterfall. It is brittle and extremely hard. In the western Alps, the ice that is encountered is glacier ice, which is compacted snow and is much softer and more porous. With the French technique, the climber on steep glacier ice ascends sideways, the feet placed firmly parallel to each other and at

Yvon Chouinard ascending with ice axe and hammer

right angles to the inclination, making as much use as possible of the ten bottom points of the crampon. To maintain his balance, a climber using the French technique drives his ice axe in point first, like an anchor, above his head—a position that the French call *piolet ancre*. Chouinard, who was climbing in Europe when he tried to learn this technique, found that unless the ice axe was placed perfectly it tended to come out of the ice as soon as one began to climb. In 1968, he wrote an article on ice climbing—with photographs by Frost—for the Sierra Club journal *Ascent*. He noted, "The designs of most of the modern ice axes have evolved into all sorts of grotesque forms with weird handles, serrated and cupped adzes, ice-pick spikes, and other abnormalities that make them more suitable for assassinations than for climbing ice. I could write an entire treatise on the subtle forms and lines of the correctly made *piolet*. Try and use the average axe in the *piolet ancre* position and you will find that as you start putting weight on it, the pick will probably pop out and hit you in the eye. I had to forge my own axe before I realized that the French technique was *not* impossible to learn."

Indeed, after almost being hit in the eye a few times Chouinard borrowed every kind of ice axe that was then being used and went out on the Bossons glacier, in the Chamonix Valley of France, to see which axes worked best and why. He then designed his own model, and Frost, who has a bachelor's degree in aircraft engineering from Stanford and is an excellent draftsman, drew up the design. In the Chouinard-Frost model, the pick is replaced by a curved blade with deep serrations. The curve is designed so that it is consistent with the arc made by the arm when the axe is swung. This axe sticks into ice of any hardness and requires some effort to remove, yet it also works well for cutting steps—the purpose for which ice axes were originally designed. The Chouinard-Frost ice axe, of chrome-nickel steel, is manufactured by an Italian cutlery firm and sells for about sixty dollars. All modern ice axes make use of the basic Chouinard-Frost design. In addition, the modern ice climber uses a second axe—a mini-axe, or ice hammer—held in the other hand. One of these implements is used as an anchor while the other is being driven into the ice above. At all times, the climber is held to the ice at three points—some combination of ice axes and crampons.

The Realized Ultimate Reality Piton grew out of an abortive attempt in 1960 by Chouinard and Frost to climb the west face of Kat Pinnacle, in Yosemite. On this face, there are no cracks large enough to hold ordinary pitons, which are metal spikes or wedges topped by a loop that a rope can be strung through. Since a crack must normally be at least a sixteenth of an inch wide to accept a piton, what was needed was something that could be hammered into incipient cracks. The RURP, which is made of chrome-nickel steel, is half an inch long and weighs half an ounce; it looks like a slightly thickened razor blade. Despite its small size, it has held substantial falls, although the Iron Works catalog warns, "A good deal of practice is necessary before one can become proficient and confident in the use of the RURP. It is a good idea to practice placing them on a boulder and standing in étriers"—ladders made from loops of webbing or with metal rungs suspended between two nylon ropes—"to see just how little a RURP will hold." Chouinard estimates that in a normal year the Iron Works will sell three thousand RURPs, but he is convinced that most of them are being bought for souvenirs or watch-fob ornaments or the like. In any event, since 1972, when the first substantial company catalog appeared (the company was then known as Chouinard Equipment, and it changed its name when it incorporated, in 1973), Chouinard has done everything he could to discourage the use of pitons altogether, in favor of the climbing implements known as chocks, which are small pieces of metal wedged, not hammered, into cracks to hold ropes. Unlike most pitons, they are easily removable. In 1971, Chouinard became an apostle of "the clean-climbing ethic," and if he had his way there would be few circumstances in which a rock climber would be allowed to hammer a piton into a rock and leave it there.

According to Doug Scott, a British climber and the author of *Big Wall Climbing*, a definitive history of the climbing of great mountain faces, the use of the chock began in 1926, on a climb of Clogwyn du'r Arddu, a rock face in Wales. The climbers carried chock stones—small rocks—which they wedged into cracks in the wall. Around these stones they looped short pieces of rope, or runners, to which, for protection, they attached carabiners—D-shaped aluminum snap-gate links that allow a rope to be attached to a piton or a chock or a runner without untying the rope or threading it through—and strung a rope as they climbed. By the 1940s, it was common practice for British climbers to stuff their pockets with pebbles from local streams before heading for the crags. There is a railroad in Wales that runs close to Clogwyn du'r Arddu, and climbers would trudge along the tracks before making an ascent. From time to time, a large nut would detach itself from the railway tracks, and in the early 1950s climbers began picking these nuts up and making use of them. The nuts were better than the chock stones, for a rope could be fitted through the hole, and the metal stuck solidly to the rock. In the early 1960s, a British blacksmith named John Brailsford began machining metal wedges of various sizes, which were even better than the railway nuts. By 1967, these wedges were fitted with wire loops, and the modern version does not differ from them greatly in basic design.

Chouinard began using chocks—his first ones were made from aluminum aircraft nuts—back in 1959 and 1960, while he was climbing in the Tetons, but it was more than a decade later that he became a really strong advocate of them. Scott quotes a response to a letter that he wrote Chouinard in 1970 asking him about the attitude of Yosemite climbers toward this technology. Chouinard replied, "I've found nuts very useful on artificial climbing"—climbs that require the use of pitons or other aids for progress or rest—"when the rock is very poor. . . . But I would never substitute a nut for a piton in a normal situation. I've climbed with nut fanatics like Robbins, who insist on using them. . . . I can assure you he spends twice as much time . . . placing them [as] if he just nailed it." Not long after that, however, Chouinard discovered that pitons in Yosemite were ruining the rock. Pitons can destroy delicate cracks in rock, and some climbs—in regions in California like Yosemite, where it is customary to remove pitons—have been ruined by piton scars. The cracks become perforated, like the edges of a postage stamp. Chouinard has said, "I always thought of rock climbing as a completely harmless sport—one that did not hurt anyone. But I came to realize that it could do great harm to the rocks." Small cracks that could once take only RURPs now needed large pitons, and soon new cracks developed every few feet. The rock was simply being beaten to pieces.

When Chouinard and Frost changed their technique, they began to manufacture a wide variety of chocks. The present Iron Works catalog lists fourteen sizes of hexentrics—chocks shaped like irregular hexagons, which can be wedged into the rock at various angles. It also lists sixteen sizes of stoppers—chocks with pyramids at the ends. There are five sizes of tube chocks, as long as six inches, which are for large cracks. And there are five sizes of crack'n-ups—tiny, anchor-shaped chocks used instead of RURPs for clean climbing in incipient cracks. Chouinard estimates that a serious rock climber should have about twenty chocks, of different sizes and shapes, along for an average artificial climb, and perhaps sixty for a major face. For a time, some of the younger climbers accused Chouinard of a certain hypocrisy, claiming that he had used pitons on all his hard routes but was now recommending to them strange and perhaps unproved practices. As an answer, in 1973 Chouinard and a Washington climber named Bruce Carson (who died during an ascent in India in 1975) climbed the Nose route on El Capitan taking only chocks along—not pitons. This is one of the hardest rock climbs in Yosemite, and the two men completed it with no serious hitches—a feat that seems to have quieted the skeptics.

The 1972 Chouinard catalog is regarded by climbers as something of a collector's item. It sold for a dollar, and ten thousand copies were printed. Not a single copy is left in the Chouinard office. On the cover is a sixteenth-century Chinese scroll painting, "Landscape in the Spirit of Verses by Tu Fu," by Wen Chia, and among the contents are quotations from a variety of notable intellects. Page 1 has a magnificent photograph of the east face of the Moose's Tooth, a mountain in Alaska, over which is printed a sentence from Albert Einstein: "A perfection of means and confusion of aims seems to be our main problem." To prevent any confusion of aims, there is an excellent fourteen-page instructional section, written by the well-known Sierra guide and alpinist Doug Robinson, on how clean-climbing equipment is to be used. Using chocks requires a more intimate relationship with the rock than hammering in a piton does. Often two or more chocks must be stacked together to provide enough of an anchor point, and frequently several such anchor points are used in conjunction—like the trusses of a bridge—to strengthen the system. All these matters are thoroughly discussed in the catalog, along with, of course, the characteristics of the equipment—and prices are not forgotten. The whole thing so much resembles a small book that it has been reviewed as one. Writing in the 1973 edition of the *American Alpine Journal*, published annually by the American Alpine Club, the climber and photographer Galen Rowell asked, "What is a commercial catalog doing in the book-review section?" He answered, "It contains more information on the ethics and style of modern climbing than any other publication in our language."

Having been a mountain climber for the past three decades, and having encountered Chouinard's reputation both in this country and abroad but never the man himself, I decided not long ago to go to California to meet him. When I called him to arrange the visit, he said that he would pick me up at the Ventura County Airport, and added, "Stay at the house. We have visitors all the time and live on the beach. It's not bad." When I arrived, I was greeted by a short, rugged-looking man in blue jeans and a wool shirt. Like many of the world's best mountain climbers, Chouinard is short—perhaps five feet five. (The Sherpas of Nepal are, on the average, about five feet three.) And, like all of them, he is exceedingly strong. Like every first-rate climber, Chouinard has very powerful hands and fingers which, for a man of his size, are unusually large. He has a broad, open tanned face.

We got into a well-worn car and after a drive of twenty minutes arrived at a white wooden cottage whose back door was only thirty-five feet from the ocean. Chouinard's wife, Malinda, whom he met some ten years ago when both were mountain climbing (they have been married for seven years), has had to put up a small wooden gate on the back porch to keep their son, Fletcher, who is almost three years old, from following his father out to sea. The beach on which the Chouinards live is known in southern California as one of the best beaches for surfing, and each morning at sunrise Chouinard gets up to examine the quality of the waves. If the waves look good, he dons a black wet-suit and selects one of two translucent surf-boards he has stored on the ceiling beams of his living room. The boards have keels like shark fins, and there is a safety cord to attach the board to a surfer's leg, to keep it from running away if he takes a spill. When I was there, gray whales were migrating south to Baja and could be seen spouting behind the congregating surfboard riders. From time to time, the phone rang in the living room, and Malinda gave out information to surfing friends who were not in a position to inspect the waves.

Probably because Chouinard has spent so much time on expeditions, he does a good deal of cooking. He is now learning Japanese cookery, and soon after I arrived he began to study a cookbook to find out how to prepare a substantial fish in Oriental style. After dinner, which featured the fish, and was excellent, I asked Chouinard if he would tell me something about his life and about how he had discovered the mountains.

"I was born in Lewiston, Maine, on November 9, 1938, of French-Canadian parents," he said. "We lived in Lisbon, Maine, a town that was almost evenly divided between French-Canadians and Yankees. Until I was seven, I went to a parochial school, where everyone spoke French. In fact, until I was eight I couldn't speak English at all. When I was seven, my father, who was a plumber, moved the family—I have two older sisters and an older brother—to Burbank, near Los Angeles. He has asth-ma, and he came out here for his health. They put me in public school—an English-speaking school—and I couldn't speak En-glish. It was traumatic. I can understand how Puerto Ricans and Chicanos feel about going to an English-speaking school. It's rough. After about a week, they took me out and put me in a parochial school, where I got along a little better. The teachers spent more time trying to get me to talk. But I became sort of a loner—a wise kid. All through that period, I was spending my time out of school outdoors in the hills—the Hollywood Hills and the like. Before the other kids were even allowed to cross the street, I was taking my bike and riding for miles to sneak in to private lakes to go fishing. My big dream was to become a trapper—my French-Canadian background—and I read every book about trapping I could get my hands on. I spent all my time either outdoors or reading about the outdoors. I couldn't adapt to high school at all. I had a few friends. All the geeks. Couldn't dance, scared to death of girls. We joined a club—the California Falconry Club—and spent our time looking for hawks' nests and trapping hawks and banding them for the government. There were some adults in the club, who taught us things and kept an eye on us—particularly Robert Klimes, who was a schoolteacher. But it was a man named Don Prentice, another member of the club, who first taught us something about climbing. We had been climbing hand over hand on ropes down to these falcon aeries on the ledges of cliffs. But he taught us how to rappel—to wrap the rope around one's body and slide down on it. We just went crazy over that. We thought that rappelling was the greatest thing in the world. I'd go out for hours and practice rappelling. We used to hop freights that went from Burbank to Chatsworth, at the other end of the San Fernando Valley. The trains had to go uphill there, and we'd jump off. There were some big cliffs at Chatsworth, and every weekend we went out there to practice rappelling. We kept pushing the limits of rappelling. We'd take a hundred-foot cliff and instead of rappelling down it in twenty hops we'd see how few hops we could do it in. We developed all-leather outfits, huge leather pads and everything, so that we could do these hot, burning rappels—just smokers—in one or two hops."

"It was lucky nobody got killed," I said.

"I nearly did get killed," Chouinard said. "I went out in the desert with a friend—Ken Weeks, with whom I did a lot of climbing later—to a prairie falcon's aerie. There was this tremendous overhanging cliff, more than four hundred feet high, and I tied three ropes together. The hanging rope was so heavy I could hardly pull it up with my arms to feed it through to rappel. Weeks grabbed the rope and wrapped it around his body and stuffed himself behind some boulders so that he could hold me. He was a tremendously strong guy. I had some rope slings around my neck, and when I hit the first knot it wouldn't go through the slings. My arms were so tired from lifting the rope that I couldn't pass the knot through. I just hung there in midair with the rope wrapped around my body. I finally reached the point where I couldn't hang there anymore. I couldn't stand it. I was going to count to ten and then let go. I started to count and got to eight and the knot came through—popped through. I slid down to the ground and went into convulsions, because my body had been so tense. Weeks, who hadn't known what was happening, found me, and said I had been hanging on the rope for three and a half hours. It was one of the closest calls I have ever had. That was the end of the rappelling. Now I hate rappelling. I'll down-climb anything before I rappel it. At the time, we thought that rappelling was the whole thing. When I was sixteen, I went out to Chatsworth one weekend and was rappelling down the cliff and there was a guy from the Sierra Club climbing *up* it. I couldn't believe it. Well, Don Prentice showed us a little about climbing—how to use ropes, and so on—and we began to climb up to falcon aeries instead of rappelling down into them."

I asked Chouinard if there had been many climbers in California at that time—in the first half of the 1950s.

"No. There were just a handful," he said. "Those were the days of wearing tennis shoes for rock climbing—there were no climbing boots, or anything like that. In fact, even five years later, if you were hiking along in a mountain area and you saw the footprint of a cleated sole, that meant a climber, and if you caught up with him you probably knew him or you both knew the same people. I got in with the rock-climbing section of the Sierra Club in Los Angeles, along with people like Royal Robbins, Bob Kamps, Mark Powell, and T. M. Herbert. Another strong climbing group was in San Francisco. They had Al Steck, one of the best American climbers, and Chuck Pratt and Warren Harding, and people who had climbed in Europe and had kept up with what was going on. In Los Angeles, we were cut off from that group. They were doing their climbing in Yosemite, and we were doing a lot of ours at Tahquitz Rock—a big rock near Palm Springs, about a thousand feet high. But it was a good area and produced some fine climbers. Between that and Chatsworth, we got to climb all the time."

At this point, the conversation was interrupted by the appearance of Fletcher, then learning to walk, who attempted a delicate traverse along a living room couch. He misjudged a maneuver between two cushions and sat down on the floor, looking puzzled. "Fletcher, you are a turkey," Chouinard said. Fletcher stood up shakily and continued.

Chouinard went on, "When I was in high school, I rebuilt an old 1940 Ford sedan—the engine and everything. The only classes I could stand were the auto mechanics and shop classes. I was a pure geek—the worst—and I couldn't stand to be among people. In the auto mechanics class, I'd just get on my creeper and crawl under a car and spend the whole class there. So I rebuilt this old car. That is when I really broke away. I remember the feeling of driving in the desert, in hundred-degree temperatures, with all those Oldsmobiles and Cadillacs stopped by the side of the road with their hoods up—overheating—and I was just tootling right by them. That summer, I drove out to the Wind River Range, in Wyoming—the Green River Lakes area— to meet Don Prentice and a few others. We were going to do Gannett Peak, which is the highest mountain in Wyoming—my first real climb. Well, there were no guidebooks, and we didn't even know which peak was which. Then when we found Gannett Peak, which was nearly fourteen thousand feet, we couldn't decide what route to take. I thought we should go up a face, and they wanted to keep in the gullies and go off in another direction. So we split up, and I soloed the face. I never dreamed that mountains were that big. I couldn't believe it. Everything looked so short, but it went on for hours and hours. As far as I know, that was a new route on Gannett Peak, but, God, I don't know where it is—somewhere on the west side. I remember doing some hairy things, not knowing what I was doing. I had some Sears, Roebuck boots on, with no cleats, and I got up onto the snowfields near the summit—these big snowfields that drop off for thousands of feet. A thunderstorm coming on. I was really psyched out, but somehow I got out of there."

It is unusual—to put it mildly—for someone to do a solo first ascent on a maiden climb. "From the beginning, you must have been very gifted at climbing," I said.

"Yes," Chouinard said. "I was sixteen, but all I had been doing for nearly sixteen years was climbing trees and hiking. Climbing was just natural to me. In fact, I went from the Wind Rivers directly to the Tetons, also in Wyoming, for my second climb. I couldn't find anyone who wanted to go with me. At that time, the only people who were traveling around to do any climbing were college kids. Climbers in California rarely got out of California, and Colorado climbers rarely got out of Colorado. The only people who got around were guys from places like Dartmouth, Harvard, and Yale. They had climbing clubs back east, and they would go west every summer. Still, when I got to the Tetons I couldn't find anyone to climb with. I had no experience, and the climbers there didn't want to fool with me at all. Finally, I got in with a couple of guys from Harvard or Dartmouth or somewhere. They were going to do a climb known as Templeton Crack, on Symmetry Spire. The crux pitch is a chimney crack—a three-sided slot where you wedge your body in and inch your way up. It is a very disagreeable climb. The crack is covered with slime, and early in the season—late June—it was about the worst thing they could have picked. Anyway, we were climbing along, and I was making believe that I knew what I was doing. They roped me up in the middle. We got up to the crux pitch, and the lead guy went up and came down, went up and came down—he really didn't want to do it. Then the other guy went up and tried it, and he couldn't do it. So they looked over at me and said, 'It looks like you're going to have to do it.' They roped me up first and said, 'Here are the pitons.' I didn't even know what pitons were. So I just faked it all and went up there and did the thing—my second climb. Pretty lucky there. You can make a lot of mistakes. And so in the next few years I went into the Tetons for three solid months every summer."

After leaving high school, Chouinard went to work for his

brother, Gerald, who was a private detective employed by Howard Hughes. (Gerald Chouinard has retired from detective work now and is employed by the Great Pacific Iron Works.) One of their jobs was to guard a yacht sixteen hours a day for several months. Hughes was thinking of buying the yacht, but before he bought it he had to inspect it, and before he was willing to inspect it it had to be germfree. So Chouinard and his brother guarded the yacht to make sure that no one who might deposit germs got on it while Hughes was thinking of buying it. Chouinard was also going to a junior college in the San Fernando Valley, and he studied geography there for two years. By that time, he had extended his climbing activities to the Canadian Rockies, where he went with Ken Weeks. "All during those years after high school, I was very, very poor, and so were the people I climbed with," Chouinard said. "We rarely got a square meal. The Alpine Club of Canada had a big base camp, and we knew that when the climbers abandoned the camp they would leave a lot of food behind. So we waited, and carted the food back to where we were, fifteen miles away—loads and loads of potatoes, carrots, and flour. We ate ground squirrels and porcupines and wild grouse. In the Tetons once, we cleaned out some old incinerators—huge concrete incinerators—and lived inside them for the summer."

Chouinard paused, and then went on. "I took a bad fall in the Tetons one summer—the only time I've really got hurt. Bob Kamps and I were trying to do the first ascent of a thing called the Crooked Thumb. The whole wall is overhanging. I had climbed up to a spot underneath one overhang and had then used ropes and étriers to do the overhang. Just above that, there was a slightly overhanging wall. I looked at it and thought I could do it. You have to decide right then and there whether you can or not, because you can't just stop in the middle of an overhanging wall and put up protection. You can't let go with your hands. I took off, and I was able to put in one runner around a rock, but that was all. I got to within about three feet of a ledge, and my arms were shot. I was just going to make it. There was a loose handhold. I knew it was loose, but if you pull on a loose handhold in the right direction, sometimes you can use it. That's what I tried to do, and it broke. So I free-fell about 160 feet, to the end of the rope. Luckily, it was a small-diameter rope—nine-millimeter. So it took up the shock, and I didn't break any ribs or anything, although I was bruised and somehow opened a big gash in my leg—down to the bone. I was hanging in midair, which would have been a pretty serious thing except that I landed directly level with our last belay spot. I got myself swinging, and I swung in until I could grab some blocks that were there. It was an unbelievable miracle. Kamps rappelled down, and I had to pull him in, the overhang was so great. It was late in the day. It was getting cold—down below freezing. We couldn't go down from there directly, because the wall below us was overhanging, too. And I was wearing shorts. I had thought that we could do the climb in one day. Luckily, we found a little finger traverse that went right along the wall and around a corner and turned into a little horizontal ledge. We were able to creep along it for something like two hundred feet, and that got us off the wall. Then we had to descend the other side of the mountain about five thousand feet into the valley at night—down-climbing snowfields and through brush. That was rough, with my bad leg. When you're going at night like that, you learn to follow your feet—they reach out. They're like eyes. So I could feel the trail at the bottom with my feet when we got to it. I relaxed and was walking along when all of a sudden I hit an aspen stump, right on my sore leg. Oh, man! I just broke down and started sobbing. The next day, I went to see a doctor, and he spent about an hour pulling pine needles and all kinds of seeds and everything else out of my leg.

"That was a really bad experience for me. It took me three years to get my mind back to where it was before the fall—three years in which I spent winter and summer, all the time, climbing. Just traveling all over the country and climbing, climbing, climbing. Taking that fall really made an impression on me. One reason was that I couldn't climb immediately afterward. My leg was bad, and I couldn't climb for about a month. Another reason was that in that climb I had made a decision. I had said, 'Well, I can do that.' I'd gone for it, and it had turned out that I couldn't do it. It would have been different if I had got hit by a rock or something like that had happened—something that wasn't my own doing. Afterward, every time I went climbing and got myself in a similar situation—small holds, face climbing, overhangs—I couldn't control myself. My legs would shake. I'd never been bothered by that before. I used to do some very, very bold leads—a hundred feet up. I couldn't do it anymore. It took three full years before I got it back. But I did."

I asked Chouinard how he was earning his living back then.

"I was doing some guiding, and odd jobs, like haying," he said. It was at about this time that Chouinard borrowed $825.35 in cash from his parents to pay for a forging die of a type sold by Alcoa in Los Angeles, which he planned to use in the manufacture of carabiners. "There was this big, fancy building in Los Angeles, and this eighteen-year-old kid—me—walked in with cash to pay for a machine. They didn't know what to do with cash—how to process it. It just wouldn't go through the system. They were laughing. I had it down to the thirty-five cents. Anyway, I got it. I had a drill press and a grinder, and I did everything by myself, just about by hand. You see, up to that time all the climbing equipment here was imported from Europe, but I thought I could make better stuff." The Chouinard carabiner, made of aluminum, has now gone through five design changes.

Next, Chouinard turned his attention to the manufacture of pitons. Up until the 1940s, climbing pitons were made of malleable iron, so that they could be more easily wedged into irregular cracks. These pitons were not meant to be used over and over, and on long climbs dozens of them had to be carried. Then, in 1946, John Salathé, a blacksmith living in Palo Alto, California, worked a radical change in the design of pitons. Salathé, who was born in 1901 in Switzerland, had taken up climbing in California in his middle forties after experiencing a series of mystic visions. Chouinard became friendly with Salathé somewhat later, and he now told me, "Salathé had some kind of weird Swiss religion and was spending all his time reinterpreting the Bible to his own liking. He thought that he was dying from some terrible disease and also that people were trying to kill him. Well, at that time an angel came down to him

Yvon Chouinard cutting steps with ice axe

while he was working at his forge and told him to stop eating meat. This angel said, 'John, look at the cows out in the field. What do they eat?' John said, 'Well, they eat grass.' The angel said, 'That's right, John. Now look at the horses out there. What do they eat?' 'Well,' John said, 'they eat grass, too.' 'That's right, John. They eat grass. And the horses are healthy, and they work all day long. Look at you. You're almost ready to die.' And Salathé became a vegetarian and became very, very healthy. He got more visitations from angels, and they told him to go into the mountains. Salathé and I got along really well together. He knew that I was a blacksmith and that I was making pitons, and we talked about that. But he couldn't communicate with most of the other young climbers at all. In 1964, when Robbins, Pratt, Frost, and I climbed the North America Wall of El Capitan, he came out to watch us. We were just dots—a thousand feet up. There were several other climbers watching from below, with binoculars and spotting scopes. On this wall, you had no idea where you were going. You can't see any cracks from below— no systems. You just have to get out on the climb and go for it. Well, a few of the climbers who recognized Salathé said to him, 'Do you want to use the binoculars, John?' And he said, 'No, I can see them.' He plotted our whole route from down below, I was told later. He would say, 'Ah, yes, from there they will go this way and this way'—and we didn't even know ourselves. With his naked eye he saw the whole route, just like that. And when we came down, he came over and congratulated us. He asked me what we had been eating. I made it sound as if we had been eating only vegetarian foods—nuts, dates, cheese, and eggs. I didn't mention the salami we had along. And Salathé said, 'Ah, that's why you did so well—vegetables.' ''

Shortly after becoming a vegetarian, Salathé had joined the rock-climbing section of the Sierra Club in San Francisco, and had begun making rock climbs in Yosemite that were then the hardest ever made in the United States. One of the most extraordinary was his climb of the Lost Arrow Spire, near Yosemite Falls. This is a spire that rises in isolation but whose peak is only a hundred feet or so from the brow of a nearby cliff. It had been considered absolutely unclimbable. Salathé made two attempts to climb the spire from the notch, and on the second one he got to within fifty feet of the summit. He was sure that he could finish the route, but before this happened a four-man party did reach the summit, by a rather strange procedure. They threw a rope over the summit from the cliff and then used this rope to climb the last pitch to the summit; they rigged a sort of aerial tramway with their ropes, and also used it to return to the cliff. Their feat was regarded by most climbers as proof that the upper part of the spire was indeed unclimbable.

Undaunted, Salathé and his climbing partner, a carpenter named Anton Nelson, trained for months, and went as long as possible without water, until they had reduced their water intake to something like a pint a day. On August 30, 1947, they set out from the base of the spire. They reached the summit 103 hours later—after five days and four bivouacs, with only rock ledges to sleep on. "It would have been nothing if there had already been a series of two- and three-bivouac climbs in this country," Chouinard told me. "This would have been just one step more. But I think there had never been more than a one-bivouac rock climb in the whole country. For them to go out and do a four-bivouac climb of that difficulty was like someone going out and suddenly doing a two-minute mile. It was incredible. And Salathé was in his late forties at the time."

Included in the climbing equipment that Salathé and Nelson had along were about eighteen pitons that Salathé had forged by hand. It turned out that the best of these were made of metal from Model A Ford front axles—a tough alloy of chrome, vanadium, and steel. Although Salathé had made these pitons for his own use, they were so good that they revolutionized the construction of the climbing piton. The reason was that these pitons were just the opposite of the classic European piton—they were not malleable. This meant that they could be used again and again. More important, they were much safer than the malleable ones. A piton is usually driven into a crack in a rock at a down-sloping angle. If a climber falls, the force applied to the piton is primarily downward, and, unless the rock breaks, the piton can come out only if it is bent by the force of the fall. The stiffer the piton, the safer it is.

I asked Chouinard whether it was an angel that had inspired Salathé to make pitons out of Model A Ford axles.

"No," he replied. "It was his experience as a blacksmith. In 1957, when I started my equipment business, Salathé had almost quit climbing, and his pitons were not available anyway. Almost no one in the country was making pitons. So I bought myself a little hand forge—a coal forge—and an anvil and some hammers and some tongs. I got some books and learned black-smithing, and started making pitons out of chrome-molyb-denum steel. All my machinery was portable, so I just loaded it all in my car and made the stuff wherever I was. I'd sell it directly to climbers. About the same time, I took up surfing, so I'd travel up and down the California coast from Big Sur to San Diego, staying in a place for a day or two and hammering out pitons before I moved on to another place to work some more. The same with the carabiners. They were almost handmade, and I had portable vises. I'd hold the carabiners in a vise and file on them or hand-drill them."

"Could you make a living doing that?" I asked.

"Yes," Chouinard answered. "By that time, there were enough climbers. I'd sell the pitons and the carabiners in climb-ing areas in the summer, and in the winter, when there wasn't anybody climbing, I'd stockpile them to sell the next summer. I'd move from one climbing area to another, just climbing and selling my gear. I could make two pitons an hour. For years, I used to sit at the forge sometimes eight hours a day making pitons. That was hard work. I sold my pitons for a dollar and a half. At first, there was a lot of resistance to paying that much for them. The European pitons were selling for something like thirty cents. It took quite a few years before people realized how good mine were and that they were worth it." Now most pitons, including European ones, are made of a tough steel alloy.

"It does not sound like an arrangement that would ever make you very rich," I remarked.

"No," Chouinard said. "I had no idea how long it was going to last. I did not think I would make it my life's work. I never knew what I wanted to do, really. I enjoyed traveling, but I never dreamed that I was going to make a business out of selling climbing equipment—although I did know that someday climbing would become popular. I had seen some sports, like skin diving, grow from just a few freaks to an incredibly technological sport, with millions being made in the business of selling equipment for it. I knew that climbing would be the same someday, even though climbing tends to be a little different from a lot of other sports. It attracts the introverts—the real oddballs. They are the people who stay in climbing. They get into it and stay in it for quite a while. But in the last few years climbing has become an 'in' thing. A lot of college kids take it up, through their outdoor clubs, and just the guy off the street wants to get into it. But they go into it and they get out of it fast, because they soon realize that it's not as glamorous as they thought it was. It's not like athletics, where you get good and do your thing in front of an audience. There are a great many athletes who need an audience to perform to, or need at least one other person—like a partner or an opponent—watching them. In climbing, at the end of the rope there, you're pretty much by yourself, and that burns a lot of people out."

Chouinard might have continued to wander in and out of the mountains and up and down the California coast for years, but in the winter of 1962 the army called him. He was in the army for two years, including thirteen months in Korea. The previous summer, he had been climbing in Wyoming and Canada, and in the autumn he had continued in the Shawangunks—a celebrated rock-climbing area near New Paltz, New York. "I had a load of hardware with me to sell, and I sold about three hundred dollars' worth," he said. "It was a lot of money for me—a lot of money—and I was going to head back to California with it." He got a "drive-away car"—a car to be driven across the country for someone else. The car kept breaking down before it could be delivered to its owner, in New Mexico. As instructed, Chouinard got it repaired each time and saved the bills. In Boulder, Colorado, he ran into Chuck Pratt, and the two of them continued. By the time they reached New Mexico, they had fifteen cents between them, which they used to buy three candy bars. When they delivered the car, the owner accused them of wrecking it and refused to pay, and also called the police, who gave the two of them five minutes to get out of town. "I had lost all my money," Chouinard recalled. "And I just sat down on the curb there and bawled."

They managed to hitchhike as far as Grants, New Mexico, where they and the driver of the car they were riding in were thrown into jail for three days, because the police thought that the car looked suspicious. By then, it was midwinter. They went on to Gallup, New Mexico, and there they were stranded. "We could not get a ride out of Gallup," Chouinard told me. "It was unbelievable. We were desperate. All the Santa Fe freights keep the doors of the empty railway cars locked, to keep hoboes out." So they found a Santa Fe train that was carrying automobiles. "We checked all the automobiles and found one that had its doors open—a station wagon," Chouinard said. "We got inside—got on the floor and went to sleep. We got as far as Winslow, Arizona, where we were awakened by a flashlight. A railroad bull. He had seen that the windows of the car we were in were foggy—meaning that there had to be someone inside. We were hauled up in front of a judge and told that if we pleaded not guilty to vagrancy we'd go to trial in a month or two but that if we pleaded guilty they'd just check us out and let us go. Well, we pleaded guilty, and they locked us up for eighteen days. They gave us one slice of Wonder bread in the morning and a bowl of oatmeal and a bowl of pinto beans at night with a slice of Wonder bread. Pratt was allergic to oatmeal, so he gave me his oatmeal and I gave him my Wonder bread. He came out of jail weighing 115 pounds; he had lost 25 pounds. After a while, they had me working on a garbage truck with some Indians, collecting garbage. That was some trip. To top it all off, when we got home we both were drafted."

Chouinard was sent to Fort Ord, in California, for basic training, and then to Huntsville, Alabama, where he studied guided-missile mechanics before being sent to Korea. At Fort Ord, he was told that he would be issued a three-day pass if he got the highest score in his company, made up of some two hundred soldiers, in a physical-training test—grenade-throwing, pushups, and the like. Such was his dislike of the army that he did get the highest score. It turned out that some of the climbers he knew—Ken Weeks, T. M. Herbert—had also won such competitions in the army. "It was not because we were physically superior," Chouinard told me. "It was just because we *had* to have those three days."Before leaving for Korea, he encountered a Korean who said that his brother was the best climber in Korea and that Chouinard should be sure to look him up. This turned out to be nearly impossible.

The army was not liberal in giving weekend passes in Korea, and the men hardly ever got off the base—in theory, at least. "To get free time to go climbing, I had to cause a lot of trouble," Chouinard said. "So I went on hunger strikes—a couple of quite long hunger strikes—and I refused to follow orders. I purposely acted eccentric—half crazy—until they finally let me alone. I would come just short of being thrown into the brig—just short, and then I'd back off. But I caused so much trouble for the company that the company commander told me to get lost. He put me in with some civilians who were working on missiles. All I had to do was to turn some generator on in the morning and then turn it off at night. The rest of the time, I went climbing."

It had never occurred to me to think of Korea as a climbing area, but apparently it is.

"There is some great climbing near Seoul—big domes and pinnacles, beautiful granite," Chouinard said. "Once I got in touch with the Korean climbers, they kept a set of civilian clothes for me at their house. I had my climbing gear sent over from the States. The climbing routes that existed in Korea then had been established by the Japanese during their occupation. The Koreans learned to climb from the Japanese. All that the Koreans wanted to do was to repeat the old Japanese routes. There was one fellow who had done the same climb seventy-five times. I asked him why he did the climb so many times, and he said that it was his favorite. 'Well,' I said, 'why don't you try some new climbs?' 'What for?' he said. 'We have all these nice climbs. Why should we do any new climbs?' There were such a lot of new routes to be done, and finally we just went out and did them. Once we started, the Koreans really got behind the idea. We did some high-quality climbing—even bivouac climbs—and everyone in the mountains got to know me. It was almost like not being in the army. So it turned out that Korea, in the end, was a pretty good experience."

When Chouinard was shipped back to the States, the army sent him to the Presidio, in San Francisco, where he was assigned to maintain a baseball diamond. A climbing friend, Douglas Tompkins, had started a climbing shop not far away, and each morning he would arrive at the base on a motorcycle. He would call up Chouinard's sergeant and shout over the phone, "This is Major So-and-So! Where the hell is that goddam Chouinard? I want him here at the library in ten minutes. *Ten minutes!* Do you hear me?" The sergeant would say, "Chouinard, get over to the library on the double. Major So-and-So wants to see you." Chouinard and Tompkins would then go off on the motorcycle for a day's outing.

Chouinard was separated from the army in July of 1964, and headed directly for Yosemite, where, with Chuck Pratt and Warren Harding, he participated in a first ascent of the south face of Mount Watkins.

That fall, Chouinard went back to making climbing equipment. "I came out with my first mail-order catalog," he told me. "It was a one-sheet mimeographed price list. At the bottom of the list, it said, 'Don't expect speedy delivery in the months of May, June, July, August, and September.' " That was the climbing season. Until 1965, Chouinard's shop was in the back yard of his parents' house, in Burbank. Then he rented some old tin shacks, also in Burbank, for a total of sixty dollars a month. But he was spending so much time driving back and forth to the beach to surf that in 1965 he decided to move to Ventura, and in 1966 he set up a small shop near a railroad siding there, next to an abandoned slaughterhouse. Now the Great Pacific Iron Works has taken over the site of both the siding and the slaughterhouse. It was at the time of the move to Ventura that Chouinard went into partnership with Frost, who was from Orange County, and with whom he had climbed in Yosemite. "Making hardware was getting a little more complex," Chouinard said. "The demand was such that I couldn't make things fast enough by hand any more. I had to go into making things by machine—designing sophisticated dies, and so on. That's where Frost came in especially handy. He had been an aeronautical engineer, and it was really valuable to have engineering experience."

Chouinard and Frost began with two or three employees, and there are currently thirty-two. In the early days, the workers were usually itinerant climbers. "They wanted to work for a while, and then they'd take off and go climbing," Chouinard told me. "Often, we'd hire British climbers who needed a few bucks. It was a very loose organization, and in some ways it still is." Perhaps the most extraordinary of the British climbers who worked for them was Donald Whillans. Books have been written about Whillans. He was born in Salford, England, in 1933, and got into climbing after the war. In the past, British climbing had been the province of a relatively upper-class segment of society. After the war, however, a number of workingmen discovered climbing as an escape from a life of drudgery, and they became known as "the hard men." Whillans, a plumber by trade, is the quintessential hard man. He is about five feet three and is constructed like a small tank. As Joe Brown, the first of the hard men, puts it in his autobiography, *The Hard Years*, Whillans's "tough reputation spread like wildfire in climbing circles." Brown goes on, "True or false, it had a salutary effect on other people. During the early fifties, for instance, when hordes of climbers slept rough in the Wall End barn in Langdale, Whillans quelled a riot of noise late at night by shouting, 'Pipe down and go to sleep.' This order was greeted by indignant comments, such as, 'Who the bloody hell do you think you are!' Whillans replied in a whip-cracking voice, 'Whillans,' and silence fell instantly upon the rowdy company."

Chouinard told me a Whillans story that I hadn't heard before. One afternoon in the 1960s, he and Whillans found themselves in a small café in the Alps. On the terrace were two substantially constructed Continental climbers with two pretty women. To pass the time, the climbers had taken the parasols out of two heavy concrete umbrella stands and stuck the stands together to make a barbell. They succeeded in lifting it a couple of times, to the admiring glances of the women. At the bar, Whillans had been drinking his pint and watching this performance with growing distaste. Finally, he put down his glass and said, "Right." He strode out on the terrace and began lifting the barbell up and down, up and down, indefinitely. Chouinard thought that Whillans might continue for the rest of the afternoon, but in time he lost interest and went back inside to finish his drink. The Continental climbers and the women went off in search of another café.

Whillans now confines his activities to lecturing, mainly to workmen's clubs in Britain. Chouinard sells something called the Whillans Sit Harness—a device made of nylon webbing which a climber wears like a parachute harness. The climbing rope is tied to the harness, so that a climber who falls will not be cut in two by the rope around his waist. Most climbers now wear harnesses of some sort, and these have all but eliminated the kind of accident in which a climber falls, is suspended in midair at the end of the rope, and suffocates within a few moments.

After several months, in which Whillans tried his hand at various sorts of shopwork, Chouinard found that his services could be dispensed with. Whillans retaliated for this affront in his autobiography, *Portrait of a Mountaineer*, by neglecting to mention Chouinard at all, even though he and Chouinard had done quite a bit of climbing together. That is the sort of risk one takes if one crosses people who write autobiographies. In any event, Chouinard's Ventura business began with a few thousand dollars in sales in 1966 and doubled its sales each year thereafter for five years in a row, and Chouinard decided that he had better look elsewhere for his work force. In 1971, he brought in the first of what eventually became half a dozen Koreans. There are now five, along with an Argentine toolmaker and several Mexican craftsmen. Malinda Chouinard also works at the Iron Works, and so does Vincent Stanley, Chouinard's nephew and sales manager. It is Stanley who is responsible for one of my favorite lines in the 1976 catalog, of which thirty-five thousand copies have been distributed. In writing of Mountain Spectacles—goggles that filter ultraviolet light—he notes, "The round shape is tasteful and makes you look like a large fly."

The atmosphere of the Great Pacific Iron Works is rather like that of a large family. Many of the employees live on the beach, close to the Chouinards. When I visited Ventura, the newest employee was Kenneth Deprez, a thirty-three-year-old business graduate of Stanford, who had been at the Iron Works for a couple of weeks. Before that, Deprez had been general manager of Camp 7, a company near Boulder that is noted for its sleeping bags and down jackets. Deprez had the task of introducing modern accounting and business methods into what had been, and still is, largely an informal company. To handle two million dollars in annual sales and all the inventory problems that such a sales volume poses, Deprez has installed a computer and has reorganized things, and he feels that everything will now run by itself. While I was there, a Ventura banker dropped in and was taken for a tour of the premises. It was his first visit, and he appeared to be rather astonished by the extent of it.

To someone like me, with a fondness for climbing equipment, a tour through the Iron Works can be an incredibly satisfying experience. There is a retail shop, in which all the Chouinard-Frost products are displayed and sold. It includes a small climbing library, and a little piton museum, in which there are some original Salathé pitons, some of the early, hand-forged Chouinard pitons, and a primitive RURP. There are row upon row of bright-colored down jackets, tents suspended from the ceiling, sleeping bags hanging from the walls, climbing shoes, ropes, and display cases full of chocks and pitons. Chouinard estimates that someone who wants to get into rock climbing will have to invest $250. The most expensive single item is a good climbing rope. Such a rope is about 150 feet long and from 9 to 11 millimeters in diameter, and costs between $80 and $120, depending on its length, thickness, and quality. It is made of nylon. A typical nylon climbing rope of 150 feet weighs perhaps seven pounds. Modern ropes stretch under tension, and do not break in falls (a prudent climber will retire a rope after it has held one severe fall, however, and, in general, will think about replacing it after a hundred hours or so of climbing), but they can be cut if they are placed over a sharp edge, like a jagged rock. Ropes must be placed so as to avoid this kind of contact.

Boots suitable for both rock and ice cost between seventy and a hundred dollars, and, next to the rope, represent a climber's biggest expense. A pair weighs about five pounds. Shoes intended only for rock climbing are lighter and cost less. Chouinard, who has himself designed a rock shoe (the Shoenard) for a bootmaker, once remarked that the best boot he knew about for rock climbing was a mountain goat's hoof. It has a hard perimeter, with a soft interior for adhesion. If he could figure out how to duplicate this in rubber, leather, or the like, he said, he might go into the shoe business. In addition to a rope and boots, the serious rock climber will need twenty or so chocks and a load of carabiners and rope slings. There are also items like étriers, for artificial climbing and similar items, called *jumars*, for climbing up the rope. All these, however, are for extreme climbing. In addition, most climbers wear a tough plastic helmet, which protects the head both from falling rocks and from impact in case of a slip. Chouinard profits by selling these products of technology, but in his own opinion the ideal climb is done solo by someone barefoot and in shorts.

After visiting the retail shop, I wandered into the factory, behind it. Chouinard's old portable forge is there, but idle. The machining is done now with stamp dies and presses. A block of metal goes in, a piton comes out. Workers were busy adjusting carabiner gates and ice-axe handles. In one corner stood a wooden board several feet long to which Chouinard had attached a large number of irregularly shaped wooden blocks, to make it resemble a rock face. It was rigged up so that he could place chocks in the fissures in all sorts of combinations, and was designed to illustrate how clean-climbing equipment works. When I saw it, it was full of chocks with bright-colored rope loops through them. (A wise climber will try to color-code his chocks, so that he can spot the right size rapidly.) While I was wandering around, I asked Chouinard about the economics of the climbing-and-back-packing industry.

"It's a funny business," he said. "It started traditionally with very, very low retail markups—20 or 30 percent. Now the markup is 40—which is still low—and it has taken a long time to reach that. If a carabiner, for example, were an item for yachting, it would cost $15.00. But it's an item for climbing, so it costs

$3.65. I don't make any money selling hardware. The best I have ever done in twenty years of business is a net profit of 2½ percent one year. That's pretty bad. I generally end up with 1½ percent or 1½ percent from the hardware. That's why I don't have much competition. Who the hell wants to get into a business where he has to compete with somebody who has already got the market pretty much cornered and is making a profit of 1½ percent?"

Chouinard shook his head and continued, "It's the clothing that subsidizes the hardware. The dies that we use to make pitons, and so on, cost thousands of dollars, and often I don't get my money back for five to ten years. We want to manufacture old-fashioned hiking and climbing clothes—the kind that never wear out." I had just bought a pair of thick corduroy hiking shorts in the retail shop, and Chouinard said, "Take that pair of climbing shorts you bought. They are made in England. There is one machine in an old mill in Lancashire—a mill that goes back to the Industrial Revolution, and used to run on water power— that turns out that kind of corduroy. Workmen's clothes were made out of it before denim was used. Well, only a handful of old men know how to make the stuff on that machine. Whenever we need some corduroy, seven of them come out of retirement and crank up the machine to run some off for us. You can't wear those shorts out. They'll last forever. That's the kind of stuff we want to make. It will cost more initially, but it will last. The climbing-and-backpacking business is not like the ski business, which is incredible. A pair of plastic ski boots that costs fourteen or fifteen dollars to make sells for a hundred dollars or more. The backpacking-and-climbing business is very ethical—very, very clean—and people are really getting their money's worth out of it. I make a comfortable living. I don't have any money in the bank, but I have a living, and that's all I want out of it."

While I was in Ventura, Chouinard decided one day to go up into the High Sierra near June Lake, not far from Yosemite, to test a new pair of crampons he had designed, and also a pair of ultralight plastic ski bindings. He asked if I would like to come along. I had no cold-weather gear with me, but he said not to worry—he would find everything I needed around the shop. He added that this would be his first time off in six weeks. I arrived at the Iron Works at noon on the appointed day, and Chouinard presented me with my gear. "This is a new synthetic-filled jacket that some manufacturer wants me to try out, and a light-weight sleeping bag we are thinking of selling," he said. "The jacket looks pretty bad to me, but you can try it." I did, and it turned out to be all but useless in keeping out the cold. The sleeping bag, however, was splendid. Kenneth St. Oegger, a retired cabinetmaker who lives in Santa Barbara, arrived in a Dodge van. St. Oegger is in his mid-fifties and is an avid ice climber. The three of us loaded the gear into the van. Eight hours later, after an extremely beautiful drive up the eastern slopes of the Sierra range, we reached the house of James Collins, in June Lake, a small mountain town. Collins, a big, amiable man in his fifties, is a highway patrolman, an alpinist, and a member of the local mountain rescue service. He has a large, comfortable house, and apparently is used to having an indefinite number of climbers bunk out on his floors. In the course of his various duties, Collins gets around the back-country a good deal, and in the winter he keeps a lookout for water ice that could make good extreme ice climbing.

The next morning, Collins told us that he had two sites spotted—one near town and the other high up on a pass that leads into Yosemite. He thought that the pass could be tackled in the morning and the nearby climb after lunch. We were joined by Doug Robinson, the professional guide and writer of articles for the Chouinard catalogs. Robinson, who is in his thirties and is about the same height as Chouinard, lives in the Mammoth Lakes area, not far from Bishop, California. He and Chouinard, between them, have accounted for most of the difficult ice climbs in the Sierra.

The day was extremely cold, with the temperature about ten degrees and gusts of icy wind that blew plumes of snow off the tops of the nearby mountains. After breakfast, we headed for the pass in Collins's pickup truck. There was room for only four of us to squeeze into the cab, so Robinson, who was heavily

Two climbers on an ice fall

YVON CHOUINARD

equipped for winter climbing, volunteered to sit outside, in the truck bed. He bundled up in his down jacket, and off we went. We stopped near the top of the pass, at about ten thousand feet. The wind was unbelievable; Chouinard and Robinson estimated that there were gusts of sixty and seventy miles an hour. I am not capable of vertical ice climbing in a sixty-mile-an-hour wind, so after they started out I stationed myself a bit down the road, where I could get a view. The four of them descended into a canyon. From the bottom of the canyon, a tiny ribbon of vertical ice led back up to the top. Chouinard, who was the first to tackle it, had an ice axe and a small ice hammer. He hit the ice above his head with the hammer until it stuck. After that, he kicked the front points of one crampon in hard, and did the same with the other foot. He next put in the other ice axe and delicately shifted his weight off one foot and kicked it in at a higher level. He moved up, repeating the process again and again. The ice looked dark blue and nearly vertical. If it had been higher, Chouinard would have put in an ice screw for protection—a piton that is literally screwed into the ice. But his confidence in his technique was such that he simply went on up to the top. I watched anxiously, knowing that there could be no checking a fall on ice like that. Chouinard made it look as easy as walking up a path. When he got to the top, he lowered a rope, so that the others could climb up more easily. I watched for a few more minutes and then, shivering with cold, retreated to the truck. A little while later, I spotted Robinson climbing the icy side of the gully alone, and soon afterward Chouinard and the rest came along and we headed back to June Lake. I was ready for lunch and the warmth of the indoors, but such matters seemed to be far from Chouinard's mind. "My favorite place to climb is Scotland in the winter," he remarked. "The weather is bad every day, and you know it's going to be bad, so you go out in it anyway. Your hair freezes, your beard freezes, and you come home like an icicle. You're always only a few miles from the pub. The climbing is one foot on ice and the other on rock. That's what I really like."

3 Two Days in the Life of a Member of the French Alpine Club

Glaciers often make groaning sounds from their depths as they move, like elderly people coming down flights of stairs, and one of the crevasses moans slightly as I step forward. This seems to me—standing there on a tiny, sharp ice ridge leading between two monster crevasses high in the French Alps—like a bad omen, and I retreat. While I am thinking what to do next, I have the sudden conviction that of all the fifty thousand members in good standing of the French Alpine Club I am the most chicken. This goad works to the extent that I try the ridge again, starting with the other foot. I now begin to wonder what will happen if I slip. This reflection is needless for clearly what will happen is that I will fall into the bottom of one of the crevasses. No doubt climbing is somewhat crazy, but there is a profound satisfaction in conquering one's deepest fears, a sort of spiritual satisfaction which in this age of televised and pre-digested experience is all but disappearing. Let me go back to the beginning of the day.

We are late. We are always late. Jacccoux somehow manages to arrive three seconds before the last train or *téléphérique* or something. It's not that we will miss the last train—the cog railroad that goes from Chamonix to Montenvers, a vantage point above the Mer de Glace glacier, at 6,300 feet. There are trains until nearly 6 P.M. But from Montenvers we still have a four-hour climb to the Couvercle climbing refuge which sits beyond the head of the glacier at about 8,800 feet. I figure that if we are on the glacier at five we will have about two and a half hours of light, and the thought of groping around the moraine with flashlights does not appeal to me very much. Just in case, I check that my flashlight is actually working. A few years ago I

49

went with a group up to the Couvercle, without Jaccoux, at night and in a rainstorm. It turned out that everyone had forgotten his flashlight except me. But I had not checked to see if mine was working. It was not, and by the time we found our way to the Couvercle in a raging storm, it was close to midnight. Well, at least my flashlight works now.

There is Jaccoux, racing up in his orange Fiat with Colette, who in a gesture of loyalty has decided to come along. Colette is wearing a pair of modish, off-orange knickerbockers and a matching riding jacket with a yellow scarf. She looks as if she is dressed for golf. I hope she has a sweater at least. Jaccoux unloads his sixty- or seventy-pound *sac du guide* which contains, among other things, two climbing ropes, some pitons, a hammer, several small rope slings, a pair of crampons, a first-aid kit complete with Alka Seltzer—Jaccoux is a bit fragile of liver—two pipes, some reading material, two flashlights (no fool he) and some extra warm clothing.

I have my sack which includes, in addition to my crampons and down jacket, my red plastic helmet for warding off falling stones and food for the expedition. The last two items have been a source of irritation. Jaccoux refuses to wear a helmet and I refuse *not* to wear one. He has several interesting rationalizations for his attitude, the latest being that it cuts down his vision. My own rationalization is very simple. I do not want to get hit on the head by a rock. As for the food, in guided climbing, at least in the French Alps, it is the client who supplies the food—and carries it, I might add. I am usually too nervous while climbing to eat and therefore have a tendency either to forget completely about buying any, or if I don't forget, to get some sort of salami which Jaccoux says is bad for his liver. On one notable occasion when I forgot to bring food, Jaccoux sat down in the snow and refused to move. We were saved by the appearance of a large party of climbers who had an extra bar of chocolate. This time I have *two* different types of salami and four bars of chocolate. Still, my provisioning compares unfavorably with the *nourriture* supplied by the rest of Jaccoux's clientele, most notably a Parisienne who usually turns up with shrimp canapes, paté du foie, and the like. At least we will eat. What Colette has in her *sac* I hesitate to think.

We are on the train. Apart from us, there is a straggle of tourists who will catch a ten-minute view of the glacier before coming back down. Some may even be planning to spend the night at the Hotel de Montenvers, an ancient solid stone affair now being run and renovated by a young French couple—the Remi de Vivis. In its present guise the hotel offers fine food, a marvelous glacial panorama, and the *coupe perrichon glace myrtille et vanille fruits vodka*. This last is a delicious vanilla ice cream sundae filled with fresh fruits, smothered in whip cream and laced with vodka. Staggering down the Mer de Glace, more dead than alive, I have often been sustained by the vision of a *coupe perrichon*, or perhaps two, which await me if I can just gather enough energy to climb the last set of metal ladders that lead off the glacier and up to the trail that goes to the hotel. Now, I am suddenly seized by the manic notion that we should simply abandon the horrible four-hour climb to the refuge and stay the night at the hotel feasting off *coupe perrichons*!

This fantasy is reinforced by the sight of Abigail, Remi de Vivi's wife, at the Montenvers station. She is seeing someone off to Chamonix, and she invites all of us to a feast at the hotel. I would accept instantly, but I know that Jaccoux is determined to climb *something* tomorrow and the only climbs accessible from the hotel are more difficult than the one we had planned. Jaccoux mutters something about staying at the hotel and doing the Brioche de l'M the next day, a ghastly route on the Aiguelle de l'M which, according to rumor, features some sort of passage of V on slick rock covered with lichen. The prospect of having to slither up lichen after a night of feasting at the hotel is too much for me and after a certain amount of grumbling from Jaccoux, we head toward the glacier.

We have descended the ladders and are now on the glacier. The Mer de Glace is an amiable old iceflow, creased with crevasses especially at the bottom end. In the winter, hundreds of people ski down the glacier, and in the summer hundreds of people, probably thousands, trudge up it. The various organizations in Chamonix responsible for the safety of climbers mark the route on the glacier with large painted metal barrels.

Toward the top there are several routes leading to various climbing refuges and each route is marked with barrels of different colors. The barrels leading to the Couvercle are painted yellow, and I can see them strung out along the glacier in a reassuring—more or less—straight line. In fact, I am beginning to feel a virtuous sense of self-satisfaction when I encounter a totally unexpected obstacle—this pair of crevasses with the tiny ice ridge leading between them. Jaccoux and Colette, having somehow negotiated the ridge, are comfortably settled on the other side. I have been over the glacier a week or so before but have no recollection of any such ice ridge. It occurs to me that Jaccoux might have taken some sort of short cut, but just behind him, there is one of the infernal yellow barrels. Glaciers change so quickly that the damn ridge must have formed in the last few days.

I put a foot tentatively on the ridge, and this is the moment at which I hear the glacier groan and quickly retreat. Overcoming my fears, I step forward again. I now remember something my father once said to me: "You don't have to be crazy to climb mountains. But it helps!" I again retreat. Jaccoux who has been watching this charade with a growing sense of impatience in view of the hour—it is now well after six—has bestirred himself and is now working his way back across the ridge knocking sizable pieces off of the top of it with his ice axe and muttering, "*Quel métier!*" The now-crenelated ridge looks reasonably inviting, and I make my way over it.

Like a rocket, Jaccoux has taken off up the glacier with Colette gamely trying to keep up. I am content to amble along at my own pace—we are not roped since all of the crevasses in the upper part of the glacier are small and clearly visible. The sun has set and the moon is doing its best to chin itself on the Col des Hirondelles, a break in the range of mountains that demarcate the Franco-Italian border. A few clouds, born in the chill of the night air, cling to the vertical architecture of the *aiguilles*. Tomorrow we are going to traverse the needle of the Nun. To the left of the Mer de Glace as we go up is a wall of

The Aiguilles of Chamonix

GASTON RÉBUFFAT

aiguilles which have all been given ecclesiastic titles—the Monk, the Nun, the Bishop, and so on. The summit of the Nun is at 11,022 feet, a small alp, and by Chamonix standards it is not much of a climb. However, we have had two weeks of really bad weather, and everything higher is pretty thoroughly plastered in snow.

It is now quite dark and we are picking our way through the upper moraine with flashlights. Soon we find the *egralets*, a series of ladders, ramps, and rock passages with footholds that have been cut out of the rock leading vertically up the trail to the Couvercle. By the time we reach the trail it is pitch black and we are all sufficiently winded to stop for a breather and a swig of tea from my canteen. After a brisk walk of a half-hour or so by flashlight, we can see the lights of the refuge above us. In the dark it looks like an ocean liner in a sea of snow. It is a friendly and reassuring sight. The Couvercle is built of solid stone bricks and, during the height of the climbing season—July 1–September

1—it can, and often does, accommodate more than 250 climbers in several large dormitories. Simple but good meals are served, and the place is constantly being resupplied by porters and helicopters from the Chamonix Valley at relatively low cost, considering the effort it takes to bring the food up. It is now past the climbing season, and as we enter the main dining room there are perhaps forty people in it. Most of them, it turns out, are young *aspirants guides* (apprentice guides) who are in the process of taking their final examinations on snow and rock from the instructors of the Ecole Nationale de Ski et d'Alpinisme, who will decide whether or not they qualify as full-fledged guides.

There is a good deal of red wine being passed around among the *aspirants* and they look as if they are out on a pleasant excursion rather than taking an examination. The thought crosses my mind that it might be an ideal time to have an accident, if one is going to have one, considering the force that is assembled for a potential rescue.

Through the murk of pipe and cigarette smoke I make out the familiar craggy features of Gerard Herzog. Gerard is the brother of Maurice Herzog, the man who led the French expedition that climbed Annapurna in Nepal. Gerard, now in his fifties, is one of the best climbers in France. He is a writer and television producer and his wife José, an actress and singer, is one of the most beautiful women I have ever seen. Happily, José is also there; not only that, they have an enormous vat of delicately seasoned noodles which they offer to share with us. We order a couple of bottles of wine—this is, after all, France, and no climb in the Alps is complete without a good dose of red wine. Gerard and José are planning to do a long snow climb, but after several glasses of wine, the ambience has become such that they too decide to climb the Nun, and, it appears, so have a large contingent of *aspirants* and instructors. By ten the wine has been exhausted, and we turn into our bunks for a few hours of sleep.

It is 3:00 A.M. The guardian of the refuge has just turned on the lights in our dormitory. It is freezing cold and my first thought is that perhaps there is a terrible storm outside and I can go back to sleep. I peer tentatively out a window. Stars and planets are flickering brightly in the night sky—no storm. *Les étoiles*, Jaccoux," I announce. Jaccoux replies indistinctly, attempting to escape the grisly implications of my discovery by burying himself deeper in his blankets. Gerard stirs, and soon the five of us are groping our way downstairs to breakfast. The night before Jaccoux had decided that we had two alternatives: to get up very early to try to beat the *aspirants* to the Nun and avoid being showered by rocks from above; or to wait until the *aspirants* had climbed the Nun and were moving onto the Bishop. We have opted for the latter since it is hopeless to try to beat the *aspirants* who are all young and strong and will be moving like crazy. This has given us an extra hour to sleep. Breakfast consists of thick fresh bread with jam and honey and coffee with milk and sugar. We will have lunch on the Nun.

By the time we leave the Couvercle the sky has turned the clear, pastel blue of the early dawn of a lovely day. Our route leads up the snowfields back of the Couvercle. The snow is hard as rock and we have put on our crampons which in the snow make the crunching sound of someone eating corn on the cob. Colette has somehow lost a crampon. It has fallen off in the snow. By the time we recover it and she is shoed up again, we have all had a splendid and welcome fifteen-minute rest. By now the sun is beginning to come up in earnest, and the red rock of the *aiguilles* is bathed in a rosy glow. We can see various groups of *aspirants* on several rock faces shouting instructions to each other. We climb a very steep snow slope and come to rest on a somewhat precarious-looking tongue of snow which abuts the rock ribs of the Nun. Jaccoux and Gerard take their ropes out of their sacks, and we rope up in groups of three and two. Jaccoux takes a last puff on a cigarette and then launches himself onto the rock. He disappears, leaving only a trail of red rope. "*A toi*," I hear him say from somewhere. I give my plastic helmet a final reassuring twist and after a few abortive flapping motions against the rock, begin to climb. It is not very difficult, but I try to be careful not to dislodge any loose stones on my friends.

I reach Jaccoux, who has now lit his pipe and is calmly puffing away on a narrow rock ledge. He has wound the rope around a protruding rock and as I move up he coils the extra rope in a neat pile on the ledge. To save time he will move up to the next ledge from which he can secure me while I protect Colette. To make sure that nothing goes wrong, Jaccoux fastens me to a rock with a rope sling so that even if Colette should fall, there is no way that she—and the rest of us—can become detached from the Nun. Colette is climbing slowly but well, and while I am coiling in the rope leading from me to her, I have a minute to look up and catch a glimpse of the last of the *aspirants* disappearing along a ridge well above.

The five of us move steadily up the Nun like a quintuped attached together by nerves of red rope. Just below the summit we reach the only really difficult passage—a delicate blade of smooth rock which juts precariously over the glacier a few thousand feet below. The smooth surface of the blade is broken by a few small indentations that will have to serve as footholds. Eight feet or so up the blade I can see a piton, a metal wedge driven into a crack and left there permanently, glinting in the sun. Jaccoux heads up the rock in the direction of the piton. Good climbers always manage to stay away from the rock with their bodies so that their center of gravity is directly above their feet, thus imparting the greatest possible traction to the rubber soles of their climbing shoes. Jaccoux is a master at this technique, and when he climbs a rock face, he gives one the impression that he is going up a ladder with deep rungs. When I try it myself I usually find that the "rungs" are almost imperceptible indentations in the rock to which his feet have somehow adhered. Jaccoux has reached the piton. He takes a metal ring with a snap that opens by pressing on it—a carabiner—from a collection that he has been carrying like cartridges on a rope sling over his shoulder. The piton has a hole in the end protruding from the rock, and Jaccoux snaps his carabiner into it and then runs the rope through the fastener into the carabiner which snaps shut with a click. Now he is protected from below, since should he fall, his drop will be stopped by the rope attached to the piton. He continues up, reaches the summit, and settles himself into a place where he can watch the rest of us ascend.

I press a toe against the slab and, by wrapping part of an arm over a ledge, manage to move my foot into another minuscule

Gaston Rébuffat climbing
a smooth vertical wall,
Chamonix   GASTON RÉBUFFAT

indentation. I now see that by stretching my leg and pushing against the edge of the slab I can maneuver myself into a position from which I can make a lunge for the piton.

Holding on to pitons is considered bad form but, as I see it, it beats falling. Now, by pushing off against the piton, I succeed in reaching a rock ledge that leads directly to the summit. During the course of all this I have managed to cut a finger and it is bleeding generously. José, who is slithering her way up the slab, shouts up to me not to worry about it as she will fix everything at the summit. The summit is a tiny point barely capable of holding us all—hanging from it in different directions. José bandages my finger and as she does so she says, "Where but in France could you find a beautiful woman on the summit of the Nun to heal your finger?" It is a fine sentiment, and, somewhat winded, I settle down on a rock finger to have lunch in the bright sun.

It is very important to avoid being out in the Alps in the late afternoon. The weather turns bad and the snow melts on the glaciers, opening the crevasses. What is a safe romp on the frozen snow in the morning can become a dangerous nightmare in the afternoon. So after a quick lunch we head down. Descending is harder, at least for most people, myself included, than going up. It is difficult to maintain the right balance and get the necessary traction. Also, one is much more conscious of height. On the other hand, there is the consoling thought that each rope length brings one closer to home, i.e., the Couvercle. The first passage leading off of the Nun is a rappel. In a rappel one loops the rope between one's legs, around the back and over a shoulder. It is easier to carry out than to describe. The net effect is that one can then slide down the rope using the feet as guides along the wall. It is as if one were walking down the wall under the control of the rope. (In fact, there is so much friction from the rope that gloves must be worn, and, after a certain amount of experience, I have taken to wearing leather-lined pants.) It is a generally safe procedure provided that the rappel rope has been carefully placed and provided that there is a good terrace to land on below. It requires, above all, willing suspension of disbelief since the walls one goes down are usually absolutely vertical.

In any case, Jaccoux goes first, protected by Gerard with a security rope. Having two strong climbers with us, we enjoy the luxury of being able to send Jaccoux down to look for a landing place, with Gerard securing the rope. If Gerard had not been along, I would have gone first. Jaccoux disappears completely, and after a few minutes it is Colette's turn. As we watch, from above, she disappears over a rock and after a minute or so it is clear from what she is shouting that she is in serious trouble.

Not being able to see her, there is nothing to do but to let her down on the rope like a package. Gerard calls, telling her to use her feet against the rock as much as possible. Then, as the rope tightens around his back, he lets her down foot by foot while José and I try to do whatever we can to help. After a few anxious minutes, the rope becomes slack and we know she is down. Next, it is my turn.

The first step of the rappel is the hardest for me. One must give up the security of a comfortable ledge and go over the edge straight down, facing in toward the rock. I take a step or two down the wall with the rope sliding around my back. I look down and my heart sinks. Below there is nothing. No wonder Colette panicked. The rock face simply disappears below the overhang from which we have been rappeling. Jaccoux shouts up that everything is all right and tells me to simply put my weight on the rope and let go. Gerard calls down with reassurance. Knowing that there is no choice and that I must keep my nerves under control, I take a deep breath and swing backwards on the rope. For an instant I dangle in midair but then the rope swings me back against the face below, and after what seems like a lifetime I can feel my feet back on the rock and can walk down the rest of the face. I feel an enormous sense of relief and elation. José and Gerard rappel down with no trouble at all. From our ledge we can see that the summit of the Nun looks like a perfect rock *capuchon*—a Nun's bonnet. Jaccoux leads us skillfully from ledge to ledge downward to the glacier below.

By the time we reach it the hard snow of the morning has

Claude Jaccoux
negotiating
an overhang,
Chamonix

turned to the consistency of cream soup, and I slosh and slide my way back to the Couvercle a bit behind the others. They are sunning themselves on the terrace of the refuge, and Colette and José, brown in the sun, look like fashion models from *Elle*. I stop for a brief drink and head for the Mer de Glace. Jaccoux and Colette are staying at the Couvercle since he has another client coming up from the valley to meet him there. Gerard and José will come down later, and I am happy to be alone with my thoughts. It is a glorious afternoon. Wildflowers peer timidly from behind patches of light snow. Streams of clear water are falling onto the glacier. I stop on a rock and the entire group of *aspirants* passes me running, literally bounding from rock to rock, on their way down to the valley. Crowds of guides and tourists make their way up the glacier, and by four in the afternoon I am at the ladders leading to the Hotel Montenvers and the *coupe perrichon*. As I stop and look out over the great walls of the French Alps, it occurs to me that never have I felt more alive or happier.

4   *Le Poids sur le Ski aval*

I first took up skiing as a child of ten or so, in the late 1930s. Rochester, New York, where I grew up, had, and still does have, heavy, severe winters, and winter sports, especially ice-skating, were exceedingly popular. I soon found out that I had weak ankles, so ice-skating was a disaster for me; hence the skis. With the aid of a Boy Scout pamphlet, a small group of us attempted to teach ourselves skiing on a broad slope in Ellison Park, near where we lived. Lifts were unknown to us, and our ski equipment was such that the user of the oldest ski yet to be discovered—the ski was found in Hoting. Sweden, and is about forty-five hundred years old—would have felt himself in familiar territory among us. ("Ski" is the Norwegian word for "snowshoe," and the Hoting ski essentially resembles a snowshoe; there are, however, Scandinavian skis over two thousand years old with turned-up, pointed tips which resemble the modern version.) We had wooden skis—mainly hickory—with a groove carved in the bottom along the axis of the ski; this groove, which produced a small raised line in the middle of each ski track, was supposed to make the skis more stable. A rule of the day was that skis, whatever the skier's proficiency, should be one's height plus the length of an outstretched arm. Some of the more mechanical-minded among us tacked metal strips along the sides of our ski bottoms. These helped to preserve the wood from abrasion—without them our skis would have been chipped away after a season or so—and they also helped in controlling descents when the terrain was icy, for they could be edged into the ice. Waxing these wooden skis was a ritual that all but approached high alchemy. Waxes came in every color and variety, and were to be applied in layers with cheesecloth whenever the snow conditions warranted—whenever the snow was wet or sticky. (As I recall, the first wax I used was my

61

mother's floor wax—a limited success.) We spent hours in basements happily applying and scraping off wax.

The attachment of skis to the feet evolved somewhat during those years. At first, there had been a system of leather straps that more or less tied the boot to the ski. One put the toe of the boot in an open iron wedge, buckled the straps over the boot, and hoped for the best. Sometime in the early thirties, the cable binding was introduced. The old toe wedge remained, but the back of the boot had a groove carved in it, and through this groove went a metal cable—spring-wound—that wedged one's foot into the toe iron. These cables had three or four possible tensions, depending on how they were adjusted. (There was a gadget in front of the binding into which the cable could be set, in various positions. One then tightened the cable by pulling forward on a lever.) In adjusting the cable tension, one was faced with an unpleasant choice: either to attach the ski so loosely that it would fall off at the slightest movement of the foot or to attach it so tightly that it could never come off and there would inevitably be a tangle of skis and feet when one fell. It is a miracle that none of us broke a leg or an ankle with this arrangement, which was extremely dangerous, but, then, children are rarely hurt in ski falls. Our ski boots were leather hiking boots with the soles modified—cut square by the manufacturer—to fit into the toe iron and with the groove cut into the heel for the cable. The system worked about as well with ordinary hiking boots, or even with gym shoes. Ski poles were made of light bamboo, and each pole had a large wheel of leather near the bottom. Special ski clothes were unknown to us.

Such skiing instruction as we were able to extract from the Boy Scout pamphlet on skiing dealt with what is now known as the Arlberg technique. This is a method of skiing that was invented by Hannes Schneider, a native of Stuben, in the Arlberg of Austria. His father had wanted him to be a cheese-maker, but in 1907 Schneider had begun teaching skiing at the Hotel Post, in St. Anton, where he worked out the details of his method. Soon he was winning races, and by the end of the First World War the Arlberg technique was essentially the standard

European ski method. Some of Schneider's disciples migrated to this country, and Schneider himself, fleeing the Nazis, came to North Conway, New Hampshire, in 1939. (He died in 1955.) In a recent issue of the *New York Times*, Michael Strauss, the paper's ski correspondent, interviewed Herbert Schneider, Hannes's son, in North Conway, where Schneider was teaching *his* son, Hannes, age six, to ski—with the Arlberg, naturally. Schneider recalled his father's giving him his first pair of skis, when he was five. "He gave me wooden skis that had no steel edges, and Huitfeldt bindings that had toe irons and leather straps with a buckle that attached to the boot with a metal snap," Schneider said. Fritz Huitfeldt, a Norwegian, introduced this system of metal bindings in 1894. " 'Herbert,' I remember him saying, 'with this kind of modern ski gear, you can conquer the *Welt*.' "

The Arlberg technique begins with the snowplow principle, which consists in placing the two skis at an angle to each other in front—the tips close together and the tails separated by several feet—with the inside edges of the skis slanted into the snow. The snowplow is an indispensable maneuver for slowing down or stopping when there is no room to turn the skis. Next, one progresses to the snowplow turn, with the skis in the basic snowplow position but with the skier's weight shifted to one ski or the other, depending on the direction he wants to turn. Basically, it is a turn in which the snowplow braking action is continuous. Then, at the next step, the braking action is released, and the skier actually picks up speed—at least momentarily—as he turns. This represents the real quantum leap in learning to ski. The first maneuver of this type one learns in the Arlberg method is the stem turn. To change direction when one is traversing a hill diagonally, one "stems" the uphill ski—slides its tail uphill—while gradually shifting the weight to it as one begins to turn. When one overcomes the sense of loss of control as one turns down into the steepness of the slope, one begins to be a true skier. The *ne plus ultra* of the Arlberg technique is the christiania turn (Christiania was an ancient name for Oslo), which is now usually called the parallel turn. Here the skier skids the skis along the snow parallel to each other, and, by maneuvering the body weight and, often, the ski poles, all but tangos down a slope.

Much of this was explained in the Boy Scout pamphlet, but because, for one thing, we had no instructors to interpret the rather arcane serial drawings, and because, for another, the slope at Ellison Park could hardly have exceeded fifteen degrees, none of us got much beyond the snowplow turn. Indeed, a typical afternoon would begin with a few snowplow descents of the hill, each one followed, since we had no tow, by a long climb. (The first patent on a mechanical ski tow was issued to a Swiss engineer, Gerhard Mueller, in 1932. He used a hemp rope and some old motorcycle parts. The first tow in North America was installed in the Laurentians, in Canada, in 1932, and the first tow in the United States was installed at Woodstock, Vermont, in 1934. It was powered by a jacked-up Model T Ford, and it used a Manila-hemp rope to tow skiers up five hundred feet, at a cost of a dollar a day.) In any event, after our snowplows, not knowing what else to do, we would simply barrel straight down the hill, falling into a snowbank at the bottom to stop. I persisted in this for several years, at the end of which I could say, with all sincerity, that I did not have the foggiest idea of how to ski.

After the early 1940s, when I made a few unsatisfactory forays with my rudimentary Boy Scout Arlberg technique, I essentially gave up skiing for twenty-five years. It was just too frustrating. During that period, I took up guided mountain climbing—primarily in the French Alps, in the summers. In Chamonix, over the years, I got to know a large number of the best alpine skiers in Europe—racers, members of various Olympic teams, guides who taught skiing in the winter. One of the more remarkable skiers among them is Sylvain Saudan, a Swiss guide, now in his late thirties, who has become world-famous for his exploits in what the French call "*ski extrême.*" In the late 1960s, Saudan got the idea of skiing down some of the most difficult snow and ice climbs in the Alps, thus giving birth to this form of skiing. He has now extended his activities to North America, and in June of 1972 he skied down the southwest face of Mount McKinley, in

Alaska—the highest mountain on this continent. (Saudan did not quite get to the top of McKinley, but since there was a hundred-mile-an-hour wind blowing that day he can be forgiven.) Most recently he skied off of the summit of Nun Kun in Kashmir which is 23,403 feet high. Saudan, now sponsored by manufacturers of various sorts of ski equipment, gives lectures about these descents, and illustrates the lectures with breathtaking films. When I first met him, at a café in Chamonix, he had just begun this enterprise. He is a charming, modest fellow, and, like many of the best skiers, he is short and compact. A friend once observed, "Sylvain has no neck." The reason he gave me for skiing down the snow slides was simple: he thought it was fun. He was always somewhat mysterious about his next project, primarily because, following his example, several other skiers began skiing down steep alpine slopes, and he didn't want a lot of competitors buzzing around him. People who have skied with Saudan note that he has a method of "windshield-wiper" turning in deep snow which enables him to control his descent by a series of zigzag traverses even when the slope exceeds sixty degrees. On a typical difficult descent, Saudan makes about two thousand turns. All the skiers kept telling me that I was missing a whole alpine world by not learning to ski correctly—that the beauty of the Alps in winter was beyond anything you could imagine from what you saw of them in the summer. My response was always that one of these years I would come to the Alps and learn to ski, but, perhaps haunted by memories of Ellison Park, I kept putting the lessons off.

A few winters ago, finding myself with a little free time, I finally decided to take up skiing again. The French Alps, where I went to learn, are dotted with ski stations. These fall into two basic categories—the "classic" ski areas, such as Chamonix, Mégève, and Val d'Isère, which are old mountain towns, and the newer areas, which the French call *"balcon,"* or "balcony," resorts. (Val d'Isère will soon celebrate its fiftieth anniversary as a ski station. Before the early 1930s, it was a peaceful mountain village occasionally visited by skiers as a way station on one of the alpine ski tours that were, and still are, frequently made in the spring. The alpine ski-touring season begins in February and lasts through the end of May.) The virtue of the old stations is that they offer more than skiing; they have something of the atmosphere of real village life, although by now this has been all but buried by skiers. The drawback is that the skiing is not necessarily very well centralized. In Chamonix, for example, the skier must rely on automobiles and buses to take him to the various ski areas up and down the valley. The newer ski resorts—the oldest of them is Courchevel, which was constructed in the 1940s and 1950s—are usually in the foothills, or natural balconies, of the really high Alps. These stations have been constructed from scratch, on what was previously pastureland. Being new, they have lent themselves to unconventional architectural experiments. Most of the stations consist of closely interconnected buildings—almost a single architectural unit that has been contoured to the terrain. At Les Arcs, one of the newer *balcon* stations, there is a hotel that is contoured so closely to the shape of the hill on which it has been built that people have used the roof as a ski run.

An experienced skier coming to the Alps would certainly want to visit one of the classic stations, to enjoy real high-mountain skiing, frequently on glaciers. But for an inexperienced or intermediate skier the *balcon* stations fill the bill. Quite simple slopes abound, along with more difficult ones, and the ski lifts begin fifty feet or so from one's hotel room. The well-known American ski writer Harvey Edwards, who has lived in Chamonix for the last twelve years, and who is not enthusiastic about the *balcon* resorts—he misses the village life—admitted in an article in the *Mountain Gazette*, a Denver-based monthly devoted to skiing and mountaineering, that "skiing at the *balcon* resorts is certainly more convenient sport." He went on, "Things are superbly organized. The lifts are close by, the slopes well groomed, ski classes are held on schedule. The *balcon* resorts are great, efficiently organized machines." And this, he adds, "is exactly one of the criticisms I level at them." In any event, considering what I wanted to do—learn to ski—a *balcon* resort seemed just right.

There are many *balcon* resorts, but I had no problem choosing the one I wanted to go to—La Plagne, above the valley of the Isère, ninety miles southeast of Geneva. Apart from considerations of convenience, I chose La Plagne because many of my closest climbing associates teach skiing there. The ski school at La Plagne had been run since its inception, in 1962, by Pierre Leroux, who is a Parisian by birth and is one of the rare Chamonix guides from outside the Chamonix Valley, having been admitted to the company for his alpine exploits. Leroux was, among other things, a member of the 1955 French expedition to Nepal, which first climbed Makalu, and later, in 1962, he was a member of the expedition that climbed Jannu, also in Nepal, (Makalu, at 27,790 feet, is the fifth-highest mountain in the world; Jannu, though it is nearly half a mile lower, is considered a more difficult climb.) Now in his early fifties, Leroux is an urbane, carefully tailored man, and he resembles an articulate, somewhat *sportif* French businessman rather than a professional mountaineer, but this impression of him changes rapidly when one sees him climb or ski. Upon coming to La Plagne, he assembled a group of ski instructors which included several mountain guides, and among them was Jaccoux. When I decided to go to La Plagne, I wrote to Jaccoux to find out whether the oil shortage had affected the place and whether there was any snow. Of oil, the French had, for the moment, plenty. (When I arrived, there were several broadcasts on the national radio network praising the *"politique Arabe,"* with its oil dividend. When I left, however, the franc had started to plummet sharply, and the price of crude oil had more than doubled, which meant a rise of 20 to 30 percent in gasoline prices. No one seemed to know what was in store for the future. Still, ski resorts were doing a record business, and one had the feeling that people were taking a fling before the bottom fell out.) Of snow, the Alps seemed to have something of a shortage, especially early in the season. This lack has occurred for several years, and possibly may be an aspect of the "greenhouse effect"—the trapping of radiation by an increasingly polluted atmosphere. But Jaccoux assured me that there would be plenty of snow for my purpose. Indeed, in its publicity brochures La Plagne offers a sort of insurance against a lack of snow:

> Si c'est blanc, vous payez;
> Si c'est vert, on vous paye.

If at any time during a skier's visit at least twenty lifts out of the thirty-nine available at La Plagne are not functioning because there isn't enough snow, the station will pay the skier's bill for each day of skiing missed. So far, no one has collected. All visitors to La Plagne reach the ski station, which has three sections, by driving up the serpentine mountain road that leads from the small Savoyard village of Aime, in the valley, to the lowest section. This is La Plagne itself, at 1,970 meters, or 6,500 feet; two separate satellite sections, at 2,100 meters, are connected to the lower level both by roads and by *téléphériques*. (A third satellite has now opened.) About six kilometers from the lower station is the entrance to an ancient lead mine. This mine and agriculture provided the sole occupations for the Savoyards in the region until the construction of the ski station began, in 1961. In consequence, young people were leaving to find jobs elsewhere. Whenever one considers the inevitable destruction of virgin alpine territory and the associated ecological damage, one must also take into account this economic reality in the mountain communities. Skiing has kept these valleys alive.

La Plagne is not especially noted as an *après-ski* resort—among the *balcon* resorts, Courchevel, about sixty kilometers away, has the greatest reputation for night life—and, as I discovered, it is quite rare to find anyone but a few hardy young souls up much after 10:00 P.M. However, the stores stay open until eight during the season—December to Easter—seven days a week. Around 7:00 P.M. the day I arrived, Jaccoux and I wandered into the Émile Allais Ski Service. (Allais, a great French ski racer of the late 1930s, pioneered one of the early successor techniques to the Arlberg.) My aim was to rent a modest assortment of equipment suitable for the task at hand.

In his film *Sleeper*, Woody Allen, wrapped in tinfoil, awakens after a two-hundred-year sleep to confront a technologically incomprehensible landscape. I know how he felt. Not only have ski techniques changed greatly since I first tried the spot but the wooden ski and the leather boot of my childhood have vanished, and in their stead *chez* Allais was an all but incomprehensible chaos of plastic, fiber glass, and metal. The basic shapes seemed familiar, but they bore roughly the relation to their predecessors that Secretariat bears to the shaggy prehistoric horses of Central Asia. With a lot of help from the *Encyclopedia of Skiing*, I was subsequently able to piece together some idea of what has happened to ski equipment in the last twenty-five years. Until the mid-1950s, most skis were still made of hickory or ash. A number of aircraft engineers—most notably Howard Head, of Baltimore, who was an engineer with the Glenn L. Martin aircraft company at the time—had been seriously experimenting with the use of modern, lightweight metals in combination with wood for skis. In 1950, after three years of experimentation, Head introduced his first production model of a kind of sandwich ski—a black plastic coating on the top and bottom, over two aluminum layers bonded to a wooden core. He sold three hundred pairs. These Head skis were both lighter and stronger than their wooden counterparts, and, moreover, they turned much more easily. By the 1960s, metal had begun to give way to plastics, especially fiber glass, which can be produced in varying degrees of resilience. Almost all skis now have a running surface of polyethylene plastic, which, as the encyclopedia points out, has the virtue of not sticking to anything— "and, in particular, not to snow"—and is thus an ideal surface for sliding. Applying wax to such a surface is an act that, under ordinary circumstances, most skiers would now regard as bordering on lunacy. (Racers still wax.) The old philosophy about ski lengths has also changed radically. With the advent of plastic skis, there developed what the French call the *"ski évolutif,"* or what is known in the United States as the G.L.M.— the graduated-length method. The beginner learns to ski on very short skis—an adult would begin with a ski of 130 to 160 centimeters, or four feet three inches to five feet three inches. The longest standard ski made is 220 centimeters, or seven feet three inches, and a typical recreational ski for a normal adult male would be 200 to 210 centimeters. The advantages of short skis for beginners are that they are extremely easy to turn and that they are the closest thing, in feel, to wearing shoes. The disadvantage is that they do not perform well in deep snow or in icy conditions, and so are unsuitable for general alpine skiing. Furthermore, once the novice begins to feel at home on his short skis, it can be nearly impossible to wean him away to the next length, which will inevitably feel strange. Considering my history, Jaccoux suggested that I start with a pair of skis 160 centimeters long, so I rented a flashy red pair of Rossignols—a standard French variety.

Next came the boots. The change in boot styles in the last twenty-five years is nearly total. Boots are now made almost entirely of plastic. Many are fastened in the front with buckles, but some open in the back with hinges. The old system of heavy woollen socks has given way to an interior molding of plastic foam or wax, which is injected into bladders inside the boots when one buys them; the hot foam or wax then cools and solidifies around the foot. (A layer of thermal insulation protects the foot and prevents one from being burned in this process.) The fit is so precise that one can, in principle, ski barefoot, but most people wear thin socks. The colors of the boots are fantastic—bright yellows, blues, and oranges. Most of the new boots come up well above the ankle, and this new length and the new bindings raise an interesting safety question. All modern bindings are of the "safety-release" type. One puts the toe of the boot into a metal clamp and presses down with the heel, which snaps a spring device shut. The spring is designed to release when it receives a violent shock, and the toe part is set on a pivot, so that the release is activated when the ski receives a shock from any direction. This has had the paradoxical consequence that practically all serious accidents—involving broken bones—now occur at slow speeds, for a skier can twist a leg enough to break it, or can dislocate a knee, without sufficient shock to release the binding. (I am speaking here not of accidents that ski racers have but of the kind of accidents that befall normal recreational skiers.) Furthermore, because of the high rise of the boots, ankle accidents rarely occur—one simply breaks a leg. During my trip, I encountered an American surgeon who specializes in ski-accident cases. We discussed the relative merits of breaking an ankle—the old-fashioned way— and breaking a leg. An ankle break, he noted, takes six or seven weeks to heal but may leave the ankle vulnerable to arthritis in later life. A leg break takes several months to heal, and the leg usually recovers, although, he said, breaks resulting from skiing accidents are now especially nasty, because of the high boots. I asked him which he would prefer, and he said, "Neither." As an afterthought, he remarked, "If skiing were a job and not a sport, it might well have been outlawed as too dangerous."

The choice of boots *chez* Allais was among five hundred or so equally bizarre-looking pairs. Finally, Jaccoux said he would lend me an old plastic pair—ankle-high, leather-colored, and large enough for a comfortable heavy woollen sock. The only piece of ski equipment that I actually owned was an ancient pair of gabardine over-the-boot pants with stirrups to hold them down. I think they had a considerable vogue only a few decades ago. Some years back, wool-nylon-Spandex stretch pants came on the scene, along with nylon parkas. The early versions of these parkas, while elegant, had a remarkable and unexpected property: they were slick that anyone who fell at the top of a moderately steep hill had a pretty good chance of sliding all the way to the bottom. The present parkas are made of materials that have rough textures to make them slide-resistant. Thus outfitted—light aluminum poles came along with the skis—I was to present myself at the ski school the next day for a diagnostic session with Jaccoux.

When I arrived, late the following morning, carrying the skis, I discovered not only Jaccoux but also Yannick Martenet, an old friend and a guide from Saint-Gervais, who is noted for his somewhat mordant alpine humor. Martenet announced that he was going to come along with us, because he hadn't had a good laugh in several days. He and Jaccoux tied into their skis and moved off in the direction of an intermediate lift called the St.-Esprit. I put on my Rossignols, and found, to my bewilderment, that they were stuck to the snow. The damn things simply would not glide. They resisted every attempt at forward or backward motion. Fortunately, another ski instructor, who had been watching me, came to the rescue. From him I learned that metal or plastic skis, polyethylene surface or not, have a property that, as a physicist, I might have anticipated: they cannot be put on the snow until they have been "refrigerated" for at least fifteen minutes after being brought out of a warm room—in this case, the ski room in the hotel. Otherwise, the warm skis melt the snow around them, and it instantly refreezes as ice; the ice takes the form of irregular lumps glued to the bottom of the skis, which will not glide. It took me about five minutes to scrape this stuff off, and afterward I could dimly make out Jaccoux and Martenet standing in the distance smoking cigarettes. Whatever the defects of our old wooden skis, they never produced a problem like that.

I learned later that there were two routes to the St.-Esprit—a gentle slope leading down from the hotels, and a "shortcut." Jaccoux and Martenet had taken the shortcut, which led along level snow and then made a sudden drop to the lift, about three hundred feet away. I don't know how steep this drop really is, but to me it appeared to be the steepest-looking snow slope I had ever been on without crampons, an ice axe, and a rope. "*La voilà*," Jaccoux remarked, pointing down to the lift station and indicating that I was meant, somehow, to get down there. A good skier can snowplow down anything, but one thing I was sure of was that *I* would never be able to snowplow straight down the thing. I headed off on a more or less horizontal trajectory, hoping that as I lost altitude something would come to mind. Shortly thereafter, I ran onto a snowbank, fell, and slid down several feet. The fall had the satisfactory consequence that my skis were now turned in the opposite direction, so I could start another horizontal traverse. I reasoned that about six of these maneuvers would get me near the bottom. After the next traverse and fall and slide, Jaccoux shouted down that I had better stop where I was. He and Martenet zipped down, and Jaccoux announced, "*Jeremy, franchement, ta position est épouvantable.*" The French technical term for "ski stance" is "*position*," and a *film d'épouvante* is the sort of movie that features Boris Karloff and Bela Lugosi. Jaccoux then demonstrated how one should perform such a traverse. The two skis are meant to be parallel to each other, with *le ski amont* (the uphill ski) slightly in advance of *le ski aval* (the ski closer to the valley). The key—and this phrase was to be repeated at least six hundred times in the next nine days—was "*le poids sur le ski aval*," meaning that one keeps the weight on the downhill ski. All control on the *trace direct en traversée*, as the French call the traverse, comes from putting weight on the downhill ski. Moreover, Jaccoux said that I was leaning backward—the most common fault of novice skiers. I should flex my knees until I could feel the backs of my ski boots pressing against the backs of my legs. (Some of the modern boots are canted forward, to lock the knees in the proper position.) Furthermore, contrary to the instinct of self-preservation, the upper part of the body should be angled out *away* from the hill; in fact, one must almost lean out over the hill and look down at the valley. This increases the pressure on the downhill ski, and hence the control. I kept wanting to lean into the hill. This releases the downhill ski, with a subsequent loss of control, and one begins to slide sidewise down the slope. To stop at the end of the traverse, Jaccoux proposed, I should try to turn uphill. This, at least, appeared to solve the problem of how to get across the hill and stop without falling down, leaving only the question of how to turn the skis around to begin the next *trace direct*. Jaccoux thought that I had enough to concentrate on for the moment without getting into moving turns—they would come later—so he proposed a *conversion*, known to Americans as the kick turn. This is a static turn in which the two poles are planted firmly in the snow; one then lifts the downhill ski—which until this point has been parallel to the uphill ski across the slope. The front of the ski is lifted entirely off the snow, with the tail planted firmly in the snow. One then pivots the ski and puts it back on the snow so that the two skis are now parallel but pointing in opposite directions. Then, in a single motion, and with all the weight on the downhill ski, one swings the uphill ski around so that it points in the desired direction; it thus becomes the downhill ski, and one plants the appropriate pole below the new downhill ski. The two skis are now pointed in the same direction and one has turned a full 180 degrees. A number of *conversions* were made by one and all, and after much tangling of skis and poles I acquired at least the rudiments of the method. By converting and traversing, I managed to arrive at the St.-Esprit without falling again. When I remarked to Jaccoux that the whole business seemed very technical to me, he said that it was. Alpine skiing, he felt, is a much more technically complex business than climbing, and, in his opinion, a person who is only normally gifted requires at least four full seasons of alpine skiing to become *convenable*, or acceptable.

The St.-Esprit is a fairly typical poma, or button lift—a device that has a metal bar suspended from a guide wire, with a button-shaped disc at the rear end of the bar. One straddles the bar, holding on to it with one hand and leaning one's buttocks against the button—an arrangement that has given the machine the common name of *"tire-fesses,"* which means one is pulled up the hill by one's tail. Martenet got aboard, and I was somewhat surprised to see him lifted suddenly, with both skis off the ground. This is apparently standard practice with the longer *tire-fresses*—the St.-Esprit is over a mile long—so one must hold on firmly and make sure that one's skis are not crossed, because if one lands after such a jump with crossed skis one risks a bad fall. On some of the button lifts, one is propelled into the air several times in the course of the trip—whenever the terrain rises sharply—and it is just as well to be prepared. Near the top was a sign instructing one to detach oneself after thirty meters— one lowers the metal bar, and slips the disc through the legs, and off one goes.

We meandered back down the broad trail—more *trace directs* and *conversions*, and an occasional snowplow—while other skiers were gliding on all sides like so many birds. The trail brought us back to La Plagne, and I was pleased to have got down—albeit very slowly—in one piece and without so very many falls. Jaccoux had an appointment with another client, but before he left he remarked that I might show some progress if I skied perhaps thirty miles a day for the next week. Then he offered a suggestion that made my heart sink. "At your stage, you should enroll in a group lesson, a *cours collectif*. It is the only way to learn," he said, "and, moreover, the atmosphere in the classes is *très sympathique*." There is nothing that I like less than group athletic lessons. The idea brings to mind the most dismal aspects of Boy Scout hikes, high school calisthenics classes, and summer camps. I told him I would consider the matter carefully, actually intending, even if it meant any number of broken legs, to get no closer than several kilometers to any group lesson. With this, the skiing ended for day one.

The next day was Sunday. It was a magnificent day, and warm sun glistened off the mountains. My first thought was to spend the day reading on the terrace in front of the hotel. Like the hotels in all the *balcon* resorts, those in La Plagne have terraces that extend out over the snow; in fact, one may ski along in front of the hotels and shops, from one terrace to another. Having rented the ski gear, though, I felt I should venture out for at least an hour or so on my skis. As I was passing the ski school, I heard a familiar voice calling. It belonged to J. L. Bernezat—known universally as Bernouze. Bernouze's wife, Odette, who is a ski instructor and one of the best women climbers in France, is known as Bernouzette. When I first met Bernezat, he was a full-time alpine guide in the summer and taught skiing at La Plagne in the winter. For the past decade, he has been living in the Sahara for six months of the year, with Odette and their camels, and organizing treks, climbs, and Land-Rover trips in the desert for all sorts of travel groups. He and his wife now climb and ski only for the fun of it, and, by chance, he had come up for the day from Grenoble, where his home office is, for some recreational skiing. He suggested that we ski together for an hour or so. I explained that I skied badly and would spoil his day, but he said that since he had not been on skis for six months, he was not sure he knew how to turn anymore. With this, we hopped a nearby button lift and took off for a relatively simple slope. Needless to say, Bernezat had not forgotten how to turn, and he repeated some of the instruction of the previous day, ending with the same advice: Join a class. A message was beginning to get through.

Normally, there are no group lessons on Sunday at La Plagne, so I decided to use the rest of the afternoon to look into the matter. I soon made several discoveries. The first was that the lessons are very reasonably priced. The fee—which is set by the national ski instructors' union—is fifty-five francs for a card of six tickets, or slightly less than two dollars a ticket. Each ticket entitles you to one lesson. When I was at La Plagne, the classes were given from 9:45 to 11:45 in the morning, and from 2:15 to 4:15 in the afternoon, so the cost came to less than a dollar an hour. There are seven levels of instruction, I learned, ranging from the *Cours accueil*, for people who have never had skis on, to

Cours 1. In addition, there is specialized instruction in racing techniques and the like. These divisions are standardized in all of France, so that a student who has moved up to a certain division may feel free to enter the same division at any ski station. The divisions also mean that a skier's degree of competence can be determined before he undertakes true cross-country alpine skiing—tours on glacial terrain lasting for several days—in which it is absolutely essential that all the skiers have a technical mastery over what the French call *"tous terrains, toutes neiges"* (any terrain in any kind of snow or ice). Jaccoux, whom I talked with later that Sunday, told me that only certified alpine guides who are also ski instructors are legally entitled to take people on glaciers, and that he will take skiers on cross-country glacier tours only if they have moved up to *Cours 3*—true parallel skiing. He also told me that the instructors in the group classes are paid every two weeks, when the money received for tickets and cards is added up and then divided, according to a union-established formula, among all the instructors in the school. This means that it is in the interest of each instructor to make sure that the school as a whole is functioning well, and it means that it is in the interest of every instructor, whatever his national reputation, to teach classes at all levels. Jaccoux was president of the Syndicat des Guides de France—the guides' national union—and has a national reputation for both guiding and skiing. Nonetheless, the week before I came to La Plagne he had instructed a *Cours 6*—the next-to-lowest level—and he said that by the end of the week his students were taking simple daylong alpine tours. When I asked him what class I should enter *if* I decided to take group lessons, he said, *"Cours 6."* By the end of the day, I had made up my mind, bought my card of six tickets, and asked who the instructor would be. "Régis Villien," I was told. *"Un jeune—très sympathique."*

The next morning, after refrigerating my skis, I made my way up a small snow hill to the area where the ski-school students were to assemble. Poles had been stuck in the snow at uniform intervals, each with a round placard on top giving the number of the *cours* whose members were to assemble at that spot. There is nothing to stop one from entering a class at any level, but a few minutes of observation will enable an instructor to weed out people who have overestimated their abilities. In the elementary classes, there can be as many as twenty skiers during the busy periods of the season, which coincide with school vacations, but since my visit was in January—between vacations—things were relatively uncrowded. Ultimately, eight of us assembled by our pole. There were a husband and wife from Paris and two girls who had come with a ski club from Paris, but the rest of us were total strangers. Yet by the end of the week we had become almost a family unit. We had got to know a good deal about one another, and whenever we encountered another group we all tried to put on a good performance on behalf of our own. There is nothing like several good falls in snow up to one's neck—and we all had plenty—to expose one's vulnerability and reveal a good deal about one's emotional state. I have never attended a group psychotherapy session, but I would not be surprised to find a similar atmosphere there. After some initial awkwardness, everyone genuinely tried to help everyone else; we all needed all the help we could get, and no one was above asking for it.

Like the French *lycées*, ski classes start on time, and at 9:40 the instructors came out of the ski school; they wear a sort of uniform with a cloth patch on the jacket indicating that they are instructors. A young man detached himself from the rest and glided up to where we were assembled. This was Régis. There was something about him that was instantly likable. He had a great shock of hair and an infectious laugh. After taking our tickets, Régis made sure that no one had any residual ice on the running surface of his skis, and then led us off to *le Baby*—the easiest button lift in La Plagne, which rises to the magnificent height of thirteen meters. There we found ourselves surrounded by babies—tiny children with miniature plastic skis, most of whom were wearing scaled-down versions of ski racers' numbered cloth bibs, which in their case bore a small deer, indicating that they, too, were in class. Leading one of these Lilliputian parades was Henri Pollet, a large Chamonix guide, looking like a serious and schoolmasterly Gulliver.

We took our turn on the lift, and when we had lined up at the top, Régis asked what at first seemed an odd question: Did we know how to fall? Most of us felt we had fallen enough to qualify for an expert falling class, but it had never occurred to me that there might be a *correct* way to fall. Régis pointed out that while no one likes to fall, emergency situations could arise in which it would be better to take a planned fall than to run out of control into, say, a tree. He shoved off, sat down on his skis to get as low to the snow as possible, leaned back, with his chin close to his chest, so that he wouldn't hit his head, and, just as he reached the snow, stretched out flat on his back, using his arms to cushion the impact. In a real fall, his safety bindings would have released, and he asked us to see that the thin elastic loops attached to our bindings were securely fastened to our lower legs. This arrangement keeps the skis from running away after the binding has been sprung. There is nothing more dangerous to skiers on a track than a loose ski coming down from above; a heavy, pointed, rapidly moving object, it can inflict serious harm. Next, of course, Régis showed us how to get up. The skis are swung downhill and placed parallel across the fall line—the line of steepest descent on the slope at a given point. By pushing on the poles, if necessary, one can eventually right oneself. We then all fell and got up several times.

Next, Régis instructed us to come down the hill one at a time, and he thereupon skied off to the bottom to study our form individually. Here the various personalities in the group began to reveal themselves. The timid inched down, clinging to the snowplow maneuver for dear life. A young Parisian named Hubert said amiably, at the top, that he tended to be somewhat *cassecou*—breakneck—and that in skiing the thing that really interested him was speed; to him, stopping and turning were minor inconveniences. With that, he pushed off in a tremendous leap, flew directly down the hill, with his skis crossed, and crashed below us—a performance that was to be repeated several dozen times a day for a week. Each time, he would rise from the snow swearing that he would never ski out of control again. After we had gone down and back to the top, Régis led off again, and we were to play follow-the-leader—all eight of us in a line doing successive snowplow turns. This was about the peak of my existing technique; all the rest would be essentially new. And, indeed, before lunch Régis gave us two new exercises to perform. The first was a snowplow, but of a different breed from any I had done. Régis went to the bottom of the slope and planted his two ski poles like a slalom gate—a few feet apart. We were to ski straight down the hill, with our skis parallel and not checking our speed (a schuss), go through the gate, and stop with a snowplow. Among skiers, perhaps the most widely appreciated of Newton's laws of motion is the one stating that an acceleration, however small, will produce, if it is applied long enough, a velocity of any magnitude. The Baby hill was fairly flat, but it was long enough so that by the time one had schussed down to Régis's gate one had worked up a respectable speed, and I, at least, had to fight the temptation to cheat by applying a little snowplow before I got to the bottom. Finally, I learned to bend my knees enough so as to edge the skis firmly, and thus use the snowplow as a braking device at higher speeds. The last exercise of the morning was a first attempt at a technique for dealing with bumps. Many bumps—especially successive ones—are taken by turning around them or moving over them and turning at the same time, but since our turning was still in a very primitive stage, Régis wanted us to practice going over a good-sized bump without falling or panicking. Just such a bump is provided on the Baby, and we were told to keep our weight forward and our knees fully bent. The fatal mistake is to lean backward at the moment of impact. The skis will go out in front, and one will sit down hard. One after another, we schussed down the hill, leaning forward for dear life and leaping perhaps three feet into the air upon hitting the bump. It was a slightly scary but not unpleasant sensation.

In the French ski resorts, the lunch break is taken seriously, for reasons apart from the obvious one. It is very important not to overwork at skiing, for fatigue is a skier's worst enemy. The *Encyclopedia of Skiing* says, "A tired skier does not ski well. In this connection, avoid taking 'one last run.' It is a superstition among skiers never to say, 'Let us take a last run.' (It may really become your last run for a while.) The superstition has a good basis in fact. If you are tired and yet tempted to take just one more run, you are stretching it; this is when you get hurt." I was meeting Jaccoux for lunch, and I decided to take the opportunity to ask him how one becomes a *moniteur*, or ski instructor, in France. It turned out to be a complex business—something like the stages one goes through to become a mountain guide—and, like that course of training, it is all nationally supervised. One must undergo at least six years of training to become a fully licensed French ski instructor. The first step, which the candidate usually takes at about eighteen, and which is open, as all the stages are, to both men and women, is to pass an examination in skiing, offered at several centers in France, that covers all technical aspects of skiing and is quite tough. Anyone who passes it is called a *capacitaire* and is entitled to do some ski teaching, but the *capacitaire* receives only a small share of the percentage of the ski-school gross. After a minimum of one season—more often it is two—the candidate goes to school for five weeks in Chamonix, at l'École Nationale de Ski et d'Alpinisme, sometimes known as the Sorbonne of the Snow. His aim is to move up to the next stage, that of *auxiliaire*. An interesting glimpse of what happens during those five weeks was given in an article in the *Mountain Gazette* by Dick Dorworth, a well-known American skier and climber. Dorworth went through the school in 1970, because, he wrote, "I was making my living as a ski instructor/coach, [so] it made sense to get all the certifications, credentials, knowledge, exposure and experience that I possibly could in that field." He went on, "Certification by the French National Ski School would . . . give me the opportunity to live and work in France if I ever wanted. Also, I was curious. It was said that the French had the best national system for ski instruction, the best teaching techniques, and the best instructors. They certainly were producing some powerful racers in those years. I really wanted to find out what the French were up to with their skiing."

Dorworth then described the working conditions that he found:

My roommate was Richard Meeker, an Aspen real estate salesman. We lived a very organized existence.

7:30 A.M. a loud bell rang, as it did for everything, and it was time to get up.

8:00 A.M. breakfast of coffee and bread and butter and jam in the single dining room.

8:40 A.M. buses took us to one of Chamonix's several ski areas, where we skied and learned the French teaching method until 12:30 P.M. when we returned to the school for lunch.

1:30 P.M. back on the buses for what was usually a different area than we were at in the morning. We skied, discussed, practiced, and demonstrated technique until 4:00 P.M. when we got back on the buses and returned to the school.

5:30 P.M. each night were lectures on avalanches, first aid, weather, high country skiing, guiding, bivouacks, rescue, and equipment, with a great emphasis on the necessity of common sense in all situations.

Dorworth added, "Saturday's schedule was the same, except that after lunch was a written examination." During the course, the trainees had four slalom races and a race that was both a downhill and a giant-slalom contest. An instructor—as often as not a former member of the French national ski team—would set the opening time; that is, he would ski the course first, and the students were required to ski three of the five races in near his time. If they did not, they failed the course. Dorworth wrote, "I stood a long time looking at the Gervasutti Couloir, which Sylvain Saudan, whom I had met that week, skiied down. I was impressed." This is understandable when one reads the description of the couloir in a standard climbing guide: "The *couloir* is very steep—45° in the lower section, rising to 55° below the wall of *séracs*. . . . The climb is very exposed to stone and ice falls and is best climbed at night and in cold weather." At the end of the five weeks, there were, according to Dorworth, "several days of tests—skiing, first aid, teaching, technical; spoken, written and practiced." The skiers were graded in five levels—*très bien, bien, assez-bien, passez,* and failing. In his session, there were 105 candidates. "One achieved '*très bien.*' Four got '*bien.*' Twenty-two were given '*assez-bien.*' And thirty-four were '*passez.*'" Forty-four failed. Dorworth got a *bien.* After three years of working as an *auxiliaire* the *moniteur* is entitled to return to Chamonix to try to pass to the highest stage—the *national*. The standards for this are even more rigorous. Further-more, every *moniteur* must pass a control examination every five years after he has qualified for any one of these divisions. As the instructor moves up the ladder, he gets a higher percentage of the total receipts of the school.

Apart from the fact that this system assures licensed ski instructors of a very high caliber, Dorworth felt that there is a definite difference in the way skiing is taught in France and in the United States. Since 1960, by the way, there has been an association of Professional Ski Instructors of America, which certifies instructors. I am in no position to say how its require-ments compare in rigor with the French system. In any event, Dorworth wrote, "Aside from things of technical, methodologi-cal and attitudinal nature, I learned one important differ-ence . . . between the place of emphasis in teaching skiing in France and in America. In America the emphasis is on explana-tion-demonstration and having the student practice a certain maneuver until he is proficient at it. . . . In France, however, the overriding attitude is that the student learns faster and better by emphasis on skiing itself, guided by a minimum of explaining and demonstrating. The French student is encour-aged, forced or cajoled into educating his physiology as much as his brain. This approach makes a lot of sense to me." Again, I am in no position to make comparisons, but I *was* struck during our instruction by the fact that Régis constantly challenged us to do a little more—frequently more than we were at first confident we could do. As Dorworth suggests, we were taught skiing by being urged to ski dozens of kilometers. A week in a ski school in France *is* one's entire ski week. There is rather little time left over after classes.

Later in the week, I asked Régis how *he* became an instructor. His history is fairly typical. (Jaccoux's is not, since he began skiing and climbing in his late teens and made the switch from teaching literature in a *lycée* to professional guiding and skiing only in his twenties.) Régis, who is now twenty-seven, was born in Aime, in the valley below La Plagne. He took up skiing at the age of four. At that time, the only ski station that was functioning in the area, except for a small lift above a village near Aime, was at Val d'Isère, seventy kilometers away. Régis learned skiing on his own, more or less, and at the age of seventeen he got a job as a *pisteur* at the newly created ski station at La Plagne. The *pisteurs* in the French ski stations are responsible for the maintenance of the *pistes*—the ski runs. Early each morning, they ski each *piste* to certify that it is free of avalanche danger. They also set up markers then to warn people against hazards—bad snow or deep gullies—and they spend the rest of the day on rescue duty. Each night, just after the lifts are closed to the public, a team of *pisteurs* skis every *piste* that has been open during the day, to make sure that no skier has been stranded because of injury or has simply lost his way—something that is quite possible, when one considers that at La Plagne, for example, there are about a hundred miles of ski trails, many connecting one village with another. When the development of the area is completed, in a few years, many of the *balcon* resorts will be linked by ski lifts and trails, so that one will be able to ski from, say, La Plagne to the neighboring station at Les Arcs and back during a day. Régis told me that it was his experience as a *pisteur* that really taught him to ski, since he was forced to go out every day, often under the worst snow and weather conditions imaginable. After three years of that, Régis passed the examination for *capacitaire* and then for *auxiliaire*. He will soon have enough experience to attempt to qualify as a *national*. During the summer, he is training to be a professional alpine guide. The *moniteurs* at La Plagne have a ski team that competes with teams made up of *moniteurs* at the other French ski stations. La Plagne has had one of the strongest teams, which includes Armand Bérard, who the local people feel could probably outrace anyone on the current French national ski team. Régis skis the slalom for the La Plagne team, and, according to the people I spoke with, is tremendously strong in this race and is still improving. During the two weeks that preceded my arrival in La Plagne, he had been assigned to train racers in the slalom. (Both the Chileans and the Argentines had sent groups of young skiers to La Plagne to train, and while I was there, I often saw them flying down various slopes.) It was just a matter of luck—good luck, we all felt—that Régis had been assigned to our lowly *Cours 6* the week that we were members of it.

After lunch the first day, we reassembled, and Régis led us toward the St.-Esprit via the shortcut. It was on the steep hill leading down to the lift that he introduced us to the technique that is the heart and soul of modern skiing—a technique that has been made possible by the introduction of plastic-and-metal skis, with their ruggedness and "slide-ability." This is what the French call *dérapage*—or, in its Franglais version, *"le sideslip-ping."* Here one begins, as in a traverse, with the skis at right angles to the fall line. Again, the uphill ski is slightly advanced, and the weight is on the downhill ski. Now, instead of edging the downhill ski and moving forward, one flattens the downhill ski so that both skis are flat and slide, still parallel, down the slope. This is the vertical sideslip, and one controls it by pressing the knees in toward the slope, thus edging the skis and bringing the slip to a stop. The method can be refined so that one slips forward or backward as conditions warrant. The importance of learning to do this cannot be exaggerated. Suddenly, the student has a method that enables him to negotiate anything. The steeper the slope, the easier it is to sideslip down, and in complete control. When in doubt, sideslip, and goodbye the snowplow forever. It takes a good deal of work to learn the control and to learn to let go with the edges. But I think that it is fair to say that in my group we all felt a sudden sense of liberation. Skiing looked no longer like a dangerous sport but like something we could do safely and with real satisfaction. In fact, we were at first all so addicted to sideslipping that Régis had his hands full to make us point our skis back down the fall line and let go. From the sideslip, all the modern turns begin. A forward sideslip is converted into a parallel turn up the hill, and so on. If one closely watches a good modern skier coming down a slope, one notices that what is happening is that the skier is slipping his skis back and forth across the fall line by the motion of his knees and upper body. Bumps are negotiated by slipping off the top, planting a ski pole, and turning. The sound this makes is a gentle hissing of the skis against the snow. It is a beautiful sound. By evening, I was so elated that I reported to Jaccoux that I thought I had become *le roi du sideslip*. He said that if it were only true I could ski anywhere.

Over the next five days, we took on increasingly steep slopes and increasingly high lifts. The next day, Régis took us out on the Biollet—one of the highest lifts at La Plagne, from which we got a view of the whole Mont Blanc range, thirty miles or so to the north. While we were skiing down—sideslipping and traversing—Régis gave us some pointers on rules of the road. In French law—and this has been the basis of judgments in legal suits—the skier farthest downhill is the presumptive innocent in any collision. One's responsibility is to all skiers below. As Régis was explaining this to us, a skier dropped in from above, bounced off Régis's skis, and landed, not much the worse for wear, several feet below. Régis was legally innocent but somewhat surprised. On one occasion, Régis showed us the measured kilometer at La Plagne—a run, reaching sixty degrees, on which a skier can be timed over a kilometer to see if he can break the current world's record of 114.411 miles an hour, held by a young Italian skier, Alessandro Casse. When I was there, the record at La Plagne was held by Armand Bérard, and was 94.1 miles an hour. Régis asked if any of us would like to try, but he got no takers. On some days, the snow was perfect and the sun shining. On other days, snow and rain fell. Whatever the weather, we skied. Heavy, wet snow is extremely difficult for skiing, and Régis said that it was a snow *"qui ne pardonne pas"*—that one must ski correctly or risk a fall. One day, he led us off the beaten track to the top of a short, steep wall covered with thick powder. He made a track straight down, and we were to follow, one at a time, One of the Parisian girls—a former competitive swimmer—led off and planted herself in the snow up to her neck. I was next, and planted myself in snow up to my neck.

Early in the afternoon of our last day, before class, I watched Régis and Armand Bérard practice the slalom. They had set up a few dozen poles on a nearby hill. They seemed to dance from turn to turn, and their skis appeared almost never to touch the ground. Powder flew up and caught the bright sun. When Régis spotted me watching, he skied up and said, "*Un slalom.*" And then, looking up at the snow-covered mountains that cradle La Plagne, he added, "*Il fait beau.*"

5   *On vous cherche*

The summer of 1971 in the Alps was one of the best in recent years—day after day of nearly perfect cloudless, sunny weather. It was also one of the worst—perhaps the worst ever—from the point of view of alpine accidents. By the end of August, in the region of Mont Blanc alone, there had been 77 deaths attributed to climbing or walking in the mountains, and 120 reported accidents involving injuries. (These were presumably injuries that were serious enough to involve some sort of mountain rescue, since minor injuries are not reported at all.) The good weather, ironically, was in part responsible for this perhaps record toll, since more people were climbing in the region than ever before. Many of these climbers were very young, and many were almost completely inexperienced and unaware of the dangers that are an inevitable part of high alpine climbing—sudden changes of weather, hidden crevasses, and, in dry weather, excessive rockfall. As if to epitomize the tragic aspect of the season, an incident took place at the end of the summer which not only resulted in the deaths of two inexperienced climbers (seven others were hospitalized with varying degrees of frostbite) but revived a demand that has been made in the past in France: that some sort of legal restrictions be placed on climbers and what they are allowed to climb.

During the last week in August, a group of eleven young people—mostly teen-agers—arrived in Chamonix with a young counselor from a nearby summer camp where they had been vacationing. The counselor had some alpine experience but was not a qualified professional guide, and none of the young people had had any real mountain experience at all. Early in the week, they hiked up to a refuge cabin, and on Thursday they set off to climb—or so it seems, since after the accident there were conflicting reports as to what they *had* intended to do—the

87

Aiguille du Tour, one of the easiest snow-and-rock climbs in the Chamonix region, but still a climb that requires care. Somehow, they found themselves on the wrong peak, and then were hit by a sudden and violent mountain storm. An experienced group would have kept moving, and, in any case, would have had suitable clothing and extra food for such an emergency. Most of these campers had, at best, light summer jackets, and there was no emergency food and no water and no equipment for melting snow. Freezing, they stopped where they were, and it was not until early the next morning that some members of the group were able to get down to the refuge, where there was telephone communication with the valley, and where, fortunately, five guides had been spending the night in preparation for their own climbs. With the help of a mountain-rescue helicopter, the guides were able to get most of the party back down to Chamonix, but not before two boys, seventeen years old and twenty-one years old, had died from exposure. It was noted after the accident that such a party should have taken at least three, and possibly four, professional guides. It was also noted that this would have cost the hikers something like two hundred dollars in guides' fees, which they could not have afforded. However, as someone remarked, "Would you allow a bunch of children with no experience and no safety equipment to go automobile racing just because they felt like doing it?"

This incident, and some of the other accidents that took place during the summer, inevitably reminded people in Chamonix of the extraordinary series of alpine accidents and rescues that took place during the famous 1965 and 1966 climbing seasons, some of which involved combinations of bad fortune, disparate personalities, courage and cowardice, generosity and avarice, put together in juxtapositions that resembled the fabric of a great, if implausible, novel. In June of that second season, a distinguished French climber, Pierre Henry, assembled some statistics on climbing accidents in the French Alps and published them in *La Montagne*, the journal of the French Alpine Club. These statistics could be gathered precisely, since rescue work there is a police function (with the help of local Guide Bureaus and the like), and accidents in the mountains, like automobile accidents, are subject to full police inquiry. Every year between 1962 and 1965, M. Henry reported, there were between 150 and 180 accidents (some involving more than one person) in the mountains of France. These annually required the intervention of from twelve hundred to two thousand rescuers and from three hundred to five hundred helicopter flights, and each year about sixty deaths resulted from these accidents. (During the same period, there was an average of eighty climbing deaths a year in the Swiss Alps, and of twenty-five a year in Britain.) In a breakdown of these statistics, M. Henry disclosed that in an average year about 75 percent of the accidents occur in good weather, and that about 40 percent are due to simple falls, the rest being divided up among avalanches, crevasses, lightning (which claims one or two victims a year), and the like. The proportion of accidents decreases with the difficulty of the climb—reflecting the fact that only very good climbers can do difficult climbing. (Their accidents, however, are more often fatal than the ones involving beginners.) At least 85 percent of the accidents occur to climbers without guides. M. Henry concluded that the number of accidents is increasing faster, in proportion, than the number of climbers, which has also been steadily increasing. Some of the increase in the accident rate, he felt, was due, ironically, to an increase in the excellence of the mountain rescue services, which has given some climbers the attitude of, in his words, *"Après tout, on viendra me chercher, et cela ne coûtera rien"* ("After all, they'll come and find me, and it won't cost me anything"). There have been some spectacular recent applications of this attitude.

In September, 1965, the alpine community was stunned by an accident that took the lives of two of the best climbers in Europe—Marc Martinetti, a young Chamonix guide, and Lionel Terray, also a Chamonix guide, whom many people regarded as the greatest expeditionary climber who ever lived. No one will ever know exactly how they were killed. Together, they had been climbing a difficult *falaise* near Grenoble, and, having negotiated the hardest part of it, they fell while doing a relatively easy passage near the summit. When a great climber does have an accident, it not uncommonly occurs while he is moving very quickly on easy terrain.) I did not know Martinetti, who was twenty-five when he died, but I had come to know Terray and his family through Jaccoux, who lived for a while in a small chalet on the Terray property in Chamonix. Terray was one of the most remarkable men I have ever met. He gave the impression of invulnerable physical strength combined with a lucid intelligence and great warmth of personality. His physical courage was legendary. During the first successful assault on Annapurna, in the Himalayas, in 1950, it was Terray who, at the risk of losing his own fingers—and thus his livelihood as a guide—undoubtedly saved the lives of his companions by massaging their limbs and giving them his gloves. Physically, he was not especially well built for climbing. He was heavy, and his arms were rather short. But at forty-four—his age when he died—he told me that he still constantly did gymnastics to improve his agility—something unheard of for a guide, who keeps fit simply by doing his job. Terray's alpine experiences, wonderfully described in his book *Les Conquérants de l'Inutile*, so often balanced him on the thinnest margin between life and death that for alpinists he became a symbol, as Jaccoux put it in a letter to me, "of the myth of invulnerability, of good fortune, of the great climber who would never be killed in the mountains."

Terray was what French climbers call "*un pur*." He simply and plainly loved the mountains, and his exploits came as a consequence of his love, and not of any desire for personal publicity or acclaim. He belonged to an old tradition of idealistic mountaineers—a tradition that, like so many traditions, is in danger of disappearing because of the temptations offered by the mass publicity media. To Americans it may seem curious that there could *be* any temptations that radio, newspapers, magazines, and television might offer an alpinist. In our country, the mountains, for most people, are far away, and what happens in them is of relatively little interest. However, in Europe tens of thousands, if not hundreds of thousands, of people climb, hike, and ski. And the number is increasing all the time. The great alpine communities like Chamonix, Zermatt, Kitzbühel, and Cortina are familiar to most Europeans, and in a place like Chamonix, where the most spectacular climbs are made and the most tragic accidents occur, many French newspapers keep "stringers"; the magazine *Paris-Match* had a full-time correspondent on hand there all summer, just in case something happened. Indeed, it has now become fashionable for European newspapers to sponsor sensational climbs. In return for financial support, a climber will sell the rights to his story and his photographs, and the editors no doubt hope that something out of the ordinary will occur. After Terray's death, the next stunning alpine accident developed out of just such a newspaper-sponsored climb. It came about on the North Wall of the Eiger.

The Eigerwand—the Eiger's North Wall—is regarded as the most dangerous of the great alpine climbs. Most of the approaches to the summit of the Eiger are over relatively easy glacial terrain, but the North Wall, which looms more than six thousand feet above the tiny village of Kleine Scheidegg, in the Bernese Oberland of Switzerland, is a fantastic, vertiginous maze of rock, snow, and ice. The Swiss, with their instinct for tourism, have constructed a cog railroad that passes *inside* the Eiger and ultimately deposits the passenger in the magnificent alpine setting of the Jungfraujoch. En route, the train occasionally stops at what is called the Eiger Station, where the passenger can get out and walk down a rather frigid illuminated tunnel to a window that has been cut in the North Wall. The window is about a third of the way up the wall, and the sight that greets the viewer is not exactly calculated to encourage him to start a career of alpinism. He is perched over a vertical expanse of rock and ice, down which flow constant streams of water, snow, and stones; these avalanches constitute one of the more dubious charms of venturing out onto the wall.

The North Wall has had a turbulent history. In 1936, after several fatal accidents—especially to German climbers, who were hoping to dedicate a victory over the wall to Hitler—the Canton of Bern made an attempt to prohibit climbing on it. One wonders how this ban was supposed to be enforced, and, indeed, it was lifted shortly thereafter. In late August, 1938, a mixed German and Austrian party made the first ascent. It was not until 1947 that the second ascent was made—by Terray and the great French climber Louis Lachenal. By March, 1966, the wall had been climbed by fifty-five different parties (about 150 people in all), and there had been twenty-six deaths. In that year, it occurred to several climbers—among them an American, John Harlin—that the Eiger's North Wall was ripe for a *"direttissima."* A *"direttissima"* (the "super-direct") has been defined as the route that a drop of water would take if it were to fall from the top of a peak to the bottom. There are no first ascents of particular peaks left in the Alps, so climbers who are interested in making a reputation specialize in pioneering difficult routes on peaks that have been climbed. The ultimate in such route-pioneering is the *direttissima*.

Harlin, who fell to his death in March, 1966, during the *direttissima* on the Eiger, was, like Terray, a remarkable physical specimen. Before taking up climbing, he had been an Air Force jet pilot. He had also studied costume designing. He once told me he had done a good deal of motorcycle racing in California, but James Ramsey Ullman, in a biography of Harlin, *Straight Up*, observed that he was not above embellishing his own myth when it suited him; since there is no mention of motorcycle racing in the book, this may have been an example. According to Mr. Ullman, Harlin had in his character a streak of violence, and, indeed, often claimed that he had killed a man in a street fight. He was married, and he and his wife taught school during the winter in the Swiss community of Leysin. Like Terray, he had had innumerable escapes in the mountains. He was thirty-one when he did. His expedition up the Eiger was sponsored by the English newspaper the *Telegraph*, which paid the cost of the equipment and also of an airplane that Harlin rented to survey the face, so that he could trace out his route. Harlin conceived of the attack as a kind of miniature Himalayan expedition. He planned to establish "camps"—really caves dug in the snow—at various places on the wall, and had decided to try the *direttissima* in the winter, since he hoped that the rockfall might be at a minimum then. When he and his group arrived at Kleine Scheidegg, they found an even larger German party, subsidized by a German publisher and accompanied by its own public-relations director, also ready to attempt the *direttissima*. Although the press built up the climb as a race for the summit, the two parties ultimately cooperated. To provision the camps, they fixed ropes on the face of the cliff and used them both for descending from the camps and for climbing back up to them. One climbs such ropes by attaching metal clamps—*jumars*—to them, which, in conjunction with a system of attachable stirrups, enable the climber to go up with relative ease. The major disadvantage of the system is that the *jumars* can abrade the ropes. That is what happened to Harlin; an abraded rope gave way under his weight, and he fell.

The deaths of Terray and Harlin, occurring as they did within a few months of each other, set the scene for the extraordinary events of the coming summer—a series of events that caused many people to wonder whether some sort of regulation should not be introduced into alpine climbing, on the order of the system in the Soviet Union. There a climber must have what amounts to a license, beginning with a "learner's permit" and gradually working up to more and more difficult climbs. Such a system unquestionably prevents many accidents, yet it also—at least, so it is argued—destroys the freedom of expression that is so important a part of mountaineering. The summer following Harlin's death offered some of the worst weather in recent European history. A few days of intermittent sunshine would be followed by a week of extremely bad weather—torrential rain in the valleys and violent snowstorms in the mountains. Mountain weather is almost impossible to predict from day to day under the best of circumstances. In those days, there were two barometers in front of the Guide Bureau in Chamonix. One was a modern, shining metallic apparatus, which, along with the atmospheric pressure, indicated by a red or a green light whether the pressure was rising or falling. It had several other dials, whose precise significance I was never able to penetrate, but I think they measured the density of water vapor, or something. The second barometer was an ancient affair in a wooden case, and it must have dated back many decades. It gave only the barometric pressure, which was marked by an inked needle on a moving paper tape. The needle traced out a curve, so that one could compare readings at different times of the day. A careful observer could note some curious kinks in this curve, which could be ascribed to a habit among the Chamonix guides of giving the instrument a kick when they were unhappy over the barometric situation. I once discussed these barometers with the *doyen* of the Chamonix guides, Armand Couttet, who was then eighty-two and in splendid shape. Our talk was prompted by the fact that Chamonix had just undergone a period of fifteen days of constant rain during which the barometers had announced everything from *"Grand Beau"* to *"Variable."* When I asked him how he felt about the matter, he said, *"On n'a plus confiance dans ces choses-là depuis très longtemps."* Now Chamonix has a weather bureau with a full-fledged meteorologist in the same building that houses the Guide Bureau. It functions during the climbing season, issuing bulletins a few times a day, and these appear to be uncannily accurate. But for an alpinist engaged in a difficult climb, an hour or two of good weather can mean the difference between life and death, and no meteorologist, however competent, can predict the tremendously rapid changes of mountain weather to such a refined degree. Unfortunately, the meteorologist was not in residence in 1966, and climbers had to rely on the two unattended barometers (which are still there, and still being kicked, by the way).

The conclusion that one might draw from all this is that it is foolish to attempt a difficult climb unless the weather conditions appear to be nearly perfect. To understand the events of that summer of 1966, then, one must realize something of the psychology of the alpinist. Most climbers are young and do not have much money. Typically, they are students who have skimped for a whole winter in order to save enough money to come to the Alps for a brief season of climbing—a season that, at best, lasts only six or eight weeks, since in June there is still too much snow for high climbing, and by the first week of September the days are getting too short. Many of the young climbers hitchhike to Chamonix or come on motor scooters, and, to save money, they pitch tents on one or another of the camping grounds nearby. For a climber, there is nothing drearier than sitting in a small tent, with the mountains all around, waiting until the weather clears. On top of this, a young climber who wants to make a reputation is under heavy pressure to do something of great difficulty. (The guides have already earned their reputations, and they can fill in the days of poor weather by taking clients of modest abilities on the numerous classic routes around the valley, from which there are easy retreats if the weather turns really bad.) In addition, a young climber has before him the countless examples of those who have done difficult climbs even in bad weather. Finally, as M. Henry noted in his report on alpine accidents, there is also in the back of the young climber's mind an awareness of the efficient rescue service in the valley—the realization that, if the worst comes to the worst, "*on vous cherche.*"

Early in the first week in August, having learned from the Geneva-airport weather service that a temporary spell of clear weather could be expected, three extremely strong French alpinists, including a first-rate guide who had come along for the fun of it, decided to attempt one of the great routes on the Italian side of Mont Blanc. From France, the flanks of Mont Blanc give the impression of a serene glacial slope, and, indeed, anyone with a modicum of experience and a fair amount of training can, with a guide, make the long trudge up with no great difficulty. The summit of Mont Blanc is so large that in bad weather it is quite easy to lose oneself on it, and for this reason alone it is important to be with someone who can find his way down under any circumstances. The Italian side is another matter altogether. From the Valley of Aosta, Mont Blanc is a giant Himalayan wall. There are several routes up the face— routes that have been given rather stirring names, like La Sentinelle Rouge, La Voie Major, and L'Innominata. Apart from the technical difficulties of these routes—which are extreme— the climber must be prepared to cope with arctic cold, winds of over a hundred miles an hour, and the physiological discomforts of the lack of oxygen. In addition, on many of these routes there is literally a point of no return in bad weather. The lower parts of the climbs involve picking one's way through vast fields of crevasses, and if the visibility is not perfect there is no hope of finding one's way back down. There is an axiom that above a certain point on the Italian routes the only way to safety is over the top and down the easy side. One cannot turn back.

The three alpinists had decided to do La Major, and they were confident that they could do it in twenty-four hours—the time during which the weather was expected to hold stable. The first stop on their route was the refuge-bivouac of La Fourche. I have never been to La Fourche, but I am told that it requires first-class alpinism to get even that far. The three men had installed themselves as comfortably as possible in a tiny, cold bivouac when, to their astonishment, they observed four other climbers, who did not seem to be very strong, making their way toward them. These turned out to be four young French climbers, who announced that they, too, were going to do La Major, even though they did not appear to have either the equipment or the training for such a difficult route. At this point, the guide with the first group told the newcomers, bluntly and plainly, to go back down. (One *can* get back down from La Fourche.) Once a guide agrees to go with a group of climbers, he is not only morally but legally responsible for their safety. In this case, however, the guide, not having been hired by the newcomers, was not in a position to *force* them to return. Something of a quarrel developed, and the first group decided that in order to establish their independence and absolve the guide of any responsibility for the second party, they would move on as soon as possible to the next bivouac. The following morning, when the three men started up, they quickly noticed, to their consternation, that the four others were following them, making use of the trail that the three men had cut in the snow. After a short time, a violent snowstorm suddenly hit Mont Blanc. (Another of the features of climbing the Italian side is that it is difficult to see the approach of bad weather if it comes, as it often does, over the top from France.) The three men decided that the best thing to do was to establish an emergency bivouac in the shelter of a shallow crevasse and to go on to the summit if the weather showed any sign of clearing. Shortly, they were joined by the four others, and the seven men spent the next forty-eight hours huddled shoulder to shoulder in the subzero temperatures of the crevasse. At the end of the forty-eight hours, there was still no sign of clearing, and the guide decided that now they *must* get to the top if they were not to die of exposure. They started up, and within twenty meters one of the young French climbers fell exhausted to the snow. Under any less desperate conditions, it might have been possible for the rest of the group to carry him, but in the near hundred-mile-an-hour winds, the freezing cold, and the heavy snow there was nothing to be done. At this point, his companion on the rope— the four young Frenchmen had been roped together in pairs— heroically decided that he would stay with his fallen comrade. After leaving the two of them with as much clothing and food as they could spare, the five remaining men pushed on to the summit. There another of the young French climbers passed out from exhaustion, and his ropemate, too, elected to stay with him. The three original climbers proceeded down the French side as fast as they could to get help, and, in the worst weather conditions imaginable, the mountain rescue service of the French police succeeded in flying a helicopter to the summit of Mont Blanc. There the crew found the two young climbers still alive but at the limit of their strength; below the summit, they found the two other climbers together, frozen to death. *On vous cherche.*

Within ten days of this tragedy, there occurred in Chamonix what was without doubt the most complicated and dramatic mountain rescue in the history of the Alps. By the time it was over, it had required the services of forty-four French alpine troops, six mountain policemen, eight Chamonix guides, and ten voluntary alpinists. It involved seventy helicopter flights and nearly a mile of climbing rope, all of it left behind. The cost of the undertaking was more than $10,000 and the life of one of the rescuers, a German climber who had volunteered his services. *On vous cherche.* In addition, the rescue operation brought to light one of the most remarkable personalities in contemporary alpinism—Gary (Gareth) Hemming, an American whom the European newspapers soon christened "the beatnik of the Alps" and who came to symbolize the drama and heroism of the rescue. In addition to everything else, Hemming proved to have an odd sense of mischief, and it was not easy, as countless interviewers found out after the rescue, to get clearcut answers from him about his life and career. He was extremely tall—perhaps six feet six. (After the rescue, he told a journalist, with great solemnity, that he was originally only six feet four but that during the war in the Pacific he had been captured by the Japanese, who had stretched him. When the journalist dutifully took this down in his notes, Hemming said that he was only kidding—the truth was that he was six feet six at birth.) Piecing together various accounts, and making a generous allowance for Bunyanesque hyperbole, one would hazard that Hemming was born in Pasadena, California, around 1933, and that he studied for a while at San Diego State College but, finding the regimentation intolerable, came to France. From what I have been able to make out, he studied philosophy for a while at the University of Grenoble, and afterward lived, one way or another, on the five dollars a week that his mother sent him. Needless to say, this regime imposed certain economies; in fact, during several winters Hemming resided under various bridges over the Seine, depending to some extent on mountaineering friends in Paris for more substantial lodging and sustenance when these were available. In the summers, he usually resided in a small tent near Chamonix. Hemming's face was absolutely remarkable. It had something of the beauty of the paintings of the Christian saints, and it was crowned with an incredible foliage of long dark-blond hair, so thick that it must have afforded not only considerable thermal insulation but also substantial protection from falling rock. In the mountains, he wore a thick red pullover and one or more pairs of ancient pants, whose multicolored patches gave something of the effect of Joseph's coat. He had a delightful smile, an air of inner strength, and great serenity.

The adventure of which Hemming became the hero began on Sunday, August 14. That day, two German climbers, Heinz Ramisch and Hermann Schridde, began the extremely difficult climb of the West Face of the Dru. The Dru—really Les Drus, since there are twin summits—is one of the most beautiful and impressive mountains in Europe. It towers over the Mer de Glace glacier, above Chamonix, like a needle reaching into the sky. It is unlikely that any climbing routes in the world offer more sustained difficulties than the ones on the faces of the Dru, and it is the ambition of every great climber to tackle them. There is no easy route. The *voie normale*, or standard route, which was fashionable with expert climbers before the war, is technically not of great difficulty, but it is very long and is constantly exposed to falling rock. It is now used mainly as a route of descent by climbers who have taken the extraordinarily difficult routes on the West and North Faces. The West Face of the Dru was first climbed in 1952 by four Frenchmen, and since then the climb has been repeated a few times each year. On that August Sunday, after being informed that the weather could be expected to hold stable for at least forty-eight hours, Ramisch, a twenty-two-year-old student from Karlsruhe, and Schridde, a thirty-year-old mechanic from Hannover, who had just met and who had never climbed anything together, set out for the West Face. They made an arrangement with some companions who remained below to signal by waving a red parka if they got into trouble. Since they expected the climb to last at least two days, they took with them an extra supply of food and some bivouac equipment. By Monday noon, they had done two-thirds of the face and were at an altitude of about ten thousand feet. There, they were struck by a violent storm—snow, hail, and lightning. (The Dru, because of its needle shape, is an especially frequent target of lightning.) Their first thought was to get down. They had just surmounted one of the principal obstacles of the route, a *dièdre*—a vertical cleft in the rock made where two faces join each other at an angle—of ninety meters, and they rappelled back down it and bivouacked at its foot, in the hope that the weather would change. At daybreak, they awoke to find the whole lower portion of the mountain covered with sheets of ice. It was at this point that, by their own admission, they made a mistake in judgment that nearly cost them their lives. Instead of continuing down, which would have been feasible, though delicate, they decided to go *up*, and so escape over the top; they felt that the part above, which they could not see, might be clear. So they went back up the *dièdre*. Above the *dièdre*, the route up the West Face takes a curious twist. The face is climbed by a series of more or less parallel vertical fissures. To go from one fissure to the next, it is necessary from time to time to displace oneself *sidewise* along the face. This is done by what is known as a "pendulum rappel." As the name implies, the climber swings from his rope, which is attached to a piton, in a series of arcs until he gets to where he wants to go. Quite clearly, this maneuver can be used only if there is a suitable landing place at the end of the arc. At this point in the route on the West Face, a pendulum rappel was called for. The landing place was a small terrace, about six feet long and three feet wide. The two Germans executed the rappel and then, to their horror, discovered that the rock above the terrace, instead of being dry and climbable, was impassable, because of a thick covering of ice. Moreover, Ramisch had developed a sore throat so painful that he could no longer swallow, and his companion had severely bruised his ribs in a fall while climbing the *dièdre*. The only possible way to get off the terrace was to make an extremely difficult, and very dangerous, traverse across the vertical face to a point where the West Face and the North Face joined, and then to climb down the North Face—which in itself is very difficult. Leading from their terrace the two Germans found some strands of rope attached to pitons that had been put into the rock in 1952, when the original French group climbed the West Face, but since it had been exposed to the weather for fourteen years, the two climbers decided that it was unlikely to support their weight. According to later reports, they disagreed about whether they should try to go on, and in the end they settled down on their terrace, ten thousand feet in the air, and prepared a bivouac, which was to last for the next *seven days*.

It was now Tuesday, August 16. Realizing that they were trapped, the two Germans signalled for help to their companions below. During the summer, mountain rescue in Chamonix is nearly a full-time job, and it is so taxing and dangerous that it used to be split up among three principal groups—the Chamonix guides, who were responsible for all rescues until August 1; the École Nationale de Ski et d'Alpinisme, in Chamonix, which trains all the guides in France and was responsible for rescues during the first two weeks of August; and the École de Haute Montagne, which trains French alpine troops and took over until the first of September, when it was again the turn of the guides. These organizations all work coöperatively with the Péleton Spécialisé de Haute Montagne, a division of the French police, which, in addition to specially trained personnel, has at its disposal several Alouette III helicopters and a radio station that maintains communications with many of the refuges in the region. This group is now responsible for *all* rescues in Chamonix. Since the accident occurred in the third week of August, under the old system the job of getting the Germans down fell to Colonel André Gonnet, the officer in charge of the alpine troops. From the valley there was no way of knowing whether the Germans were injured, or even—since the weather had by now turned so bad that one could not even see the Dru from Chamonix—whether they were still alive. The first thing to do was to dispatch a helicopter to the Dru to find out what their condition was. (*Paris-Match* later published some remarkable photographs showing the Alouette hovering like a forlorn lost insect a few meters from the terrace where the climbers were trapped.) In good weather, the rescue might have been accomplished by helicopter—or, at least, provisions might have been dropped to the climbers. As it was, the only thing the helicopter crew was able to do was to catch intermittent glimpses of the Germans and so ascertain that they were still alive. Not knowing their physical condition, Colonel Gonnet had to assume the worst. He therefore dispatched a platoon—over forty alpine troops, with their own guides—to the base of the Dru. The idea was to get a strong group of climbers to the summit by the *voie normale* and then drop a steel cable down the face. Rescuers could be lowered to the terrace by the cable, and the two climbers winched up. This plan meant that the troops had to carry very heavy equipment up the *voie normale*, which was covered with snow and ice, and along which there were violent discharges of lightning. (Several of the soldiers received minor electrical burns during this part of the operation.) Moreover, the terrace on which the climbers were trapped was situated under some enormous overhanging rocks—*les grands surplombs*— which meant that any cable lowered down the face would be beyond their reach. On Wednesday and Thursday, Colonel Gonnet proceeded with what the newspapers came to call "the invasion of the Dru." By this time, Chamonix itself had been invaded—by newspapermen from all over Europe, by television crews, and by a team from O.R.T.F., the French national radio-and-television network, who came equipped with their own helicopter. Every newspaper in Western Europe carried details of the rescue operation on its front pages.

At noon on Thursday, August 18, Gary Hemming was sitting in a café in Courmayeur, the delightful alpine town at the Italian end of the tunnel that leads under Mont Blanc. With him was a young German friend, Lothar Mauch, with whom he had driven from Chamonix. They were planning to do a climb together, but Hemming was reading an account of the accident on the Dru in the *Dauphiné Libéré*, a paper published in the French department of the Haute-Savoie. Suddenly he turned to Mauch and said that he had to go back to Chamonix. Among all climbers, Hemming was one of the greatest experts on the West Face of the Dru. He had been on it many times, and had even pioneered a new route; above all, he knew how to get down the face in any kind of weather. He felt that he could not stand by and watch two men gradually die of exposure when he had the technical skill to save their lives. Mauch did not need much persuasion, and soon the two of them were heading back to Chamonix.

At three o'clock that afternoon, Hemming presented himself to Colonel Gonnet. The Colonel apparently had a little difficulty recognizing Hemming, since he had recently shaved off his beard. The beard had become an issue a year or so before, when Hemming was invited to join a specially selected group of alpinists for a training course at the École Nationale. When he showed up, he was told that he would not be admitted to the course unless he got a shave and a haircut, which he refused to do. He was not admitted, but sometime after the course was over he removed his beard anyway. In any case, the Colonel was pleased to accept his offer of help and, in return, supplied Hemming with army equipment, including a light two-way radio and some specially prepared rucksacks containing provisions for the two Germans, if they could be reached in time. Hemming recruited four very strong alpinists in addition to Mauch: another German, named Gehrad; an English specialist on the Dru named Mick Burke, who later died on Mount Everest; and two French climbers. By seven that evening, Hemming and his team were on the cog railroad that winds upward to a point above the Mer de Glace glacier, which must be crossed to reach the foothills that lead to the Dru, and by three the following morning they were on the glacier itself. (Hemming was offered the use of helicopters to transport his group to the base of the Dru, but he was afraid that flying might be delayed by the bad weather, and he knew that the Germans were fighting a losing battle against time.) At ten in the morning, they began the climb up the long and very dangerous Couloir du Dru, a corridor that leads to the West Face and is notorious for rockfall and avalanches. By two in the afternoon, they were on the West Face itself, and it had begun to snow heavily.

Meanwhile, in Chamonix, another bizarre aspect of the story was unfolding. A renowned French climber and Chamonix guide, René Desmaison—also a leading expert on the Dru—had set forth on his own, without making contact with any of the professional rescue groups in the valley, to undertake what amounted to an independent rescue mission up the West Face. Both Hemming and Desmaison had independently reached the conclusion that the only way to save the climbers was to follow the route that the climbers themselves had used, and then bring them down by the same route. One cannot fault Desmaison's skill and courage—nothing is more dangerous than a rescue in bad weather—but he was severely criticized for undertaking such a private operation without consulting the authorities in the valley; indeed, shortly after the rescue the Company of Chamonix Guides voted to exclude him for what was regarded as an intolerable breach of discipline.

Ironically, in February, 1971, Desmaison was himself the subject of a dramatic helicopter rescue. On the tenth of the month, accompanied by a twenty-four-year-old fellow-guide, Serge Gousseault, he set out to establish a new route on the north face of the Grandes Jorasses, near Chamonix—one of the most difficult climbing faces in all the Alps. The winter had been marked by rather little snowfall, and the conditions were especially favorable for winter climbing, with long periods of rather mild, stable weather. As luck would have it, by the thirteenth, the pair, now halfway up the face, were caught in a severe snowstorm, which slowed them down and which was followed by a second storm on the fifteenth. By the sixteenth, Gousseault's hands were so severely frostbitten that he could no longer use them, and Desmaison was literally dragging him up the mountain, rope length after rope length. The pair still had radio communication with Desmaison's wife, in the valley, and as late as the sixteenth Desmaison gave no indication that anything was wrong. On the night of the seventeenth, there was a third storm, and by the nineteenth, although the two men were nearly at the summit, Gousseault could not continue farther. By this time, a helicopter had been dispatched from Chamonix to investigate, and although the pilot succeeded in flying close to the pair, he did not get any signal from Desmaison that he could interpret as an S.O.S. (In the subsequent inquiry, there was a difference of opinion between Desmaison and the pilot as to what signals had, in fact, been given.) In any case, despite a brief spell of very good weather on the twentieth, no rescue attempt was called for, and on the night of the twenty-first Gousseault died of exposure. By this time, Desmaison was so exhausted that he could not get to the summit alone. Bad weather set in again, and no helicopter could set down near the summit until the morning of the twenty-fifth. Then a rescue team was lowered from the summit by cable, and in less than three hours Desmaison was brought up and transported to the hospital in Chamonix. As a commentator in the February, 1971, issue of *La Montagne* noted, "It was just in time. He would not have survived another night." The commentator went on, "Once more, René Desmaison has exhibited his exceptional physical resistance and his courage in adversity. But many Alpinists wonder about his choice of a companion for such an enterprise in such a season [Gousseault had never done any serious winter climbing], and about his decision to continue despite the fact that the conditions had become unfavorable." The commentator also went on to criticize the various newspapers and magazines that had treated the whole matter as if it somehow merited respect: *"On eût souhaité plus de pudeur,"* he wrote. He concluded, "These dramatic events in the Jorasses should be carefully studied both by individual Alpinists and by the mountain rescue organizations; there are many lessons to be learned on each side." *On vous cherche.*

Whatever Desmaison's motives may have been in undertaking to rescue the two Germans, there was no doubt but that the journalists and television people exerted all sorts of persuasion, monetary and otherwise, on the principals in the rescue in order to obtain exclusive reports and pictures. Recently, Lothar Mauch (who now owns a very successful chain of Mod boutiques in France) told me that a respresentative of an important magazine had at one point physically tried to shove a camera and some film into the hands of the Hemming people as they were leaving for the Mer de Glace. Mauch said that they finally told the man that they would smash his camera if he did not take it back. Like all alpinists, Hemming had a small camera with him, but he and Mauch agreed that if they did not find the climbers alive and safe they would destroy the film without showing it to anyone.

In any case, at five o'clock on the afternoon of Friday, August 19, Hemming, camped on the West Face, observed Desmaison and a companion, Vincent Mercié, moving up the face somewhat below. Hemming immediately decided to join forces, and when Desmaison arrived the next morning the group split into two units of four, with the strongest climbers going ahead and the others following to equip the face with fixed ropes as a line of retreat. That night, the eight men bivouacked together on the wall. Originally, Hemming had thought that he might be able to reach the Germans in a day, but, as he later admitted, he had not even imagined the severity of conditions on the Dru. At noon on Saturday, nobody knew when—or even whether—the Germans could be reached from the West Face. Consequently, the École Nationale and the Guide Bureau decided that they would send a group of guides, chosen from the best and most

rapid climbers available, up the North Face, with the idea of
reaching the Germans from slightly above their terrace. The
army was still engaged in its steel-cable operation at the
summit, and among the dangers that beset the climbers on both
faces was the fall of blocks of ice unavoidably kicked loose by the
soldiers as they installed their heavy equipment. It was during
one of these maneuvers that the German climber Wolfgang
Egle, who was a friend of the trapped men, and who had
volunteered to help, lost his life. As nearly as one can tell, while
doing a rappel from the top, he somehow became snarled in one
of his ropes and was strangled.

By 6:00 A.M. on Sunday, August 21, Hemming was close
enough to the Germans to talk to them. "We are coming," is
what he said, and by noon he and Desmaison were there. For
six days, the Germans had been living on a tiny ration of nuts,
one of the last of which they peeled and offered to Hemming,
who remarked to Desmaison that if the stranded men had been
French they would have eaten everything the first day. About
five minutes later, the head of one of the Chamonix guides who
had been going up the North Wall appeared just above the
terrace. A discussion ensued as to the safest way to get everyone
back down; the guides on the North Wall favored lowering a
rope to the terrace and maneuvering the two exhausted Germans onto their wall, which they had equipped for the descent.
Hemming said that he would feel more comfortable taking the
men down the route *he* had come up. Since he had reached the
trapped men first, it was decided that it was up to him to bring
them down as he saw fit. After giving the Germans some solid
food and warm clothing, the entire group began the hazardous
descent of the West Face. It was not until Monday, after still
another bivouac on the Dru, that the party reached the safety of
the glacier below. The following morning—when, as one of the
newspaper reporters somewhat cynically observed, the light
was bright enough so that the O.R.T.F. television cameras could
obtain excellent pictures—the two Germans and their rescuers
were transported to Chamonix by helicopter.

Ramisch, the younger of the two men, appeared to be almost
untouched by the effects of spending nine days on the Dru, and

The end of a successful alpine rescue. Gary Hemming is at the right of
the photograph, wearing a long scarf and cap; René Desmaison is above
and to the left of Hemming, and just to the left of Desmaison are the two
rescued German climbers, Hermann Schridde and Heinz Ramisch.
Lothar Mauch is at the far left of the photograph, with his leg stretched
forward.   *Paris-Match*

Schridde, in the hospital in Chamonix, soon recovered from his rib injury and exposure. In one of the interviews Ramisch gave, he said that the only thing he regretted about the whole adventure was the loss of his friend Egle. (In the October, 1967, issue of *La Montagne*, there was a brief postscript on the accident published in "La Chronique Alpine"—a periodic summary of alpine events. The "Chronique" noted that in August, 1967, a well-known French guide, Yannick Seigneur, and a client found themselves in a storm on exactly the same ledge as the Germans. They were, however, able to make—unaided—the traverse to the North Face, which they said was not especially difficult except perhaps psychologically, since the passage takes place over "*le vide impressionnant.*" The note concluded, "This illustrates the incompetence of the German climbers, who did absolutely nothing to get out of the dangerous predicament they found themselves in.")

In 1971, Desmaison, who still has a large and active climbing clientele, published his autobiography, *La Montagne à Mains Nues.* In it, he writes of the events on the Dru as he views them. He is, as one might imagine, rather bitter about his expulsion from the Company of Chamonix Guides. He writes, "One heard certain writers who took themselves to be guides, or certain guides who took themselves to be writers, making pompous declarations when they probably had never once taken part in any rescue worthy of the name. *L'occasion était vraiment trop belle.*" He adds, "Helping someone in danger is not only a duty but an obligation. For a guide, it is a question of honor. . . . If the same situation were to arise again, and if my intervention would be helpful, *eh bien, ce que j'ai fait je le recommencerais.*"

As for Hemming, he suddenly became an internationally acclaimed hero. Some time after the rescue Jaccoux and I were riding the 6:15 A.M. *téléphérique* up into the Aiguilles of Chamonix, and there in the car was Hemming, in his red sweater and his ancient pair of mountain pants. He and Jaccoux were close friends. "*Où tu vas?*" asked Jaccoux. "For a little walk," Hemming answered, with a mischievous smile. Later, Jaccoux told me that Hemming never informed anyone where he was going, so that "a little walk" really could have been a little walk or, as had been the case earlier that summer, an attempt to make a very difficult first ascent. I had heard that Hemming was writing a book, so I asked him how it was coming along. "Oh, the book," he said vaguely. "The book is something I tell people about who ask me what I do. It's curious that people who ask you that sort of question seem to be particularly pleased if you tell them that you're writing a book." The *téléphérique* came to a stop, and we all got off, Jaccoux and I to proceed on foot, and Hemming to take the connecting *téléphérique "vers le haut."* When he left us, he said softly, perhaps as much to himself as to us, using one of the kindest farewells that climbers exchange before going into the mountains, *"Allez, et bonne course."*

On August 6, 1969, Hemming was found shot to death in Grand Teton Park, in Wyoming. It is presumed that he had committed suicide. He had spent the preceding winter in Chamonix working at removing the snow from the roofs of the taller buildings in the valley. In the spring, he set off to hitch-hike to Alaska, where he planned to work in the forests. Many of his friends in Chamonix received postcards from him from Alaska—postcards full of his usual irreverence and gaiety. After his death, some of his closest friends said that Hemming had often talked of a day when he might lose his love for the mountains and his love for life. Why such a day should have come among the great mountains of Wyoming no one will ever really know.

6 *Une Bonne Ballade*

On July 19, 1965, the tunnel under Mont Blanc between Chamonix, in France, and Courmayeur, in Italy, was opened to the public a few days after General de Gaulle, who had come to Chamonix for *la grande ouverture*, figured in a splendid ceremony culminating in a trip through the tunnel with the president of Italy. I myself traveled through the tunnel a few weeks later. It is a slick affair—two comfortable lanes, air-conditioned all the way, with flashing lights that tell you that you are going too fast or too slow, or are too close to the car in front of you. In ten minutes you are in Italy. The tunnel is good for the tourist trade and it dramatically shortens the time it takes a businessman to drive from Geneva to Rome. And it represents the end of an era.

Before the tunnel, the only way to go directly from Chamonix to Italy was by crossing a high mountain pass. To be sure, in recent years one could make the trip over the glaciers by *téléphérique*, but until then the only way to go was on foot. Alpine literature is full of accounts of crisscrossings of these passes. Ever since I began mountain climbing in and around the Chamonix Valley, I have been reading chronicles of the early climbs and pass crossings, and it occurred to me that just before the tunnel opened might be a good time to make a complete circuit of Mont Blanc by means of the glacial passes and valleys that surround it. The trip takes about five days, winding its way through seven valleys in three countries, and it would be a kind of tribute to the pioneers as well as a chance to see some completely new landscape.

As soon as I got to Geneva, where I was going to be working during the summer, I phoned Jaccoux, and asked him whether he would be interested in making such a trip. He was delighted with the idea and said, to my surprise, that although he had been climbing around Chamonix for nearly fifteen years, he had never done *le tour de Mont Blanc*. He also said that if he could garage his then six-year-old daughter with her grandparents, he was sure that his wife Michèle, a former Olympic skier and now a ski instructor, would be glad to come along, too. A few days later, he phoned back to say that Michèle could come, and we fixed the first of July as the date on which to begin the trip. Shortly after *that*, I found myself in La Hutte, a sports shop in Chamonix, buying all sorts of equipment.

To get some idea of what we had in mind, and to see why the equipment was necessary, it is helpful to review a little of the geography of the Mont Blanc region. The Mont Blanc massif itself is a high glacial plateau about thirty miles long and ten miles wide. It runs from the southwest to the northeast, starting in France and ending in Switzerland, and the Franco-Italian border is traced along most of its length. It is ringed by a system of seven valleys—a giant ice castle surrounded by a moat. The classic tour of the massif involves following a well-marked trail through the valleys, and it would be nothing if it were not that at several points on the circuit the headwall that separates one valley from the next blocks the track. Many of these headwalls, reaching out radially, like the spokes of a wheel, are more than ten thousand feet high and are covered with snow all year long. Still, to traverse them requires no alpinism; the trip is simply a good hard walk. There are elaborate alpine refuges spaced at a comfortable day's march apart, and the whole thing takes about a week. That, at least, is the usual routine; we wanted to do something different. We wanted to make the circuit while staying as high on the shoulder of the massif as possible. This meant that we would be moving almost all the time among the glaciers that tumble down the sides of Mont Blanc. On the Italian sector, however, where the valley walls are impossibly steep, we would join the usual trail until we reached Switzerland, and then move back up on the glaciers. Our trip, like all glacier traveling, *would* involve some alpinism, and Jaccoux thought that we might bag en route a few of the peaks that border some of the high passes we expected to cross. He was not sure of the exact course we would follow, and while I was

Le tour de Mont Blanc

buying the equipment he talked it over with Roger Frison-Roche, the guide and mountain writer whose book, *Mont Blanc and the Seven Valleys*, had given me the idea for the expedition in the first place.

There had been an especially heavy snowfall the previous winter, and since we were making our tour early in the season, before the snow had had much chance to melt, we expected that the conditions would be rather wintry. In addition, we were not sure that the refuges would be open, and to be on the safe side we planned to carry enough food so that if we arrived at a closed refuge (even if the refuges are officially closed, a door or window is usually left open, so that people can use them unofficially if they have to), we would not go hungry. Jaccoux reasoned that if worst came to worst, we would be able to drop down to one of the tiny villages in the valleys below and find shelter. I made sure that I had at least two of everything—two pairs of gloves, two sweaters, two sets of *stop-tout* (cloth puttees that fit over the tops of one's climbing boots to keep out the snow)—and a new pair of boots. Buying a pair of climbing boots at the beginning of the season is a ceremonial occasion. New boots are things of beauty, wonderfully made out of thick leather and carefully lined with a spongy material to make walking as comfortable as possible. As I was trying on something like the fifth pair and answering innumerable questions about our plans asked by various guides and climbers who had wandered into La Hutte and whose curiosity was aroused by where I might be going with so much equipment so early in the season, Jaccoux appeared, full of optimism about the trip after his talk with Frison-Roche. He suggested that I buy a pair of boots named after a well-known Swiss guide, Michel Darbellay, and this turned out to be a prophetic choice, since we ran into Darbellay himself, in one of the Swiss valleys along our route. Everyone told us that we were going to enjoy *"une bonne ballade,"* and that we would come back bronzed and fit. I don't regret the trip for a second, but, as it turned out, it was not what I would call a *ballade*.

After collecting our gear, Jaccoux and I drove to the small farmhouse where he and Michèle were living. We had lunch with Claude's father, who had come to pick up his granddaughter, and were soon driving down the Chamonix Valley. We were going to start our circuit from the village of Les Contamines in the adjoining Vallée de Montjoie. The pioneers, no doubt, would have done this lap of the trip on foot, but there is a superhighway that leads out of the Chamonix Valley, and it seemed rather silly not to take advantage of it. Our first stop was to be a refuge on the edge of the Glacier de Trélatête—a walk of a few hours from Les Contamines. We planned to cross over the glaciers at the southwestern end of the massif, crossing the Italian border at the same time; it was a shortcut that would save us a two-day march around the end of the massif. On the way to Les Contamines, Jaccoux had the happy notion of stopping at the home of the guardian of the refuge to see if he was at his post. The guardian answered the door himself and told Jaccoux that the refuge was untended, adding that he had left a window open and that we should have no trouble finding it and climbing through. It was fortunate that we had stopped. In Chamonix we had been told that the refuge, which operates as a small hotel during the season, would almost certainly be open; now we added some extra food for that evening's dinner and for breakfast the next morning.

We left the car at the highest point we could drive it to and began the long climb up the slopes to the refuge. Early along, we passed a sign saying that it would take an hour and a half to get there. Jaccoux moves very quickly in the mountains, and Michèle, who was in superb condition after a winter of daily skiing, walks as fast as he does. They soon left me behind. My only previous outing that season had been a brief climb the week before with Jaccoux in the Vercors, near Grenoble. We had done Mont Aiguille—a remarkable tower, about seven thousand feet high, that was known in the Middle Ages as one of "the Seven Miracles of the Dauphiny." All its walls are perfectly vertical, while the top is a level pasture large enough to graze cattle—if one could get them up there. Only one route to the summit can be negotiated without the most advanced techniques, and this route, which involves some middling rock climbing, was done on June 28, 1492, by one Antoine de Ville, lord of Domjulien and of Beaupré. According to a contemporary account, de Ville made use of ladders and "sobtilz engins"—no one seems to know what these were—and he camped on the top for three days in a hut he built. The climbing of Mont Aiguille is the first recorded instance of a serious rock climb, and it is one of the remarkable incidents in the history of alpinism.

As we moved up the trail, clouds began to form, and it was clear that we were in for a storm. Before long, lightning began playing over the ridges above me, and every once in a while I could make out Claude and Michèle along the trail in the distance. It was a good two and a half hours before we reached the refuge. (Jaccoux figured that the time on the sign had probably been deliberately shortened to lure tourists to the refuge, which is privately owned.) By now, it was raining solidly, and we were making our way by flashlight. The refuge consists of two stone buildings, and in the smaller of the two we found the unlocked window. Jaccoux climbed in, then Michèle. I handed our packs in through the window and went to a nearby trough to fill our canteens with icy water. By the time I climbed through the window, Michèle had already begun to straighten up the barnlike room that we found ourselves in. There were long wooden decks on which straw mattresses could be placed for sleeping, and we found a vast number of dusty mattresses and comfortable-looking blankets stacked in every corner of the room. Each of us fixed up a bed, and then Michèle got dinner, Jaccoux studied our maps, and I rested. After dinner, a tremendous electrical storm broke over the refuge, and we turned in for the night to the accompaniment of the rolling echoes of thunder.

After what seemed like a very short time, I heard Jaccoux calling, "*Debout, mes pauvres! On y va!*" I struggled up from my nest of blankets and, looking sleepily out the window, saw that the sky was thickly overcast. It was not actually raining, but the air had the heavy smell of ozone produced by the lightning of the previous night. We had breakfast, straightened up the room, packed our gear, and climbed back out the window. A narrow, stony trail led onto the glacier. When we reached the ice and snow, at perhaps six in the morning, Jaccoux stopped, took out a climbing rope, and tied Michèle in the middle of it and me on the end. In the gray half-light, the glacier, about five miles long, was not a very appealing sight, and I felt some sympathy with a noted French alpinist who wrote, "Then, at the very first peep of dawn, I discovered the glacier of Trélatête. Through all the Alps I know of no more solitary or more forbidding glacier. And that was what I felt when I saw it in the wan light of early morning. It did not resemble at all what I expected. It looked like a gigantic dead beast—some dragon drowned forever between desolate banks. The whole landscape was deeply inhuman and hostile, as if distorted by the light dripping from the dull sky. It was cold, and the cold permeated my whole being, gripping my heart and numbing my body. I felt terribly lost, miserable, a prey to blind but prodigious powers. And I felt terrified." Claude and Michèle and I were cold, all right, but the slope was gentle and the crevasses easily crossed, so we moved steadily ahead. On all sides, we could see the murky outlines of the great mountains, their summits covered with clouds. We were in a narrow glacial valley, and the sides looked so steep that I did not see how we could possibly get out, but after an hour or so, Jaccoux began navigating toward a steep snow slope leading to the Mont Tondu col, or pass, and by kicking out steps in the hard snow we got up to a rock outcropping that overlooked the glacier. Jaccoux sat down heavily, and I asked him whether he had stopped to take pictures or something, since he normally stops only to keep his clients from collapsing. *"Je m'arrête pour m'arrêter,"* he responded dourly. The heavy atmosphere had made hard work of walking and climbing, and I was pleased to see that I was not the only one to get tired. Jaccoux decided that we would move more easily if we put on our crampons and this we did. It was now beginning to snow lightly, and by the time we reached the top of the pass we were being doused by a mixture of snow and rain.

The sight that greeted us there was as desolate as anything one could imagine. To our right there was a long, dark rock ridge that led up to the summit of Mont Tondu (ten thousand feet), and every few minutes the whole ridge appeared to shake when it got hit by lightning. (Later, when we finally returned to Chamonix, I was gratified to read in Edward Whymper's great alpine classic, *Scrambles Amongst the Alps*, that he had crossed the Col du Mont Tondu 101 years before us, almost to the day, and also in a severe lightning storm.) Ahead of us, across several snow slopes broken up by long rock ridges, we could make out another col—the Col de la Seigne, which marked the Italian frontier. But to move on from the crest of our pass involved dropping down a steep rock wall. It would not have been particularly difficult under normal conditions, but now the rock was slippery and wet and covered with new snow. I inched my way down as far as the rope would let me, while Claude and Michèle anchored me from above. Then I pulled the rope in taut while we got Michèle down, and we both gave Jaccoux whatever security we could while he came down to join us. Finally, I was able to jump out onto the snow, and soon we were together on what appeared to be easy terrain. The only trouble was that the snow was soft, and every few steps one of us would fall through the crust up to the waist. Since there was no real danger, Claude unroped us so we could move somewhat faster. The Jaccoux began to ski down the slopes on their feet, using their ice axes as brakes whenever necessary. I tried to imitate them, but on the first attempt I slipped and began sailing down the long slope on my back, experiencing a sort of sense of suspended animation while the terrain floated past. After sliding for a hundred feet or so, I managed to roll over on my stomach, dig my ice axe into the snow, and come to a gradual stop. One of my gloves had come off and gone hurtling down to the Vallée des Glaciers below. I picked myself up, fished a second glove out of my rucksack, and, feeling rather foolish, made the rest of the descent by putting one foot after the other. By the time I reached the Jaccoux, they had found shelter from the rain in a small crevasse by the side of a rock ridge, and as I climbed in to join them Jaccoux said, "What sort of game were you trying to play?" Michèle proposed that we have a little breakfast in the crevasse before going on, and by the time we had finished the rain had subsided considerably, although there was still a good deal of lightning on the ridges above us. We emerged from our crevasse and mounted a small rock pinnacle just in time to witness an absolutely breathtaking sight—right above us, a whole herd of wild, beautiful mountain chamois, terrified by the lightning, were leaping over the rocks, literally gliding in the air from boulder to boulder until they finally disappeared from view. We had now reached the last real obstacle before the frontier—a steep grass slope, made as slick as ice by the rain— and here again we helped each other along foot by foot. Jaccoux kicked steps up a snow wall in front of us, and by the time

Michèle and I reached him he was stretched out on the turf, smoking his pipe, eating a piece of cheese, and calmly regarding the magnificent Italian valley that lay spread out before us.

The Col de la Seigne, on which we now stood, separates France from Italy. It is rich in the traditions of the Savoy. Until a hundred years ago, the Savoy—the whole of the Mont Blanc massif—was a single political unit; now it is divided among France, Italy, and Switzerland. In his delightful book *The Alps in Nature and History*, the Victorian climber W.A.B. Coolidge notes that even the summit of Mont Blanc (now placed, according to the latest Michelin map, in France) has been the subject of dispute: "As regards the actual summit of Mont Blanc, the French (and their official maps) draw the frontier line slightly to the S. (over the Mont Blanc de Courmayeur) of the culminating point. But the Italians (and their official maps) make the frontier line follow the watershed, and so pass over the actual top, and not to its S. Some of the older maps seem to be in favor of the French contention, as well as, apparently, the map annexed to the report of the Boundary Commission of 1861; but this last map is declared by the Italians to reproduce a mistake of the original Sardinian map, published in 1854 but later corrected. The text of the Report favours the Italian contention, stating that the boundary follows the watershed, and so passes over the summit of Mont Blanc." Needless to say, there are no customs officials on the summit of Mont Blanc, and Coolidge concludes: "It is amusing to think that the great Alpine summits have thus had divers political fates. This, however, was not due to any action on their part, but to the struggles of the human midgets at their feet, who were perhaps regarded by the cloud-capped mountains as intruders dividing up that to which they had no right save force. Till very recently, too, these midgets never dared to come within the range of the heavy artillery (such as avalanches) of the Alpine giants, which came into existence geologically before man, and may perhaps long survive his extinction."

The common language of the region a hundred years ago was French patois, and the language of the Italian Savoy is still largely French. Under Mussolini, the people of the Savoy were required to abandon French as an official language, but, as in the Italian Tyrol, where the people were required to abandon German, the policy was not very successful. The Savoyards, even with the political division, thought of themselves as a unified people, and among their most cherished rights was the right to transport goods over the mountain passes from one part of the Savoy to another. After the political division, this, of course, became smuggling, and the Col de la Seigne was one of the great way stations for smugglers. Indeed, Frison-Roche, in his book, recalls that in his youth he often stood lookout for smugglers passing in and out of France, and would receive a pack of cards or a box of matches as a reward. Now the col is on the regular route of the classic valley tour of Mont Blanc. By making our way to it over the glaciers rather than via the Vallée des Glaciers, we had replaced the two-day march around the end of the massif by a climb of only seven hours.

Our destination for the night was the Elisabetta, a beautiful alpine hut about two miles from the Col de la Seigne, run by the Italian Alpine Club. We were now on a broad footpath leading down the Val Veni, and soon we passed the Italian frontier station, a small stone outpost that was completely deserted and all but lost in the snow. When we got near the Elisabetta, we could see that it, too, was closed, and that we had no choice but to go on down the valley to the alpine village of Courmayeur, which is situated at the Italian end of the Mont Blanc tunnel. Between the Elisabetta and Courmayeur there is a jeep road, and we would have been delighted to hitch a ride, but much of the road was covered with melting snow and there was no traffic. A few miles from Courmayeur, we saw our first car—a small Fiat, crowded with people, coming toward us. It stopped almost at once, however, and they all got out and stood in a circle while a priest among them said a blessing over the mountains. He was standing on the shores of a small lake, which, I later learned, was created by a giant rock fall from Mont Blanc in the 1920s. Hoping that they could transport our heavy, rain-soaked packs into Courmayeur, we hurried to reach the car, but the group climbed back in and sped away without seeing us. In a moment, we came to a winding concrete road, and Claude and Michèle, arm in arm, set off down it at such a tremendous pace that I soon lost sight of them. When I caught up, they were stretched out on two wooden benches in front of a tiny Italian inn. It, too, was closed, but we cajoled a couple of bottles of sweet Italian beer from a girl who had been left in charge. A few minutes later, a rather magnificent-looking Alfa Romeo came along, and I managed to flag it down.

Until the opening of the tunnel, Courmayeur was an isolated village with a reputation as a summer retreat for the aristocracy. Frison-Roche points out that the Italian court used to go there for summers, and that young members of the Italian nobility were sent to the valley to learn climbing from the local guides. The occupants of the Alfa Romeo—a middle-aged man and an elderly woman—seemed to belong to this tradition, for they were extremely elegant-looking. But they had the air of people who had spent a lot of time in the mountains and, dishevelled as we were, they were happy to crowd us into the back seat of their spotless machine, especially when they learned that Jaccoux was a Chamonix guide with whom they could discuss the mountains. There are guides in Courmayeur, but, as Jaccoux told me, it is a dwindling profession there. One of the reasons is that until recently the Italian guide rates were so low, compared to the rates in Chamonix, that a guide could earn a much better living, even in the summer, by teaching skiing. (There is year-round skiing on the glaciers above Courmayeur.)

The Alfa deposited us at the bus station in Courmayeur, and we decided to spend a few hours wandering around the village. It is, or was, a lovely, tranquil alpine resort in the valley, full of charming hotels and restaurants and small cafés. Above the town we could make out the rather ugly road that leads into the tunnel, and we could see the dark gash of the tunnel itself cut harshly into the granite wall. No traffic was moving through, and the village appeared to me to be living on the frontier between its past and a future that would transform it completely. As it happened, we soon had the first half of an experience that enabled us to measure the change during the summer. We knew of a nearby restaurant that was famous among European alpinists for its marvellous Italian-French cooking and for its simplicity—the Restaurant of the Brenva, named after one of the glaciers that come down from Mont Blanc into Italy. After our hard day—we had been walking for nearly twelve hours—we felt entitled to a good dinner and we went there. The food was absolutely brilliant—platter after platter of hot and cold sausages, ham, special cheeses in herb sauces, roast veal and broiled chicken, red wine, mountains of wild strawberries, and, finally, coffee mixed with *eau-de-vie* and sugar and served out of a wooden bowl with three spouts, which we passed around until it was empty. The restaurant was filled with guides, tunnel workers, frontier guards, and alpinists, and the price was half of what one would have paid in a typical restaurant in Chamonix. The other part of our experience came at the end of the summer, when we visited the restaurant again on the *fête des guides*, about a month after the tunnel had been opened. The proprietor told us, with great pride, that he had opened a second restaurant, with the same cooking but with more stylish décor, for the new patrons that the tunnel was bringing through. We went to visit it. It was designed in excellent taste in the style of a country inn, with wooden beams that crossed under the roof and small dining rooms in every corner. The diners were so fashionably dressed that we felt a little odd in our mountain clothes. At one point, a parade of people who looked as though they had stepped out of a Fellini movie came down the stairs, and each of them took a turn swinging on the wooden ceiling beams. The sight of a beautiful Roman lady, dressed in the latest fashion, with her lovely, dark face illuminated by candlelight, swinging back and forth on a wooden beam said everything that could be said about what the opening of the Mont Blanc tunnel will mean to the massif.

After a warm bath and a splendid night's sleep in a modest hotel, we awoke to a brilliant sunlit morning. Jaccoux had promised us a relatively easy day. We were to take the bus as far as it went down the Italian sector of the Val Ferret toward Switzerland, and then we were to climb the headwall of the valley—the Col Ferret—dropping down into La Fouly, at the top of the Swiss Val Ferret. All began well. The bus careered along the valley, and we could look out at small country inns, tiny streams, and wooded fields spread before the vertical wall of the Italian side of the Grandes Jorasses, one of the highest mountains in the range. The bus reached the end of its run at a small inn, and we were able to persuade a family in a car to take our packs all the way to the head of the valley, while we followed on foot. As is so often the case in the mountains, the wall of the Col Ferret appeared, from head on, to be absolutely vertical. We could make out the beginning of an abandoned road that wound up the lower part of the face and then disappeared abruptly, as if its builders had suddenly thought better of their project. (In his book, Coolidge refers to the start of the construction of this road, which was to be a rival to the route over the historic St. Bernard Pass, a little to the southeast. I have not been able to discover why or when the project was abandoned.) We followed this road and then headed up the face, which was certainly steep enough, although hardly vertical. It was miserable terrain for climbing—loose turf that slid back after each step, giving one a disheartening sense of insecurity. Claude and Michèle were ahead, and when we were well up on the wall I noticed that they had stopped and that Michèle was sobbing uncontrollably; when I got closer, I could hear her saying to Claude that she was too frightened to go on. Claude was shouting at her to give him her hand, but she was too scared to do anything but cling to the earth. He finally had to wrench her hand away and all but drag her on. As they started up, he turned and said to me, in no uncertain terms, *"Je veux que tu ne panique pas!"* I indeed felt anxious, but I was able to get to the top with no real difficulty.

Later, I asked Michèle why she had panicked. I knew that she had been born in the mountains—in Mégève, in the Haute-Savoie—and that, as a member of the French national ski team, she had specialized in the most dangerous of all skiing events, the downhill run, or *la descente*. It is a race against the clock in which the skier goes straight down, or as nearly straight down as possible. (The downhill seems to run in Michèle's family. Her brother, Pierre Stamos, was on the French Olympic team and was one of the best *descendeurs* in the world.) When Michèle was skiing in competition, she would often attain speeds of over sixty miles an hour on terrain that was easily as steep as anything we had climbed that day. She told me that she had an absolute confidence in her technique on skis, and that on skis she would certainly have been able to go down the terrain that we had climbed up. But the sight of the long, vertiginous drop to the valley, combined with the unfamiliar, treacherous feeling of the terrain, had made her panic. I asked her if she ever got frightened on the downhill. She said that very often she was frightened, but that it gave her a special sense of exhilaration, which made her ski even better; this fear today, on the other hand, simply paralyzed her. The following winter she climbed up to this pass and skied back down with no difficulty at all.

At the top of the col, we sat down for a long rest and something to eat. We were now on the frontier between Italy and Switzerland. Behind us, to the west, the whole of the Italian valley stretched out, and to the south the countryside fell away into plains. In front of us was a gentle snow slope leading down to the town of La Fouly, which we could make out in the distance. We slid down the first snow slope, and Jaccoux spotted a system of snow névés—corridors of snow—which we were able to use, thus avoiding the rather tedious walk down on loose rocks. It was beautiful country, with huge cliffs and water-falls and a rushing glacial stream that led into town. We took a path through some woods, and almost before we knew it we were inside a comfortable hotel run by a well-known Swiss guide named Xavier Kalt.

La Fouly is a town that still lives largely in the past. Kalt no longer takes climbers out himself, but he manages a guide bureau for climbers who come into the valley. Most of the people in La Fouly are herdsmen. As is typical of the small Swiss mountain towns in the Valais, they live in *mazots*—log cabins that can be taken apart, like Lincoln Logs, and moved. The Jaccoux had recently purchased a small plot of land near Chamonix and wanted to buy some *mazots* to move onto their land; every time Michèle passed an especially pretty one, she wanted to rush inside to see if it was for sale. Claude introduced us to Kalt, who turned out to be a portly middle-aged gentleman with an impressive beard. Apart from running his hotel, he was well known as a restaurateur, the specialty of his hotel being *raclettes*, a dish that is native to the canton of Valais—the area around the Rhone Valley. *Raclettes* are made from a yellow *demi-gras* Gruyère cheese, which is manufactured in the shape of a large wheel. To make them, the wheel is cut in half across a diameter, and the open edge is heated. The warm face is scraped off in a thin layer and deposited on small wooden plates. It requires a good deal of mechanical skill and physical strength on the part of the chef to keep turning out *raclettes* as fast as the guests can consume them. Traditionally, they are eaten with boiled potatoes, small pickles, and a white wine known as Fendant, and the chef stands by to dish up more *raclettes* as soon as anyone has finished his plate. I have seen people down as many as nineteen servings, but I myself find that nine or ten are more than enough. Jaccoux persuaded Kalt to make us *raclettes*, and after we had installed ourselves in a comfortable dormitorylike bedroom and had a bath, we came down to dinner.

In the dining room, we met Michel Darbellay—the guide of the boots. Although then quite young, Darbellay was already one of the most famous of the Swiss guides. He looks for all the world like the Hollywood notion of a guide—strikingly handsome, with an air of bravado—and he is known to mountain climbers all over the world as the first man to make the ascent of the North Wall of the Eiger alone. The North Wall of the Eiger is considered by many to be the most dangerous climb in Europe. It has been climbed many times—even in the winter now—but it still takes its toll of climbers each year. Three summers ago, Darbellay succeeded in doing it alone, and in a single day. Overnight, he became famous throughout Europe, and as one consequence he had a pair of mountain boots named after him. I was able to tell him that I had enjoyed wearing his boots but that they shipped water in deep snow. He and Jaccoux agreed that no climbing boots will keep out water indefinitely, and with that we settled down to consuming Kalt's *raclettes*.

Jaccoux had planned a very hard run for us the next day. However, Michèle's morale was low after her experience on the Col Ferret, and I was feeling a real sense of fatigue after three days of hiking and climbing following a long winter of relative inactivity. But nothing would put Jaccoux off, and the three of us settled in our bunks in the dormitory, prepared to get up at four the next morning, with Michèle and me jointly praying for rain; we had extracted an agreement from Jaccoux that if it was raining when we got up he would modify his plan. The next day, I was awakened early by Jaccoux, and after a silent and somewhat gloomy breakfast we strapped on our packs and went outside, Michèle and I being resigned to the worst. No sooner had we put our noses out the door than it began to rain. Michèle and I leaped around like two schoolchildren given a sudden reprieve, while Jaccoux peered sullenly at the dark clouds that were pouring over the high mountain ridges all around us. Jaccoux decided that we would wait for the first bus, travel down the valley to Orsières, and then take a second bus to the resort town of Champex, from which, weather permitting, we would climb up to another alpine refuge. From there we could make the trip back into France over the Glacier du Trient.

The trip by bus was through country as beautiful as any I have seen in Switzerland. This part of the Valais lacks the drama of the better-known Swiss alpine settings like Zermatt and Grindelwald, but it presents a wonderful panorama of deep valleys, richly wooded slopes covered with wild flowers, and always, in the distance, the great snow peaks. The town of Orsières is an attractive collection of cafés and *mazots*, while Champex, our last stop by bus, is a slick-looking resort set on the shore of a lake. By the time we got to Champex, the weather had improved to such an extent that we immediately took a swaying chair lift that carried us up over the woods to the base of a trail leading onto the Glacier du Trient. We expected to take about five hours to climb to the Cabine du Trient, a huge refuge run by the Swiss Alpine Club, and we broke the trip in half at a lower refuge that was filled with a large group of elderly Swiss alpinists up for a Sunday outing and in high spirits. We had a light lunch with them and then headed up the glacier to the upper cabin.

The trip to the upper refuge was along a gently sloping glacier. Normally, one ropes up on glaciers, but this one was so carefully traced out—a well-trodden path through the snow—

that each of us went along at his own pace, which meant, inevitably, that the Jaccoux arrived at the cabin long before I did. "Cabin" here is an understatement. Like many of the modern refuges, this one was a huge stone structure capable of sleeping at least two hundred people in dormitories. It had an enormous dining room with a small alpine library, and like many such places, served simple but excellent meals. It dominated the glacier, and from the long balcony in front we could get a magnificent view of the peaks that marked the French frontier— peaks that I had climbed in and that Jaccoux knew like the back of his hand. Until we reached the Trient, we had had a sense of having the mountains almost to ourselves; it was so early in the season that we had met almost no one. However, the Glacier du Trient was full of people. The principal reason was that a unit of the Swiss Army—young men serving out a few weeks of compulsory duty in the summer—had come up to learn climb- ing techniques from a group of guides. I have been told by Swiss guides that this military training is one of the major reasons that guiding is a dying profession in Switzerland; so many potential climbers have had such excellent training in the army that they feel no need to climb with guides when they get out. While we were eating, the recruits, from all over Switzerland, began to troop in. Besides being boisterous, they committed a basic faux pas in climbing-refuge life, which is to leave the door of the refuge open. We were at about ten thousand feet, and each blast of cold air from the open door chilled one to the bone. Jaccoux spent several minutes ranting at the new arrivals, but finally he put on another sweater and did his best to ignore the chaos. In all, there were well over eighty soldiers, and since there was already a rather large group of people in the refuge, finding a bunk to sleep in became a problem. We were crowded in so tightly that I was constantly being jammed by someone's elbow or foot. About three in the morning, I gave up and went downstairs to take a walk outside. After some difficulty in unlocking the massive front door, I walked out on the terrace and was struck by the strange, heavy, hot atmosphere. The weather had changed again, and it was unnaturally warm.

Lightning began to strike some of the peaks nearby, and when one bolt sizzld off a ridge not far from where I was standing, I beat a retreat inside to wait it out until morning.

With sunrise, the rain clouds lifted, and now the glacier was alive with light. Every few minutes, a gust of loose snow would be sent flying somewhere in the distance; clearly, a high wind was blowing. We had breakfast and, with a sense that we were now in our home territory, we roped up to cross the glacier. Jaccoux set his compass on the Col du Tour, by which we planned to cross into France, and the terrain looked so simple that, in defiance of fate, I said, "*C'est de la tarte*"—a remark that I soon regretted. About midway on the glacier, we were hit by the wind. Jaccoux was leading, and suddenly I saw him tilt forward for no apparent reason, and then right himself. Next came Michèle's turn, and finally an icy blast hit me, bringing with it tiny needles of ice and snow that stung my face fiercely. At one point, Jaccoux stopped and yelled back at me, "*C'est de la tarte, eh, Jérémie?*" When we reached the Col du Tour, we found ourselves in the middle of a raging storm. I have never seen anything quite like it. All the colors were reduced to black and white—black granite and black clouds and white snow driven in great bursts by the wind, then rain with lightning flashes. The wind was incredibly strong, and it was all we could do to fight our way over the top of the col. Fortunately, the other side of the col, although steep rock and covered with loose snow and ice, was not terribly difficult, so that we were able to get down to the glacier below fairly quickly. Once we were off the ridge and again in France, the whole climate changed again. We were now immersed in a fog—a fog so thick, that no one could not see ten feet. Everything was absolutely white and totally silent. I had no sense of where I was or where we were going. Jaccoux, on the other hand, moved off with complete certainty. It was a virtuoso performance of blind navigation. Sometimes he would stop to look at the compass and sometimes at a pocket altimeter, although an altimeter is hard to use in bad weather, since the low atmospheric pressure simulates changes in altitude; even if one stands perfectly still, the altimeter will read different heights while the pressure is changing. Most of all, Jaccoux relied on his sense of direction and on the fact that he had been over this glacier hundreds of times. (He later told me that he had guided people in the fog over glaciers that he did not know by using a map, a compass, and an altimeter, and by measuring out distances and angles by moving one climbing-rope length at a time and counting how many rope lengths he had traveled in a given direction.) At one point, the fog lifted for a minute or so, and we saw that we had been following a perfectly straight path along the edge of a huge bed of ugly-looking, massive crevasses; Jaccoux knew that they were there, and he knew just how far away he had to stay from them. We were constantly losing altitude, and soon the snow turned into a heavy rain. Jaccoux began moving at almost a run, to get out of the storm. I was wearing sunglasses because of the strong glare from the glacier, which can oppress one even in the fog, and they had steamed up so badly that I could hardly see. I kept falling up to my knees into small, loose pockets of snow and being hauled out like a fish by Jaccoux. At one point, Michèle looked back and said of her husband, *"Il a du zèle."* Puffing and staggering, I found myself being dragged over a small pile of rocks, and then, out of the fog right below us, appeared the Refuge Albert Premier, above the Chamonix Valley. We ran inside the front door and out of the storm.

The rest of the trip back to Chamonix really was *"de la tarte."* We had lunch at the Albert Premier and, as a private joke, finished it off with *tartes aux myrtilles*, a specialty of the refuge. When we had finished lunch, it was still raining, but the wind had died down, and there were no signs of lightning. An easy trail led from the refuge to the top of a ski lift, and the ski lift took us down to the town of Le Tour, near the head of the Chamonix Valley. We stopped at a small café in Le Tour, and the proprietress, a friend of the Jaccoux, after hearing of our adventures, offered us a free coffee with cognac. In an ultimate manifestation of *la tarte*, we called a taxi from Chamonix and drove back to town in high style. A few hours later, we recovered the car from where it had been left in Les Contamines five days earlier.

Why make such a trip? In his book, written just before

construction began on the Mont Blanc tunnel, Frison-Roche wrote, "The Mont Blanc tunnel is going to be built—we have seen the first hole dug on the Italian side. We must hurry, then, We must hasten to speak once more of Mont Blanc, with its valleys which are so dissimilar in appearance and yet so similar at heart, before it is too late and before nothing is left of what made the homogeneity of the range, its old traditions. . . . To be frank, it is already too late! In the Chamonix Valley, tourism has triumphed and the cowbells are silent!" In a few years, with the tunnel, the cowbells will be silent in all seven of the valleys that surround the Mont Blanc massif, and our trip will be a reminder for us of the strength of nature and its weakness before the hand of man.

7   A Sense of Something Forbidding

When I first visited the Chamonix Valley of France, at the foot of Mont Blanc, in the fall of 1959, it was just under two centuries after the Swiss aristocrat Horace-Bénédict de Saussure came from Geneva to visit the valley, in 1760. While hiking to a subsidiary peak—the Brévent—de Saussure conceived the idea that Mont Blanc, which is 4,807 meters, or 15,771 feet, high and is the highest mountain in Western Europe, could be climbed, and he offered a large cash reward—about sixty dollars—to the first person to do so. (The reward was claimed by a Chamonix physician, Dr. Michel-Gabriel Paccard, and a chamois hunter, crystal collector, and alpine guide, Jacques Balmat, after they climbed the peak, on August 8, 1786.) With de Saussure's dream, alpinism was created, and, along with it, the mountain aesthetic was invented. To feel that mountains are beautiful, and that snow-covered mountains are the most beautiful of all, is now part of our conditioning. But this is a fairly modern idea. Until the nineteenth century—with rare exceptions—people of the Western world regarded mountains as terrifying, ugly, and an obstacle to travel and commerce, and anyone living in or near them as subhuman. The change came about largely through Englishmen like John Ruskin, who, after reading de Saussure's *Voyages dans les Alpes*, first visited the valley in 1833, when he was fourteen. He was captivated by its beauty, and revisited it frequently, and his subsequent sketches and commentaries attracted generations of Englishmen to the Alps. The English transformed climbing from an expeditionary activity with an ostensibly scientific purpose (the pioneers like de Saussure felt, correctly, that they were exploring a new medium—high altitude—and took great pains to measure and describe everything they saw) to a sport practiced simply for the pleasure and satis-faction of it. By 1865, when the twenty-five-year-old British climber and graphic artist Edward Whymper, with a party of seven, climbed the Matterhorn, almost all the major alpine peaks had been scaled by at least one route. And almost all had been scaled by Englishmen with Continental guides—mainly Swiss. Whymper and his party were accompanied by three guides—a Frenchman and two Swiss. On the descent from the Matterhorn, four members of Whymper's party were killed in a fall, and this accident, on July 14, 1865, marked the end of the Golden Age of discovery of the Alps.

By an irony, surely unintended, future alpine historians may well come to regard July 19, 1965—a century after Whymper's climb—as the end of the Golden Age of the Alps themselves. On that date, the tunnel some seven miles long, drilled through Mont Blanc and connecting Chamonix to its Italian counterpart, Courmayeur, was opened to the public. The formal opening ceremony, which I attended, had occurred a few days earlier. General de Gaulle had been present, along with hundreds of tourists and Chamoniards. Some of the latter were apprehen-sive, partly because they thought the tunnel might jeopardize the alpine environment, and partly because many of them, like my friends the Morand brothers, who now own three major hotels in Chamonix, had borrowed large sums of money to expand their premises in anticipation of the new influx of tourists. (At that time, they owned only one, the Hôtel Mont Blanc; soon after the bonanza, they bought another, the Croix Blanche; and they recently built a third, the Beausite.) I recall the eldest of the three Morand brothers, a former professor of mathematics, who died of cancer in 1971, telling me in 1965 that if the family's gamble on the increased tourist trade did not pay off they would be in serious financial trouble. He need not have worried. In July of 1977 alone, 174,427 vehicles of all descrip-tions passed through the tunnel, and since the tunnel opened more than 10,300,000 vehicles, of which nearly 80 percent were private cars, have made the trip. The *Guide Michelin* of 1965 puts the permanent population of Chamonix that year at 7,966; it has since risen to 9,002. All the other people in the valley—hundreds of thousands in any given summer or winter season—are tourists. I doubt if there has been a single night since 1965 when any major hotel in Chamonix had a spare room during a vacation period, and for August, the peak summer month, many of the hotels are booked up a full year in advance. And at all seasons of the year the hotels and motor lodges accommodate numbers of people who are on their way somewhere else.

The Chamonix Valley that I wandered into in 1959, although I did not realize it at the time, bore at least some resemblance to the one that de Saussure, Ruskin, and Whymper had known. The names of the early alpine guides—Balmat, Charlet, Couttet, Dévouassoud, Payot, Ravanel, Tournier—were still the family names of the Chamonix guides, and were also the most common names on the local banks and stores. On the trail to the Brévent, a stone that Ruskin sat on while he sketched had been established as a sort of monument, although few people seemed to stop off to look at it, and fewer still to understand what it commemorated. The Brévent, to be sure, could be reached in a few minutes by a system of *téléphériques* instead of by a walk of a few hours. However, the major *téléphérique*, which reached the summit of the Aiguille du Midi, across the valley, was still a novelty, having been put into service only in 1954. There is now one other large *téléphérique*, which has opened up the Lognan-Grands Montets slope, five miles farther up the valley at Argentière, to thousands of skiers and hikers. The aiguilles—the granite needles of Chamonix—resembled, as they still do, the incredible spires of Gothic churches. By 1959, however, the alpine glaciers had shrunk since Ruskin's day to an almost pitiable state. As recently as seventy-five years ago, someone who wanted to walk on the Mer de Glace, a glacier that runs alongside some of the aiguilles, could step out of the Montenvers, a nearby hotel, and be almost on the ice. Now a tourist visiting the Montenvers must descend a few hundred feet by a series of iron ladders and fixed railings in order to reach the glacier. At that time, too, ice blocks from the Mer de Glace would occasionally break off the glacier and come sliding down to the Rue du Dr. Paccard, the main street of Chamonix. Today, the glaciers are once again on the move—rising and advanc-

ing—and if they attain anything like their former size they will
offer more of a threat to the dozens of new hotels that have
sprung up all over the valley than any army of creditors. What
did most to preserve the alpine character of Chamonix in 1959
was the fact that the two roads that led into the valley—one
from Geneva, following the route that de Saussure took, and
the other a steep, winding affair from the Swiss town of
Martigny—led only into the valley. The Chamonix Valley was a
cul-de-sac. Anyone who took these roads did so to see the
mountains. The roads led nowhere else. Then came the tunnel.

With the opening of the tunnel, the Rue du Dr. Paccard—or at
least that part of it which goes through the center of Chamonix
—was converted into a one-way street. It is a narrow street, in
many places just wide enough for two cars. One summer afternoon recently, as I was standing at the curb and waiting to
cross, an incessant stream of automobiles, side by side, in pairs,
waved on by uniformed policemen, swept down the street and
off toward Geneva. They were bumper to bumper—all makes,
with license plates from all over Europe. Because of automobile
exhaust, a gray cloud of smog now hangs over parts of the
valley. While I stood there, I recalled a rather acerbic observation of Ruskin, who as he grew older came to hate the tourists
his own art work had helped bring to Chamonix. In *Modern
Painters*, he wrote, "I would that the enlightened population of
Paris and London were content with doing nothing—that they
were satisfied with expenditure upon their idle pleasures in
their idle way. . . . The valley of Chamouni . . . is rapidly being
turned into a kind of Cremorne Gardens." Ruskin was a
thoroughgoing snob, and, to put it mildly, he failed to understand that the people coming to Chamonix in his day were there
to study and appreciate "his" mountains. Most of the people
inching down the Rue du Dr. Paccard last August were fleeing
the mountains as fast as possible. For them, Chamonix had
become just another way station on the map, and the mountains
were, as they had been until the time of de Saussure's inspiration, simply a hindrance to travel.

If one sees a friend regularly over many years, one may not
notice aging and other slow changes taking place in him until so

much of the process has been completed as to make the change qualitative rather than quantitative. Since 1959, I have been paying visits of several weeks to various alpine regions of Europe at least once a year: often enough so that slow changes— a new hotel here, a new parking lot there—did not strike me until recently as introducing qualitative changes in the alpine communities. But recently, realizing that I had not really been paying attention, I decided to try to get a feeling for what has happened to the Alps. I was shocked. In Whymper's five great alpine seasons—from 1861 through 1865—he frequently trav- eled on foot from Chamonix to what is now the Italian alpine village of Cervinia. Cervinia, which was known to Whymper by its French name, Breuil, is at the base of the Italian side of the Matterhorn, known in French as the Cervin and in Italian as the Monte Cervini. Cervinia is about sixty miles from Chamonix, and Whymper, who covered about thirty miles a day in high mountain country, would make the trip in two days. Such was the rarity of a foreigner in those parts that on one occasion Whymper, having heard of the presence of a fellow-countryman in a French alpine town he was passing through on his walk, had only to ask the locals "Where is the Englishman?" to be led straight to his compatriot. I would like to be present to hear the answer if someone asked that question in a French alpine town today. Whymper used to walk over the glaciers from Chamonix southeast to Courmayeur and Aosta, from there due east to Châtillon, and then due north into the Val Tournanche and on up this valley to Cervinia—a somewhat roundabout route dic- tated by the mountain terrain. Whymper was very fond of the Val Tournanche. In his classic account of his struggle with the Matterhorn—*Scrambles Amongst the Alps*—he wrote:

The Val Tournanche is one of the most charming valleys in the Italian Alps; it is a paradise to an artist, and if the space at my command were greater, I would willingly linger over its groves of chestnuts, its bright trickling rills and its roaring torrents, its upland unsuspected valleys and its noble cliffs. The path rises steeply from Châtillon, but it is well shaded, and the heat of the summer sun is tempered by cool air and spray which comes off the ice-cold streams. One sees from the path, at several places on the right bank of the valley, groups of arches which have been built high up against the faces of the cliffs. Guide-books repeat—on whose authority I know not—that they are the remains of a Roman aqueduct.

The present version of Whymper's trek takes about two hours. I made it not long ago in the company of Jaccoux and Colette. Our notion was to leave Chamonix in the early morning, drive to Cervinia, take a series of ski lifts which leads up to the Col de Théodule, and climb the Breithorn, above Cervinia, which is widely—and rightly—regarded as the easiest four-thousand-meter mountain in the Alps. At 3:30 A.M. on what promised to be a fine hot day, we arrived at the French entrance to the Mont Blanc Tunnel. The tunnel is open twenty-four hours a day. Tickets are sold at both ends, but all the customs and immigration formalities occur at the Italian end. (Taking the tunnel is not cheap. The lowest-priced round-trip ticket available, for the smallest class of automobile, is thirty-six new French francs, or, at the present exchange rate, something over seven dollars. The tunnel, which cost seventy million dollars and took six and a half years to build, has already paid for itself and is now making money for both France and Italy, which divide the revenues.) At that hour of the morning, we were more or less alone, but if we had waited until eight or nine o'clock we would quite likely have been part of a line of several dozen cars, trucks, and buses waiting to get through. In August, the lines can extend for several miles on either side. The tunnel is reasonably well lit, is air-conditioned, and has a single lane of traffic moving in each direction. It takes about ten minutes to get to the other end. From the Italian end of the tunnel a sort of superhighway leads down to Courmayeur. When I first saw Courmayeur, it was a lovely antique alpine town with a long tradition of mountaineering. The highway now runs practically over Courmayeur. The town is still there, to be sure, but it has become a sort of appendage of the highway. It is full of gasoline stations, motels, hotels, and night clubs. Courmayeur is for most people a stopover on the way east to Venice or the Yugoslavian coast. Beyond Courmayeur, the road narrows and heads toward Aosta. We passed a turnoff to the Val di Rhême.

This valley is one of the few places in the Alps where a government—in this case, the Italian government—has done something significant to preserve the alpine environment. The valley is a *parco nazionale*, or nature preserve, with no more in the way of development than one would find in one of our national parks. It is named for the mountain that dominates it—the Gran Paradiso (4,061 meters), a mountain often done on skis—and only a stone refuge constructed at its base indicates the hand of man. How long this state of affairs will last I do not know.

Aosta is now a dreary semimodern town, dominated by the sort of apartment houses so dear to city planners. After Aosta, one takes the superhighway—a toll road that leads to Milan and the south. The second exit from the toll road is Châtillon, where Whymper's steeply rising path to Breuil (Cervinia) began. Châtillon represents a more typical alpine village, torn between its ancient structure—narrow streets and old stone houses—and the exigencies of modern vehicular traffic. Whymper's steep path has become a steep, winding road overburdened with cars, and Châtillon is now a series of one-way streets designed to lead the motorist as quickly as possible out of the town and onto the highway. I was driving, and so did not have much chance to watch for Whymper's roaring torrents and upland unsuspected valleys. I was mainly watching for unsuspected cars, buses, and trucks carrying tourists and merchandise down from Cervinia on the narrow, twisting road. In fact, I was so absorbed in this activity that I would have missed the first view of the Matterhorn—it can be seen almost as soon as one starts up toward Cervinia—if Jaccoux had not called my attention to it.

When one makes the trip on the Swiss side, to Zermatt, one does not see the mountain until just before one arrives at the village. The development of Zermatt is an interesting example of the kind of compromise that can be made to control the unbridled exploitation of an alpine valley in the face of an enormous tourist influx. Recently, the citizens of Zermatt voted to continue a ban on automobiles in their village. It is true that, with the exception of doctors' cars, emergency vehicles, and the like, automobiles are prohibited in the center of the village. But there is a huge parking lot a few hundred meters from the center, next to the cog-railway station. This lot, which is open to citizens of the village and to outsiders with permits, is nearly always filled with hundreds of cars; other motorists can park their cars six kilometers down the valley, at Tasch, which is connected to Visp, at the lower end of the valley, by a super-highway. Moreover, there is a bypass road around Zermatt, which is frequented by large trucks carrying men and materials to hydroelectric power projects being constructed and maintained in the lower glacial valleys above the village. Almost every available square foot of flatland around Zermatt has been or is being developed for hotel and apartment construction. The sound of the jackhammer is heard throughout the valley. Nevertheless, Zermatt has retained much of its original charm. The simple fact that the main street of Zermatt is a pedestrian walkway makes all the difference. It seems to me that where some restriction has been placed on automobiles people achieve a kind of harmony with the environment. The mystery and the beauty of the high mountains work wonders on the human spirit if they are given half a chance.

Cervinia itself presents a view that must quicken the pulse of any real estate developer. The town looks like one large hotel surrounded by parking lots and tourist shops. The reason for all this activity is skiing. Cervinia is one of the major winter ski resorts and *the* major summer ski station in Europe. One might say that no guide from Cervinia who was in his right mind would go mountain climbing, for there is a fortune to be made, at no risk to life and limb, teaching people to ski in summer, and the number of mountain guides has been steadily dwindling. When we arrived at the parking area near the lower ski lift, it was about 7:00 A.M. The place was almost literally crawling with skiers and their cars—hundreds of beautiful sun-tanned girls in the latest ski fashions, and whole families with their private ski instructors. I don't know how Jaccoux felt, but I felt like some sort of Martian, carrying a relatively heavy pack, with crampons, ice axe, and other climbing gear in it. Anyway, off we went, and two lifts later we found ourselves at the Breithorn Plateau, 3,500 meters up and 700 meters from the summit. The major hazard in climbing the Breithorn is not to get clobbered by a skier on the lower slopes. There were so many skiers that it was hard to see how they could avoid running into one another. The final slope of the Breithorn is quite steep—perhaps forty degrees—and by 10:30 we were on the summit, along with about thirty other climbers. The day was perfect, and we could look over to the Italian side of the Matterhorn and study the route that had defeated Whymper again and again, until he finally turned to the Swiss ridge. On the descent, Jaccoux, who for the fun of it had twice skied off the summit of the Breithorn the previous spring, kept muttering as we floundered along in now blazing heat and melting snow, "My kingdom for a pair of skis." We then took the two lifts back down, had lunch, and returned to Chamonix through the tunnel.

A few days later, Jaccoux and I made a similar climb above Courmayeur. This time, our nominal goal was the Tour Ronde (3,792 meters), which is a somewhat steeper version of the Breithorn, and which Mont Blanc overlooks. Again through the tunnel, and then to the lifts up to the Col du Géant, from which the climb begins. At the lift station here, the density of automobiles, climbers, and skiers was such that the lift operators had assigned each passenger a number to indicate which trip of the lift he was to take. When we got there, at 7:00 A.M. the second lift load—about forty passengers—had gone. By the time I was able to buy the lift tickets, the number was nine, and that meant about an hour's wait. By the time we got to the Col du Géant, it was 8:30. When we arrived at the base of the Tour Ronde, we were greeted by a bizarre spectacle. About a hundred alpinists— an enormous number for a small mountain—could be seen toiling up and down the snow face like so many ants on a snow-covered anthill. There was only a single path in the steep snow, so all the climbers were sort of in a line, roped together in twos and threes. It seemed as if there were a single human entity stretching from the base to the summit. (Not only the Tour Ronde but all the standard alpine routes are now overloaded. The highest refuge in the French Alps that provides restaurant service is the Goûter refuge, on the normal route up Mont Blanc. It is situated at 3,817 meters, and was designed to sleep seventy in relative comfort. About the time we were trying the Tour Ronde, a guide told me that he had spent the night at the Goûter and that 256 climbers were there. They were sleeping two and three to a straw mattress, and many were on the floor of the dining room.) Not wishing to become part of a human chain, I persuaded Jaccoux to tackle a neighboring Alp, on which, for some reason, there was only a party of three ahead of us.

While we were perched on the summit, it occurred to me that there must be some place in the area—apart from climbs that are impossibly difficult—so remote that one could find relative solitude. The previous year, I had acquired *Selected Climbs in the Mont Blanc Range*, a two-volume British treatise describing more than two hundred routes, all over the range. I am a little wary of British climbing manuals, because most of them have a tendency toward understatement. Following Whymper, I suppose, a number of British climbing writers use the word "scramble" to describe routes that for me are fairly taxing. After some study of the British manuals, however, I found an area that looked promising. This, too, was on the Italian side of the Mont Blanc range, and involved still another trip through the tunnel. So be it. The area I had in mind, above the relatively untrammelled Frébouze glacier, had no refuges with restaurant service but, rather, two bivouac huts—that is, small structures, usually quonset huts. The one I had in mind—the Gervasutti Hut, named after a celebrated Italian climber who lost his life climbing in the range—was constructed to hold twelve people. I took it as a favorable sign that none of the Chamonix guides I talked with—not even Jaccoux—had ever heard of the place, let alone visited it.

Jaccoux is always eager to explore the unknown, and so it was only a few days after I mentioned the Gervasutti Hut to him that we found ourselves heading through the tunnel again—this time in the afternoon, amid very heavy traffic—and up a small road off the main highway leading into the Italian Val Ferret which I had first visited in 1965, just before the opening of the tunnel, as part of our walking trip around the seven valleys that encircle the Mont Blanc massif. It was at that time a beautiful, fairly primitive valley, scarcely occupied, in which one seldom encountered a car. I expected some changes to have taken place, but nothing like what actually has happened. The lower sections of the valley are now built up with shoddy motels, night clubs, and restaurants. This was probably inevitable. It was the upper section—the more remote part of the valley—that really stunned me. The flat alpine prairies and fragile woodlands have been turned into tent cities—hundreds of tents attached to cars, with their occupants wandering up and down the road looking for distraction. Occasionally, one of these tent colonies was interspersed with dozens of automobile trailers. No one appeared to be dressed in any sort of hiking clothes; these were herds of city people in city clothes, who had left the cities to create a sort of tent colony in the mountains.

Our path to the bivouac started from one of these tent colonies, where, with some difficulty, I found a place to park. The disadvantage of visiting one of these bivouacs is that one must carry all the food and cooking gear up on one's back, along with the usual array of climbing equipment. My pack was so heavy that when I put it on I tilted backward. I gave it to Jaccoux to lift, hoping he would feel that a terrible injustice had been done in the distribution of weight and would relieve me of some of the hardware. After lifting it, he said *"C'est correct,"* and back it went on my shoulders. Jaccoux was carrying in his own pack, along with his personal gear, two ropes and a large assortment of metal hardware—rock and ice pitons, a hammer, and the rest—which he takes when he ventures into parts unknown; he was in no mood to carry anything more. After a half hour of walking, we reached the edge of the glacial moraine, and what had been a faint trail was replaced by a few isolated cairns. We met a group of young Italians coming down, but they told us they had not got very far up, and they had never heard of our bivouac, either. The British manual makes mention of "glacier confluents"—streams—and we had forded two small ones. Jaccoux had gone on ahead, and when I looked up I could see him sitting on a small ice hill and calmly smoking a cigarette. Not knowing how to interpret this curious sight—Jaccoux usually moves on at full speed—I made my way up to where he was sitting. He pointed, and there in front of us was what appeared to me to be a sort of Amazon among glacier confluents, swollen by snow melted in an exceptionally hot August. Above was a steep cliff leading to a sort of steep glacier. Somewhere on that glacier was the Gervasutti Hut. I knew we had had it. I recalled coming upon a similar torrent in Nepal, near the base of Mount Everest, where a team of Tibetans and Sherpas had helped us build an improvised stone bridge, on which we crossed. Where were the Tibetans in our present hour of need? I sat down on the ice and looked out over the Val Ferret. The sun was setting, and we could make out the tent colonies in the valley. Just across the valley, in a lovely meadow perhaps twenty minutes' walk from the road, were two isolated tents—people with enough originality to find a perfect campsite for themselves. To my right, below, I could make out the highway leading from the tunnel; it was lined with cars bumper to bumper. "Where are they all going?" I asked Jaccoux. "Nowhere," he answered, and we got up and walked back down to our own car. Another summer, we did make it up to another bivouac hut on the Italian side. It had bunks for nine people. Jaccoux and I were, as it turned out, the eighth and ninth. The hut was so small that we had to eat in turns. I had carted up the food—a couple of steaks and vegetable soup—which Jaccoux cooked on a butane stove. It was a marvellous place—conserved, no doubt, by the fact that one has to climb some twelve hundred meters to get there.

The Golden Age of the Alps was in fact a Golden Age for the very few. Whymper was conscious of this, although the *Scrambles*—which he published when he was thirty-one years old—has, when it comes to descriptions of the lives of alpine villagers of the nineteenth century, a certain hauteur. From time to time, one comes upon a passage that offers a real glimpse of what life in the mountains was like for the many. Toward the end of the book, there is a chapter about the ascent of the Grandes Jorasses—the very mountain under whose shadow Jaccoux and I had been standing. Whymper's chapter begins:

The Valley of Aosta is famous for its Bouquetins, and infamous for its Crétins. The Bouquetin, Steinbock, or Ibex, was formerly widely distributed throughout the Alps. It is now confined almost entirely to a small district on the south of the Valley of Aosta, and fears have been repeatedly expressed in late years that it will speedily become extinct.

The most sanguine person does not imagine that Crétinism will be eradicated for many generations. It is widely spread throughout the Alps; it is by no means peculiar to the Valley of Aosta; but nowhere does it thrust itself more frequently upon the attention of the traveller, and in no valley where "every prospect pleases," is one so often and so painfully reminded that "only man is vile."

Whymper knew that what was missing in the valley of Aosta was iodine, which is leached from the soil by erosion. This lack of iodine caused goiter—an almost universal condition at that time in these valleys—and the children of parents with goiter tended to be cretins. (Friends of mine who grew up in the region remember being sent to the seashore "for their health" at least once a year when they were children; they were sent there for iodine.) This condition still prevails in the high Himalayan valleys. Now that the problem has been recognized, both goiter and its consequent cretinism are being rapidly eradicated.

Two other conditions common to the lives of the people in these mountain villages were grinding poverty and monotony. The Italian climber Guido Rey, who was born in 1861 and died in 1935, had a clear view of such matters. In his book *The Matterhorn*, he wrote:

I can see in my mind's eye one of those romantic travellers of the first half of the century, come from afar to venture among the Alps, in the days when they were known only through the studies of a few men of science or the vision of certain poets. I can see him climbing for the first time up the lonely valley path, his mind filled with the dream of an idyllic peace, of a free and primitive life, awakened in him by the writings of Haller and Rousseau. . . . And already he dreams that the happiness of the pastoral life is about to be revealed to him. . . .

But, when he enters the village street, he sees that things are not as the poet has portrayed them; a sense of something forbidding, almost akin to terror, is conveyed by the sight of the low, dark houses, huddled one against the other for purposes of mutual protection against the cold and of resistance to the shock of the winds; the garments of the hill-folk are poor and ragged [some of my friends in the region remember their grandmothers' saying that they, or their mothers, had had only one dress, which was worn every day from marriage to burial]; their forbidding faces are never lit up by a smile; their life is a hard one, as is that of all things which live and grow in those high places, and man's fate up there is like that of the pines, which fill the fissures of the rocks with their deep-burrowing roots, suck up their nourishment from the barren soil, and grow in serried groups strong enough to stand the weight of the snows, and live till the hurricane uproots them or the avalanche sweeps them away; or else die slowly of old age when the sap of life is in them no more. No man notices that there is a pine the less in the forest, or a cross the more in the little cemetery.

. . . Perhaps the troubles and the worries that pertain to town life are not apparent in the mountains, but there is instead a sort of stupor, of dull, continuous suffering.

The summer is short: the rest of the year is winter, and the mountain dweller patiently awaits in his closed stable the sun's return; the time for harvest is short, and the work of gathering it in is heavy; the placid joys of labour do not seem to brighten men's lives in these high places, but hopeless resignation to fate shapes their course.

Today, one would have to go a long way in the Val Tournanche—the valley that Rey was writing about—or any other alpine valley to find a mountain dweller patiently awaiting in his closed stable the sun's return. That mountain dweller is, needless to say, teaching skiing or working in a bar in Cervinia or some such place for what his parents or grandparents might well have regarded as a fortune, and who can say which offers a more attractive prospect—the tent colonies and motels of the modern Val Ferret or the closed stable? Such is the peculiarity of human beings that it is this comparison, vividly apparent in the mountains, that confronts us in different guises wherever the automobile has been allowed to proliferate.

In the spring of 1975, something happened that, while it was minor in itself, may have set off a chain of political and emotional reactions leading to what happened in Chamonix during the very recent past. That spring, a group of eighty-seven young French restaurateurs attempted, as a publicity stunt, to organize a feast on the summit of Mont Blanc. The idea was that these young people, dressed in costumes like those of the early-nineteenth-century alpinists—who frequently climbed Mont Blanc with whole legions of guides and porters, carrying fantastic culinary provisions—would be flown to the summit in helicopters for an elaborate banquet. At best, the whole thing appeared rather silly. At worst, because there are often seventy-mile-an-hour winds on Mont Blanc, it might have ended in tragedy. In any case, almost the entire French climbing community reacted to the plan violently and negatively. Sabotage threats against the helicopters were reported, and in the end the whole project was abandoned, ostensibly because of bad weather. A great deal of heated debate in the newspapers developed over the project, much of it involving the mayor of Chamonix—Maurice Herzog, the noted French climber, who was originally from Lyon, and who led the 1950 French expedition to the summit of Anna-purna and wrote a best-selling book about it. Herzog took the position that the alpine climbers—the French Alpine Club, the Chamonix guides—did not own Mont Blanc and so had no right to forbid the banquet. Be that as it may, because of the visibility of the project and the simplicity of the issue, the banquet proposal brought out all the frustrations that the people concerned with what had been happening to the Chamonix Valley had been feeling. Here was a small issue that people could get involved with, apparently to the extent of altering the outcome.

The banquet issue was trivial indeed compared with what was being contemplated for the valley itself. On its south side are the Chamonix aiguilles—the rock and snow needles that kindled Ruskin's imagination—and Mont Blanc. This side is heavily glaciated, and not well suited to ordinary hiking or to further hotel and skiing development. All the great climbing routes are on this side. The north side of the valley is dominated by the Aiguilles Rouges, a lesser set of rock needles, with little or no snow and ice. There are some small lakes at the base of the Aiguilles Rouges, and the whole area is ideal for hiking and low-altitude rock climbing. Some of it has now been set aside as a small park, and recently a good deal of effort has gone into preserving its environmental charm. The superhighway leading to the tunnel runs down the south side of the valley and connects with a small, badly outdated mountain road, which, in turn, joins a superhighway system leading to Geneva. Improvements to this stretch of road will be completed in 1983. The alpine environment of the southern side of the Chamonix Valley near the highway is already destroyed. A number of large apartment and other buildings appropriate to a large metropolis have been built there and elsewhere in recent years, and many people find them extremely ugly. Most visitors to the valley drive down the superhighway, park their cars alongside it, get out and stare at the mountains for a while, and then attempt to drive into town, where—especially in the summer months—they create an impossible traffic bottleneck.

To deal with this traffic problem, the municipal government decided a few years ago to build a *rocade*, or bypass—another large highway, some fifty feet wide, that would avoid the center of Chamonix. The planners proposed that the center of Chamonix would become a pedestrian zone—something that the local merchants originally objected to but, according to recent polls, now favor. The *rocade*, however, would run over the relatively untouched north side of Chamonix, the only part of the community that still looks something like an alpine village. On paper, the *rocade* looks quite neat, but its construction would destroy the last remaining parklike areas in Chamonix, and trees a century old would have to be cut down. The *rocade* would pass just behind the wonderful old Roman Catholic church of Chamonix, and then skirt an adjacent tranquil plaza where, in an old stone building, are housed the Chamonix Bureau des Guides, a weather bureau, and a municipal office that dispenses climbing information. There was even a plan to run another highway through the Aiguilles Rouges, to bypass the valley altogether; this would destroy the whole area. If all this took place, Chamonix would be turned into one large highway with a pedestrian zone in the middle. And for what? Simply to make the area more accessible to automobiles—as if this were the basic objective in planning the development of an alpine resort community.

When I left Chamonix in September of 1976, the *rocade* looked like an absolute certainty. I was told that the bulldozers would begin—and nearly complete—their work that fall. But in the spring of 1977 Jaccoux wrote to say that municipal elections held in March had completely changed the local government. Herzog was replaced by Christian Couttet, a native of the valley, and there were now four Chamonix guides on the twenty-one-person Municipal Council, along with a young Chamonix architect. The *rocade* project was being suspended. When I returned to Chamonix, I was eager to find out why, and what it meant for the future.

The answer to these questions is not simple. But one theme did recur in my conversations with friends in Chamonix: the people of the valley have had enough development. Apart from anything else, the development has been expensive for the community: the elaborate public buildings that were constructed were costly, and Chamonix now has one of the largest public debts of any community of its size in France. There is simply not enough money to build a *rocade*, even if anyone still wanted it. In the past, a *rocade* and similar projects meant "progress," and the general attitude was that such development was inevitable. But now there is a new spirit, indicating a change in the public conscience. I read, for example, a long discussion in a regional newspaper about the building of a new ski lift in the Aiguilles Rouges—a project that had been contemplated for a long time. The discussion began with the fact that the new lift would carry thousand people an hour to the top—three thousand people by noon. The article went on to ask some questions: What are these three thousand people supposed to do? Where will they park their cars? Will there be enough room for them to ski? What additional facilities will be needed once they have arrived at the top of the lift? The report concluded that if such questions were not satisfactorily answered, the community would be better off if it did not build a new lift but merely made a few improvements in the old one. It was the first time I had seen such a discussion in the newspaper. And even if there had been one in years past, the conclusion then would no doubt have been in favor of the new lift.

None of this solves the problem of what to do with the cars and their occupants during the peak of the tourist season, but it does suggest new possibilities and new ideas. Perhaps giant parking lots can be constructed at the end of the valley, on the model of Zermatt. (In looking into this possibility, the Municipal Council made the remarkable discovery that under one of the newer Chamonix hotels a parking lot for nearly two hundred cars had been built and never used.) Central to all this discussion is the question raised on the occasion of the proposed banquet on Mont Blanc: Who does own these mountains? The answer lies in another question: Who does *not* own these mountains? The Alps were "discovered" just over two centuries ago, and the mountain aesthetic was invented. They have served the imagination of millions of men and women during all that time. It is clear to me that, whatever else can be said about who owns them, they do *not* belong to the present generation alone. We are holding them in trust, and, as trustees, do we have the right to destroy in a few decades an environment with such a history, and to destroy it in such a way that future generations can never turn to it to be enriched, ennobled, and solaced?

8   A Passage to Pakistan, Part I: Passage

Sometime, late in the summer of 1969, I met a Czech alpinist who had come to Chamonix for the climbing season. He is trained as a biochemist, and he told me about a new Czech computer now functioning in Prague which will answer any question put to it. One of the questions it was asked recently concerned the Russian Moskvitch automobile. "Will the Moskvitch do 150 miles an hour?" it was asked. "Yes," it replied, "but only once." Shortly after hearing this tale I left Chamonix, via the Mont Blanc tunnel that connects France to Italy, on the first lap of a six-thousand-mile, twenty-five-day automobile trip from France to Pakistan, not in a Moskvitch, but in a Land Rover Dormobile—a long-wheel-base Land Rover specially outfitted so that it will sleep four people. (The roof pops up revealing two bunks, while the seats can be rearranged to form two lower berths. There is also a gas stove and sink as well as a picnic table attached to the rear door.) Our route, essentially the only one that avoids the Arab countries of the Middle East, took us south through Italy to Trieste, into Yugoslavia, the eastern tip of Greece, to Istanbul, across the Dardanelles into Asia, through first northern Turkey and the Black Sea, then eastern Turkey, past Mount Ararat, into Iran, through Teheran, north to the Caspian, south to the Afghan border, south to Herat and Kandahar, north to Kabul, and east to Pakistan and the Khyber Pass. All of the north-south maneuvering is forced on one by the terrain and the state of the roads. Our route made use of the best available roads which, even so, forced us to do over a thousand miles of driving on dirt, some of it in the desert (at one point in the Iranian desert the interior temperature of the car, which was moving at sixty miles an hour, was 104°), and some

149

Passage to Pakistan

of it in the mountains. Each morning I found myself thinking of the Czech computer's laconic response and wondering if, at some point, the Land Rover would simply call it a day, leaving us in the middle of nowhere. Apart from a few minor repairs and a collision with a truck in Greece, it functioned perfectly and arrived at the Pakistan border town of Torkham, at the foot of the Khyber Pass, in much the same condition as when it left France.

A trip of this complexity is not something that one can organize overnight—each country, for example, has its own rules about the importation of automobiles, and it took the better part of a month to arrange all of the documents. The planning for this one took, as it turned out, nearly a year. While not much given to diaries and journals, the only way to explain

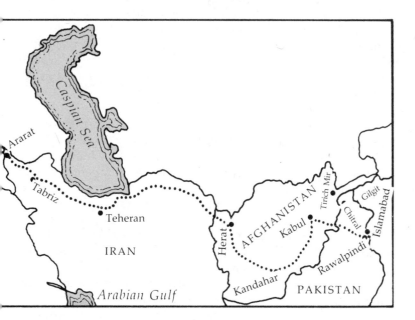

why this was so, and to unfold the details of the trip without generating a total chaos of countries, languages, personalities, and dates, is for me to arrange them in chronological order—a journal after all. The first entry is:

Brookhaven National Laboratory—June 1968

The laboratory, set in among the farm lands of eastern Long Island, is pretty much as I remembered it from eight years ago when I left it to take up my first university teaching job. Many of the people I knew then are still here. We are all eight years older. I am thirty-eight. I have come out here for one of the six-week summer sessions that bring together physicists from all over the country for lectures and study. It is an agreeable and productive time, but for people without families it is somewhat isolated and solitary. Knowing this in advance, I have brought a library full of the sorts of books one means to read if one has time. There is time. About half of the books have to do with mountains and Asia. The previous fall I spent three months in Nepal, and the magic of that land has not worn off. So I spend the evenings in the flatlands of Long Island reading about the "roof of the world."

One of the books is one that I have had since 1964. I have a vague recollection that it was given to me by a climber just returned from Asia who muttered something about it being a "great book." It deals with a part of Asia—the Hindu Kush in Pakistan near the Afghan border—that I was not familiar with and on first glance seems to be uninvitingly dense with philosophy and history and unfamiliar geography. It has been lying, unread, in a bookcase for four years. Now, after reading the first chapter it has already become clear to me that Fosco Maraini's *Where Four Worlds Meet* is just about the best travel book that I have ever read. Maraini is a Florentine who traveled to Tibet in 1937. Afterward he moved to Japan where he was interned during the war by the Japanese for antifascist activities. He had been a lecturer in Italian at the University of Kyoto. In 1953 he wrote a well-known book on Japan, *Meeting with Japan*. He is also an alpinist of distinction and the ostensible subject of *Where Four Worlds Meet* is the first ascent of Mount Saraghar, by a 1959 Italian expedition of which Maraini was the leader, a relatively unknown 24,000-foot peak located near the Afghan frontier. Maraini's book has the usual descriptions of Camp III and Camp IV, the inevitable avalanche that nearly swept everyone away, and all the rest; the sort of thing that drives nonclimbers who try to read such books to distraction and which is so nicely satirized in Auden and Isherwood's play—*The Ascent of F–6*. (There is a K–6 in the Karakoram Range in Pakistan which as far as I know is still unclimbed.) But this is mercifully confined to a chapter or so. For the most part, Maraini's book is a brilliantly successful illumination of a part of the world—the Hindu Kush—which has been fought over by armies that have included Greeks (the army of Alexander the Great), Hindus, Moslems, and, with the coming of the British, Christians. The three great religions, and Buddhism which was driven out of the Hindu Kush with the Moslem invasions, are Maraini's four worlds. Every foot of Maraini's voyage is over ground that is drenched in history, and his narrative alternates between a history and a description of his trek, often very difficult, that takes on deeper and deeper meaning as he proceeds.

Maraini is also a wonderfully evocative writer, and somewhere near the middle of the book I have come upon a page of narrative that threatens to disrupt the contemplative tranquility of my summer. The expedition has just spent one week negotiating a 150-odd miles from Peshawar, a large city in northern Pakistan, to Chitral, a small village, the capital of Chitral, which at the time the book was written was an essentially autonomous "tribal area" located nominally within Pakistan. (Maraini is at pains to point out that "tribal area" does not mean that the area is populated by half-naked savages with bows and arrows, but rather that the government of Pakistan does not accept responsibility for travelers in such areas. They are subject to the local laws which in this case were administered, at least in theory, by the *Methar*, or ruling prince, a lively boy of twelve.) The trip has been a harrowing one. It was to have been made by truck, but the trucks were caught in the late spring floods that have swollen the rivers and, in the end, the men and material were transported by a variety of improvisations involving men, animals, and machines of varying antiquity and decrepitude. (A 10,600-foot high pass, the Lowari, had to be crossed by foot, as no motorable road then existed. Maraini gives an interesting aside about the Lowari. He writes, "In 1960 Professor A. J. Toynbee, not withstanding his seventy-one years, made a trip through Afghanistan and Pakistan, much of it in the path of Alexander the Great. On 28th May he was obliged to give up his attempt to reach the Lowari Pass because of a violent snowstorm!" The Italians crossed the Lowari on the eighth of July and had better luck. Indeed, on the same day they reached Chitral, some forty miles further on, by motorized transport which was originally carried across the pass in pieces and reassembled on the other side.)

The expedition spent the night at the "rest house" in Chitral, one of the ubiquitous bungalows that dot the frontier area and were originally built to house transient British officials. Then comes the passage that is causing my unease. Maraini writes: "We could certainly not have foreseen the gleaming, fantastic spectacle that greeted us on the morning of 9th July, when we opened our window at the rest house. Any temptation we might have had to grumble about the irritating accidents which had befallen us on our journey at once vanished: if we had arrived here on our knees it would have been worth it. The air was mild and bracing: the panorama before us of unparalleled splendour. In the foreground we saw masses of flowers: great fleshy blooms that made me think of Hawaii; beyond and above them were the green, luxuriant treetops encircling the villas and houses of Chitral city, all set against a background of ancient crumbling, rock-strewn hills, yellowish-orange in colour, with outcrops that resembled the shattered ruins of prehistoric temples; and last of all, remote and imminent at once, gleaming white and azure in the sunlight, rose the fabulous, the incredible peak of Tirich Mir, towering some 20,000 feet above us." Tirich Mir is the highest peak in the region at 25,426 feet. It was first climbed by a Norwegian expedition in 1951.

Maraini goes on, "My companions went mad with excitement at the sight: for me, however, it was not only a marvellous spectacle in itself, it was one which evoked old memories. Quite unexpectedly, I found myself re-living the emotions associated with 'the first time'—that special, intangible magic which springs from the impact, on one's virgin mind, of some truly significant experience. For me, that 'first time' had been the sight of Kanchenjunga's mighty peak, more than 28,000 feet above sea level, as I glimpsed it from the tropical forests of Sikkim. Naturally, I also thought of Mt. Chomo Lhari in Tibet, as well as K–2 in the Karakoram group. Yet I must admit that this panoramic view of Tirich Mir possessed many qualities which tempted me to rate it above all the rest. The perfect way in which those flying buttresses led the eye on and up as though by magic towards the remote and supreme focal point of vision; the dewy, crystalline harmony of colour permeating the whole;

the mystical feeling conveyed by that great glacier-clad peak, whose massy rock-ribbed base was lost in a sea of blue-grey haze floating down the valley—all these things, like some cherished piece of music, combined to evoke the most profound aesthetic and religious feelings in me.''

And Maraini concludes, ''K–2, certainly is a breathtaking spectacle; and the sight of Kanchenjunga from the tropical forests of Tista is both fantastic and awe-inspiring; but this view of Tirich also embraced houses and gardens, paddy-fields, winding roads—it possessed a touching human element, a breath of poetry, a sense of pattern and proportion which called to mind a background by Mantegna or Benozzo Gozzoli. This titanic mountain towering up aloft there resembled some pagan angel's throne. It did not, like K–2 and the giants of Karakoram, reach out in fellowship towards the frozen interstellar spaces. When I contemplated it, I did not feel an infinitely small, lost creature, trembling as much with terror as with wonder. I greeted it as one might greet some mighty yet exquisite friend who has invited one to a banquet as his guest.''

As I put down Maraini's book the sun is gingerly lowering itself behind the scrub pines and the flat, sandy farm lands of eastern Long Island. Try as I might, I cannot erase this vision of the high mountains, and the question of why I am here and not there begins to ferment uneasily in my mind. As I fall asleep, I make the somewhat lunatic vow that, somehow, and as soon as possible, I am going to Chitral to see Tirich Mir.

Among the other books and papers that I have brought to Brookhaven are several rather ancient issues of the *Himalayan Journal*, a periodical put out by the Himalayan Society, a club of Himalayan climbers and explorers, a periodical that is devoted to the mountain lore of Asia. I found these issues, somewhat worse for the wear, in a bookstall in Kathmandu, but it is only now that I have found time to read them. In one of them there is the account of the Norwegian expedition to Tirich Mir, along with several other articles about exploration in the Hindu Kush and the Karakoram. These are very interesting but what has struck me is the number of expeditions, especially the British, that have come overland to Pakistan, by Land Rover. (Maraini's group flew to Karachi from Rome.) Indeed, these accounts give the impression of fleets of Land Rovers loaded down with climbing equipment happily toiling through the deserts of Asia Minor. In actual fact, the only first-hand experience I have had with a Land Rover was on a somewhat madcap Sunday outing with Boris Lissanevitch, the celebrated proprietor of the Royal Hotel in Kathmandu, in which Boris took me to see a wall decorated with sixteenth-century Newar wood friezes that he had purchased in a nearby billage. On this trip Boris's Land Rover, which *he* had driven overland from England, collapsed, and he had to send word back to the hotel for a taxi. Despite this rather inauspicious introduction, I had been very favorably impressed by the size of the machine, and, I now reasoned, if one began the trip with a *new* Land Rover, one could load all of one's material possessions into it and have every chance of reaching the Hindu Kush in one piece. Furthermore, Maraini, in his account of the Lowari Pass crossing of 1959, speaks of a road under construction that is meant to accommodate trucks and hence, a fortiori Land Rovers, even of the largest size. It is nearly ten years since Maraini wrote his book, and even at the pace at which construction moves in Asia, it seems to me that there is every chance that the road must by now be built. And even if it isn't built one could always walk.

Needless to say, I do not have a Land Rover, nor do I see any immediate prospect of acquiring one. But quite apart from that, there is the principal question of finding time and money to go to the Hindu Kush. I have just changed universities, and according to the usual academic ground rules I will not be entitled to any kind of sabbatical leave until 1974. I have only been at my new institution some six months, and it does not seem very likely that a dean, under those circumstances, would be very favorably inclined to grant me a leave of absence to see Tirich Mir from Chitral. Nonetheless, by early July, when my six weeks at Brookhaven are up, I have made a firm decision to drive to Pakistan in a Land Rover, and certainly before 1974, dean or no dean.

New York City—September–October 1968

The project has made one important forward step. I have recruited two other "expedition" members. These are Jaccoux and his wife Michèle. The Jaccoux and I traveled in Nepal together. Now it seems perfectly reasonable to him to drive to Pakistan, and, indeed, he knows several people who have done part of the drive, and several others who have been on expeditions in Pakistan, and he is already beginning to collect maps and information. His free season between climbing and skiing is the fall, which more or less fixes the time for the trip. Maraini left the Hindu Kush in late September and does not mention any adverse weather. And from our own experience in Nepal we know that the fall, even late fall, is a season that is clear—the monsoon is over—if cold. Jaccoux does not have a Land Rover either, but promises to look into the matter.

By early October the prospects for the trip have acquired a sharp upward boost, and it now begins to look as if we may actually go. This has come about by one of those happy coincidences that life sometimes produces—"Chance favoring the prepared mind." My closest colleague in physics, a professor at Rockefeller University in New York, is an emigrated Pakistani. He maintains contact with the physics community in Pakistan, and he tells me about an excellent group, newly formed, of elementary particle theorists, my field, at the University of Islamabad, the new capital of Pakistan. Moreover, the university has a large grant from the Ford Foundation, part of which is being used to bring foreign scientists to Pakistan to give courses. (The grant also helps to pay for the repatriation of Pakistani scientists, trained abroad, who provide the university's regular staff.) My colleague agrees to act as a marriage broker between myself and the Ford Foundation, and, indeed, by early October the first letters of courtship have arrived from Indiana University, where the Ford contract is administered. (My Pakistani colleague is unalterably opposed to the notion of driving through Asia Minor which he regards as "pure madness." As nearly as I can make out this has to do with his impression that there are murderous bandits and dacoits that infest the route, leap upon

the unwary, and subject them to all sorts of indescribable out-
rages. None of Jaccoux's friends has been subject to such
attacks, and I have decided to dismiss them as products of my
colleague's hyperactive imagination.) It appears as if the Ford-
sponsored *geheimrats* are armed with the title of Visiting Distinguished Professor, surely elegant enough to favorably impress
any dean, and, although my relationship with the foundation
has not actually been consummated with a firm agreement, I
feel things have reached an advanced enough stage to ask the
university for a six-month leave of absence without pay, to
begin in September of 1969. This has been granted forthwith
and, indeed, shortly thereafter, the departmental money that
would have paid my salary for the fall semester has been
committed to hire a replacement. This has the interesting
consequence that should the trip fall through for some reason, I
would find myself jobless for six months. The die has been cast.

New York City—Winter 1968–69

There have been several developments, some favorable and
some unfavorable. In the first place, I have received a letter from
one of my future colleagues at the University of Islamabad, a
young Pakistani trained at the University of Chicago. He has
made the trip overland to Pakistan in eighteen days from
Munich in a Volkswagen, and he has been kind enough to send
along his itinerary. It all looks so clear and simple. One item
catches my eye—a brief reference to a marvelous view of Mount
Ararat on the Turko-Iranian frontier. Mount Ararat is not Tirich
Mir—but still. The Land Rover has been ordered. It has turned
out that a mere three-hundred-dollar deposit is all that is
necessary to get the great Rover factories in Solihull, Warwick-
shire into production. (Actually, the conversion to the Dormobile is done by the Martin Walter Company in Folkestone.) Five
months appear to be required to fabricate the machine. I have
requested the fifteenth of August in Chamonix as the time and
the place of delivery. The fifteenth of August is not chosen at
random. It is the Fête des Guides in Chamonix and it is a day on
which Jaccoux is sure to be in the valley. I reason that we may as
well confront the beast together. In the heady excitement of the

moment I have ordered all sorts of auxilliary equipment—an extra wheel, giving us six, a fire extinguisher, a complete kit of spare parts, a steel towing cable, and the like. The bill is mounting up, but there are five months before it must be paid. I have decided to adopt the maxim of one of the French expeditionary leaders—*"Tous qu'il y du meilleur est tout juste suffisamment bon pour une expedition Française."*

On the other hand, the news from Pakistan is very disturbing. From here it would appear as if the country is undergoing a full-scale civil war. There are riots, deaths in the hundreds, student revolts, and looting and burning. Finally, Ayub Khan is forced to resign, and his place is taken by the martial law government of Yahya Khan. What has happened to the universities? Will there *be* any physics program next fall in Pakistan? Will there be a Pakistan? We can only hold our breaths and wait.

New York City—Spring 1969

The situation in Pakistan appears to have returned to something like normal. My Pakistani colleague in New York has heard from his family in Karachi. "The trains are running on time since President Yahya Khan has taken over."

Meanwhile back at Indiana University there has been fluctuating progress. At first the Ford people there have told me that they have not been able to get "clearance" for any of their visitors for next year. (All the visiting professors need clearance from the government of Pakistan before they are allowed to take up their posts.) No one in Indiana seems to know what this means. It is not that we have been refused clearance; it is simply that no action has been taken. I have no choice but to assume that the proper officials have something on their minds of more significance to the country than the visit of an itinerant physics professor and that sooner or later something will happen. On this rather tenuous basis I have completed a ferocious round of vaccinations. I may not have a job next fall but at least I will be immune to tetanus, typhoid, and typhus. Finally, in June, the clearance comes through, and I feel sufficiently emboldened to disclose to the people in Indiana that I am driving to Pakistan. They remark that this is the first instance in the history of the program of a visiting professor driving to his post, but, so long as I get to Islamabad by October 1, there is no objection and, indeed, they will contribute to the travel expenses. This, plus some savings and some borrowed money, will pay for the machine.

New York City—July 1969

July has been just about the worst month that I have ever been through. In the first place, the city is hot enough to melt. In the second, and more important, place every possible thing has gone wrong. It begins in the first week of July. A casual call to my local Rover dealer reveals that our vehicle will not be ready in time to be delivered in Chamonix on the fifteenth of August. The phrase "material shortages," whatever that means, keeps cropping up in the conversation like a weed. Indeed, according to the dealer, it is unlikely that the machine can be delivered to Chamonix at all, and I would be "well advised" to take delivery at the factory in Solihull. This means an extra trip to England, a nuisance, but not fatal. However, a second, less casual call, reveals the all but incredible news that there will be no Land Rover at all! Delivery canot be guaranteed *anywhere* before the fifteenth of October which means, as far as we are concerned, there might as well be no Land Rover. The local dealer is a somewhat harassed lady who can offer no explanation of how this could have happened. She has been getting *her* information from the Rover people in New Jersey who have a telex connection to Solihull. It is clear that the first step is for me to phone New Jersey. After some confusion I manage to establish contact with an urbane British voice—clearly a voice of authority. "Yes, I find your records. Everything seems to have been in perfect order until June. Something must have gone wrong. . . ." He will dispatch a telex.

Next I begin to make the rounds of the consulates in Manhattan, something that I have fatuously put off doing until the last month. (My flight to Geneva leaves the thirty-first of July.) I have decided to work backwards, geographically, from Pakistan—Pakistan, Afghanistan, Iran, Turkey. My reasoning is that if I cannot get a visa to Pakistan then there is no point in getting one to Afghanistan, ad infinitum. In accordance with this logic, my first visit is to the Pakistan Consulate. It turns out to be located in an elegant-looking building in the East sixties just off Central Park. (The building appears to have been willed to the government of Pakistan by the late Aly Khan and, at one point, was his personal residence in the city.) However, the interior reveals the comfortable disarray of a well-worn shoe. I am ushered into an office cluttered with papers and forms of every description. Its walls are decorated with faded travel posters, including one that shows a rather formidable view of the Khyber Pass. At a desk, a silent, angular, bald Pakistani appears to be in the process of wading through the day's accumulation of completed forms—a brief vision of Sisyphus elevating his rock through the aeons crosses my mind. I interrupt his labors long enough to present my case, my passport, and an "official-looking letter" from the people in Indiana. I am given a form, mercifully brief, to fill in for myself and another for the still hypothetical Land Rover. The latter cannot be filled out since it requires the specifics of the machine—its license number for one thing—and since there is no machine there are no specifics. However, he assures me that if and when these are acquired the document can be completed and "the permission will be granted in one day." Thus reassured, I surrender my passport and, as promised, two days later, I pick it up suitably stamped. (Upon my return, the bald functionary is nowhere to be found, but another one manages to unearth my passport in the bottom of a desk drawer after a somewhat frantic search.) Needless to say, there is still no Land Rover in sight.

Next, I am off to the Afghans. The Afghan Consulate in New York is located on the top floor of a loft building in the West thirties, not far from Macy's. There is a quiet serious atmosphere about the place, and I am ushered into an office to be interviewed by a pleasant, youthful man, perhaps the consul—the first Afghan I have ever met. It turns out that there are two, not terribly difficult, requirements for an Afghan visa that I have not met: three photographs and a letter from some person of responsibility that will, in effect, guarantee that I will not become a public charge in Afghanistan. (The Afghans had been plagued with hippies at that time as hashish was relatively difficult to come by in Nepal and Pakistan, two of their favorite former haunts, and many of them, once there, do not have money either to live in or leave Afghanistan.) He directs me to the Herald Square subway station where a machine will take three pictures for a quarter, and when I return he tells me that he will process my visa if I will promise to produce the letter when I pick it up. He also hands me a short, informative pamphlet on Afghanistan which notes, among other things, that the price of gasoline is twenty-five Afghanis per gallon. There are, it says, seventy to seventy-five Afghanis to the dollar. When I return, two days later, with a letter from the chairman of my physics department, my visa is ready. There are no special documents needed to bring an automobile into Afghanistan, which is just as well, since there is still no sign of a Land Rover.

Next come the Iranians. The Iran Consulate is located in an elegant suite of offices in the International Building on Fifth Avenue. One enters a paneled door and is greeted by a stunning if icy blonde, not Persian, who takes one's passport without ado. The visa will be forthcoming later in the day. "And the automobile?" "To bring an automobile into Iran you must have an international driver's license and a *carnet de passages*," she informs me. I have, of course, neither, and, in fact, do not even know what the latter is. It is clear to me that whatever it is, it is not going to be easy to get for an, as yet, nonexistent automobile, and so I explain to her that I am only *transiting* through Iran and ask if something might be arranged. I am ushered into the office of the legal consul, an incredibly elegant young man, whose perfect and constant smile is only slightly marred by the presence of one or two gilded teeth. A *carnet de passages*, he informs me, is a document issued by the American Automobile Association which in effect guarantees that the automobile will not be sold in a foreign country without meeting that country's requirements as to import duties and the like. There is nothing farther from my intentions, needless to say, than to sell our Land Rover, if we ever get one, in Iran. Indeed, it is my intention, I explain, to use the machine to get through Iran. He calls, he says,

Washington. At least he calls someone, and speaks at great length in Persian, a conversation that is frequently dotted with the words *carnet de passages*, but to no avail. No *carnet* . . . no passage through Iran, period.

The offices of the American Automobile Association in New York are located in the Statler Hilton Hotel, also near Macy's. The atmosphere in the AAA in the summer, the height of the travel season, is something like that of a consular office in a country that is about to be invaded—everyone is obviously desperate to go somewhere. (In such a circumstance I am reminded of the refugee, who, when told to come back in a year, replied, "morning or afternoon?") We all, dozens of us (or is it hundreds?), have put our names on slips of paper which have been placed in wooden boxes. Most of my immediate neighbors on the benches in the antechamber seem to want to know the shortest route to eastern Long Island. Since I have just come from eastern Long Island I would be glad to supply them with this information, but it is doubtful they would believe me and even if they did believe me it is even more doubtful that we could arrange to have their names removed from the wooden boxes. After a wait that seems like many years, my name is called and I am ushered to the desk of a composed, albeit wilted, gentleman. He informs me that obtaining an international driver's license, also issued by the AAA (how the AAA has got itself into the business of issuing international documents at relatively high prices is a question that is beginning to intrigue me), is a bagatelle. Two photographs—by this time I have learned my lesson and never go *anywhere* without several photographs—and a couple of dollars, along with a New York State driver's license, will get you the necessary document in a trice. However, the *carnet de passages* is issued in Washington by something called World Wide Travel Inc., also a part of the AAA. It costs one hundred and fifty-five dollars—*one hundred and fifty-five dollars*—and, in addition, the applicant must place in escrow with his bank, two-thousand dollars, against which a letter of credit is issued to the AAA. This sum is lost if the automobile is sold in violation of the provisions of the *carnet*. Oh Maraini, what have you wrought! My head begins to reel at the prospect of extracting two-thousand dollars out of our rapidly diminishing expeditionary treasury as well as attempting to deal in Washington with an application for a document for a nonexistent car. At this point I am almost ready to give up. However, a letter has just arrived from the Jaccoux announcing that they have begun getting their vaccinations and visas, so I certainly owe them at least a try.

The Washington office of the AAA is open by 8:30 the following morning when I phone. Fortunately I have extracted the name of someone there from the man in New York and, when he is located, I explain as clearly as I can the nature of the situation. He agrees to process the document without the details of the automobile. I will then have to have it completed in Paris at the AAA office there. This appears to mean an extra trip to England to get the car, if and when it is ready, and an extra trip to Paris to get the *carnet* or vice versa. I then withdraw the money from my savings account and arrange, or at least I think I have arranged, for the letter of credit to be written. There are two weeks left before I leave, and time is getting desperately short. To add to everything else, the bank informs me that somehow it has lost my *carnet* application form which means another trip to the AAA, another wait, and another form. All of this has been done and the letter of credit has gone to Washington. It now occurs to me that I have forgotten Turkey, to say nothing of the European countries. A phone call to the Turkish Consulate reveals the happy fact that the Turks require no visa and no document for the automobile except the international driver's license, although they too advise the *carnet*. Reasoning, perhaps fallaciously, that things must become easier as one goes west into Europe, I have simply decided not to find out what the European countries require. In the worst case I will deal with them in Geneva.

It is now the last week in July and, *mirabile dictu*, a new Land Rover Dormobile has been "located" somewhere in England. It is being sent to Solihull for servicing. No one as yet knows what its license number is but the Rover people are kind enough to propose that they will contact Washington with the specifics, "as soon as the car is safely in the garage at Solihull," and that the *carnet* will be sent from there. Moreover, they will deliver the car to Chamonix on the fifteenth of August as promised! This leaves, as the only loose end, the road permit for bringing the automobile into Pakistan. A phone call to the Pakistan Consulate reveals the rather disquieting news that all such applications must be sent to Pakistan—my first information had apparently been wrong—and that several weeks will be necessary. The suggestion is made that I deal with the embassy in Berne, and I am given a name of someone there to phone.

Strangely enough—perhaps it was a subconscious feeling that we would never get there—during the whole planning stage I have never looked at a map to see what the route really looked like. When I take out my atlas I am overwhelmed by what we seem about to do. Thin red lines, sometimes dashed indicating no real road, stretch endlessly through deserts and mountains, and pause, from time to time, at black dots indicating unfamiliar cities. When I think of the miles and miles to go from dot to dot, a sense of melancholy comes over me, and it is in this mood that, at midnight, on the thirty-first of July, I board the plane to Geneva.

Chamonix—August 1969

This season has been one of the best seen in the Alps for many years. Brilliant days filled with sunshine follow one after the other. Jaccoux is rarely to be found in the valley. As he puts it, *"Je bosse comme une âne,"* and Michèle seems to have vanished altogether. In Jaccoux's absence she is hibernating in a ski resort somewhere near Grenoble. Their chalet, rented from one of Jaccoux's Swiss clients, is occupied by a large assortment of visitors including the Czech alpinist with his tale of the computer and a former French racing car driver. The latter has volunteered to examine the Land Rover scrupulously for mechanical deficiencies when it arrives. The *sacré carnet* has appeared, an imposing document, with a pinkish cover, filled with slips to be torn out and filled in by various customs officials. From it I learn that our Land Rover is green and has the license plate HXC 146 H. A cable has been received from Solihull confirming the delivery date as August 15. The Pakistan Embassy in Berne has been phoned and written to and heard from. The second secretary, one Gul Haneef writes, "I regret that we are unable to give you the road permit, but you will be able to obtain it from the Embassy of Pakistan in either Iran or Afghanistan. In this connection, please see Item Six of the enclosed circular." It is with a good deal of foreboding that I study Item Six. It reads, in part, "Tourists intending to transit/visit Pakistan through land routes to/from India would, however, need a road permit issued by Pakistan High Commission in New Delhi or Pakistan Missions in Iran or Afghanistan." It begins to dawn on me that we may not need the road permit at all since we do not plan to cross the Indian border. However, there has been so much contradictory information about the permit that I make a note to visit one of the above-mentioned missions when we get within hailing distance.

As planned, we are all gathering for the fifteenth of August, the Fête des Guides. Our festivities begin on the night of the fourteenth, when in a large band, we descend on Père Bise, that celebrated temple of gastronomy in Talloires, some fifty miles from Chamonix. It is a splendid occasion (the aged Père Bise, himself, was in the dining room, for one of the last times, it turned out, as unfortunately he died only a day or so later). Among the guests in our group was Dr. Guy de Haynin, the chief surgeon of the Civil Hospital in Pfastait, near Muhlhouse. In addition to being a distinguished surgeon, de Haynin is an avid alpinist and had been the expedition doctor for two French National Expeditions, one to Nepal and the other to Peru. He had, in fact, given us our pharmacy for our trip to Nepal and had kindly offered to give us another one for this trip. I had not met him before, and he turned out to be a cultivated, witty, and extremely youthful man in his late forties. He had, just the previous summer, driven over much the same route that we were going to take and was a fount of valuable information. He and the other people we spoke to who had driven in Asia Minor all admonished: "Absolutely do not drive at night." My mind instantly leapt to visions of the dacoits described by my Pakistani colleague in New York, and while it is true that there have been instances of nocturnal highway robbery along the routes of

Asia Minor, these are not common. The real problems are the trucks and the caravans of people who use the roads at night. We were told, again and again, that it is very common for trucks to drive at full speed with either no lights at all or with a single light which conceals their size. What the explanation for this is, outside of simply faulty equipment, no one professed to know. On the other hand, caravans of people and animals use the roads very frequently at night, especially in the desert, where daytime travel is almost excluded for foot passengers because of the heat. These caravans also have no lights, needless to say, and are, in the main, heavily armed. De Haynin remarked that if, by bad fortune, one did travel at night and did hit even an animal belonging to such a nomadic group, one had better keep on going, since stopping under such circumstances was worth one's life. Clearly, the way to avoid such incidents was to plan one's itinerary day by day, so that one would get to one's destination by sundown, even if it meant starting the day's drive at four in the morning.

By the time we had finished the last of the wine and driven back to Chamonix, it was well into early hours of the fifteenth. When I returned to the Hotel Mont Blanc in Chamonix, the somewhat sleepy night concierge mumbled something about *"un monsieur avec une voiture pour vous,"* and I went to sleep reassured that the Land Rover had arrived ahead of schedule. At what seemed to be midnight, actually about 7:30 the next morning, the phone in the hotel room sounded and a very polite English voice excused itself. "Must make an 8:30 train for Calais, could you come down as soon as possible and take possession of your automobile." I dressed hastily and, in the hotel lobby, found an immaculately liveried English driver. Together we went to the hotel parking lot and there, indeed, was a gleaming blue Land Rover. After the first euphoria wore off it occurred to me that the *carnet* had mentioned a *green* Land Rover. With a somewhat somber intuition I decided that, while the driver was still at hand, we might have a look over the machine to see if everything was there. A cursory inspection revealed that we were in some trouble, although it was nothing fatal. The radio which had been ordered, as well as the automobile heater, were nowhere to be found. And more seriously the spare parts kit also did not appear to exist. In any event, the license and chassis numbers matched those in the *carnet* so, I reasoned, if some particularly meticulous custom's official questioned the color I would simply tell him that I had had the car repainted blue. As for the rest, we were not planning to leave Chamonix until September 5 which left a couple of weeks to locate what was missing at the nearest Rover garage. Remarking that the machine had performed splendidly on the trip from England, the chauffeur took his leave, and I returned to bed.

Toward noon I reemerged from the hotel and made my way to the machine. Never having driven a Land Rover I was not very clear either how one started it, or how the gear system was operated. To complicate matters a little further, I had been given a set of six keys which at first glance appeared to be all different. After some experimentation I found two sets of two that opened the side and rear doors, leaving two, by elimination, that fitted the ignition. After a cursory study of the Rover manual I managed to locate neutral, to start the engine, and to make a few tentative fore and aft maneuvers in the parking lot. I then set sail for the Jaccoux's chalet, a few miles from Chamonix, and perhaps because of the tentative character of my driving and the enormous bulk of the machine compared to the typical French car, had the perverse satisfaction of observing several French drivers, notoriously the most aggressive in Europe, ducking for cover. The entire Jaccoux ménage was at the chalet and were clearly very favorably impressed by the machine. Jaccoux and his racing car driver friend set about inspecting it from stem to stern. In no time at all they had its roof up, revealing the upper bunks, one of which Jaccoux tested and found satisfactory. To illuminate the gas stove was a much more difficult exercise requiring lifting out the front seat, revealing a canister of cooking gas lodged, one hoped, securely underneath. A stop cock was then released along with some other valve near the stove, whence a knob attached to one of the burners, there were two, could be turned, releasing a goodly flow of gas which was illuminated with a match. A very satisfactory flame resulted, and it was quite clear to Michèle that any number of splendid *repas* could be prepared thereon. A list of useful spare parts had been compiled, and the Rover Garage in Lausanne contacted, and an appointment had been made for the following week.

The remainder of the month of August has passed in a miasma of fevered preparations. On each of Jaccoux's descents into the valley he has presented me with various shopping lists. We are now in possession of a complete set of camping cookware, two lightweight portable gas stoves for camping, two mountain tents, three specially fabricated down sleeping bags, a climbing rope and several pitons in case we climb something, three ice axes, enough food to cook at least twenty-five diverse meals, complete with tins of foie gras and truffles, cod liver oil supplied by de Haynin—*"on ne sait jamais"*—a porcelain filter and pump for purifying water (ordered at de Haynin's suggestion from a dealer in tropical equipment in Paris), twelve gas cigarette lighters and twenty packages of Swiss tobacco, Cuban cigars purchased in Geneva, two sizeable sealed plastic tubes of distilled water (these were included after we read a rather sinister report of a group of European tourists who had, the previous month, found themselves in the height of a cholera outbreak stranded in no-man's-land between Afghanistan and Iran. They had come from the former and had been refused admittance to the latter on the grounds that they might be carrying cholera and then had been refused readmittance to Afghanistan. They were blocked, in the desert, between the two countries, without food and water, and when, finally in desperation they had attempted to cross one of the borders by force had been shot at and one German had been killed. If we were going to get stranded, we reasoned, at least it would be in comfort), a considerable amount of reading matter, five flashlights complete with extra batteries and bulbs, chlorine pills, in case any viri escaped the porcelain filter, and twelve cans of the Swiss insecticide that had served us so valiantly in Nepal. How we are going to fit all of this into the Land Rover, even as large as it is, is unclear to me, but the Rover garage has provided us with a specially made roof rack that fits in front of the plastic top of the machine and does not interfere with opening it. (The garage has also supplied us with fog lights. We do not expect to run into any fog, but they give us a backup lighting system in case by malchance we should be forced to drive at night.)

Towards the end of August Jaccoux has announced that he is bringing along a *"flingue."* At first I thought this was some sort of dessert mix and greeted the suggestion with happy anticipation until it was pointed out to me that *"flingue"* is a French slang word for "gun." Guns in French comic strips go *"fingue-flingue."* Some acquaintance in the valley had offered Jaccoux his pistol to protect us against unwanted intrusions. It seemed to me to be asking for trouble to have such an instrument in our possession, to say nothing of the fact that it is illegal to transport it across most borders. However, once Jaccoux has set his mind on something it takes more oratorical powers than I possess to change it and finally the *flingue*, an ancient Colt .45, and a box of *cartouches* are hidden in the bottom of one of the sleeping bags which, in turn, is locked inside a steel trunk, which in turn is placed upon the roof rack under a white plastic tarpaulin. (It is difficult to imagine how the *flingue* would, under these circumstances, be brought to bear against any marauders, but that is how the French are.) It is at this point that I remember to turn my waning energies to the matter of automobile insurance and visas for the European countries. The problem of insurance, as far as I can make out, is essentially unsolvable once one leaves Turkey. The European countries are covered by a standard policy which is registered on the *carte verte*, well-known to any motorist who has tried to enter Switzerland. (The Swiss *douaniers* seem to make a specialty out of studying the *carte verte*, while the French, at least on the borders of Switzerland, specialize in looking for undeclared tobacco.) Turkey can be dealt with by something called Europe Assistance, an outfit located in Paris which, for a modest consideration, issues one a coverage for really major accidents. They will fly you home and they will even fly impossible to find spare parts anywhere in Europe and Turkey. After Turkey one finds oneself uninsured and uninsurable as far as I can tell. (Maybe something can be worked out with Lloyd's of London.) The Pakistanis will only accept insurance issued by one of the companies in Pakistan, and this is unavailable until, and if, one arrives there. Hence, in

Iran and Afghanistan we will simply have to take our chances. After some study, the Jaccoux have discovered that the French need no visas for any of the European countries on our route and, indeed, no visas until Afghanistan. I have naively assumed that this applies, at least in Europe, to Americans as well. However a chance encounter with a physicist at CERN in Geneva, who is about to lecture in Yugoslavia, produces the information that the Yugoslavs have had a change in policy recently and Americans *do* need a visa to enter that country. This has resulted in an early morning visit to the Yugoslavian Consulate in Geneva, where the consul, as I learn from over-hearing a phone call while in his office, is busily attempting to arrange for the shipment of the mortal remains of one of his countrymen, just expired in Switzerland, back to his native land for burial. This unhappy matter having been disposed of, he can then turn his full attention to the problem of stamping my passport which, by now, is so full of printed matter of all sorts that there is hardly room for anything more.

We have opted for Greece over Bulgaria. That is to say, one may enter Turkey by road either from Greece or Bulgaria. We have weighed the matter roughly as follows: to go through Bulgaria means avoiding Greece, which, considering what was then the political state of affairs in that country, we would be happy to do. It also appears to mean better roads, and most of the people that we have spoken to about the trip who have done something like it have commended the Bulgarian highway system. On the other hand, to go through Greece is to avoid Bulgaria, and above all, and in particular, to avoid another visit to another consul. I do not know what the Bulgarians want from American visitors and, by this time, I am in no mood to find out. Moreover, Michèle has produced the clincher. She has re-minded us that Greece is her *pays natal*. Her maiden name is Stamos, and some distant descendant had migrated from Greece to the French Alps. Michèle was born in Mégève and has never set foot in Greece, but she has decided that she would welcome the chance to see the land of her forefathers, and moved by her sentiments we have chosen Greece. We have, somewhat fatuously, decided not to buy any gasoline in Greece, and it is our intention to fill the two large matching blue jerry-cans, also supplied by the garage in Lausanne, and also stowed on the roof rack, in Yugoslavia. In any event, by the fourth of September all of our preparations have been completed, and the Land Rover stuffed to capacity, and the last goodbyes said.

September 5 and 6: Italy

We have gotten off to a late start. It is noon in Chamonix, hence one in the afternoon in Entreves in Italy, before we enter the tunnel under the Mont Blanc that connects the two. We have decided that since the machine is registered in my name we may be able to minimize the complications that we expect to encounter in transporting it, and its contents, across seven national boundaries, if I drive it to and from the frontiers. We have arranged the interior so that the two front seats are free, as well as the back seat, which is wide enough so that one can stretch out on it and go to sleep. Michèle has made a comfortable nest in the back seat out of several down jackets and a sleeping bag, with luck not the one containing the *flingue*, and has settled herself therein. While negotiating the gloom of the tunnel, I notice that an amber light begins to flicker on the dashboard, but having other things on my mind, especially lunch, which we have not yet eaten, I decide to ignore it. The Italian frontier is readily crossed. Jaccoux is a familiar sight to the *douaniers* there as he makes at least half of his climbs from the Italian side of the Mont Blanc massif. Apart from a few admiring comments on the machine, nothing else is said.

By the time we finish lunch in Entreves, known well to climbers for its excellent North Italian cuisine, it is 3:00 P.M. local time, and we have covered the impressive distance of about nine miles. It was our original notion to get as far as Trieste, or at least Venice, the first day, but this is now clearly out of the question. We make our way reasonably slowly (the machine is still *en rodage*, as the French say, and the service manual is rather categoric about not pushing it over forty until it reaches 1,500 miles), through the small Italian mountain villages to the great freeway that runs down the spine of Italy. We have purchased enough in the way of gas coupons (coupons that entitle tourists to a substantial discount on gasoline in Italy) to get us through the country, and my sense of well-being is only troubled by the continual blinking of the amber light on the dashboard which seems to regard us like the red eye of HAL, Stanley Kubrick's savant computer in *2001*. Jaccoux has also noticed it and has begun searching through the Land Rover Owner's Instruction Manual to see if he can turn up something relevant. (Neither Jaccoux nor I, nor Michèle for that matter, knows a great deal about automobiles, but Jaccoux is what the French call *bricoleur*—he has a sort of green thumb for repairing things which we hope will be adequate to see us through, since I am decidedly *non-bricoleur* and can never repair much of anything.) Finally Jaccoux has turned up a paragraph that may well be relevant. "Brake warning light. As applicable. The main and important purpose of the amber warning light marked 'brake' is to warn you that fluid level in the brake reservoir is too low or that there is insufficient vacuum in the servo unit to give braking assistance." Our amber light is not marked "brake" or anything else, but we stop the car and Jaccoux examines what he is led to believe after a cursory study of the manual is the brake fluid level. This he pronounced adequate. Neither of us has the foggiest notion of what the "servo unit" is, but I recall from my brief and unsatisfactory encounter with experimental physics, that testing for a vacuum leak is likely to be non-trivial even if we should happen on the "servo unit." In any event, the brakes appear to be functioning impeccably so we decide merely to ignore the whole matter and to let the damn thing continue blinking. In the worst case, we reason, we will simply put some tape over the light, something that did not appear to have occurred to Kubrick's astronauts, and rid ourselves of it. By nightfall we arrive in Verona and share a meal with two dazzling girls, Swiss models, who have happened onto the same hotel. One of them, a magnificent blonde who is either afflicted with Saint Vitus's dance or an overexposure to *Blow Up*, jumps up from the table every few minutes to break into song which she accompanies with a sort of solitary tango. By midnight we are all off to sleep.

September 6 to 8: Yugoslavia

The route from Venice to Trieste is perfectly awful; a small, winding road charged to capacity with trucks, cars, and random human beings and animals. Although we have left Verona at a reasonably early hour of the morning, it is noon before we arrive in Miramare, a suburb of Trieste on the shores of the Adriatic. It is a lovely warm fall day, and we have decided to stop in Miramare for lunch and a swim. I also want to pay a visit to a physics center there, operated by UNESCO, which caters in the main to physicists from the developing countries. It gives a chance for young physicists from Asia, the Middle East, and South America to come in contact with the latest ideas in physics and to return to their home countries with, one hopes, renewed research programs. It was founded largely as an inspiration of a distinguished Pakistani physicist Abdus Salam who is also a professor at Imperial College in London. I have never been to the institute, but Salam is an old friend, and we stop by the elegant modern buildings in Miramare with the hope, even though it is the weekend, that he might be there. Salam is, in fact, working in his offices and is pleased to see us, and pleased that I am going to be teaching in Pakistan. On the other hand, he is profoundly troubled by the situation in the Middle East. It is just after the Aqsa Mosque fire in Jerusalem, and the tension in the Middle East is almost at a boiling point. He appears to be somewhat concerned for my welfare traveling across the Muslim countries of Asia Minor. I tell him that I will speak nothing but French and that, perhaps, the protective cover of General de Gaulle's umbrella will see me through.

We have our swim and a couple of toasted cheese sandwiches and head for the border. The border station has been completely transformed in the ten years since I last visited it. It then consisted of a few wooden sheds manned by uniformed guards who spoke a little German but no other European language. There are now several modern buildings presided over by attractive Yugoslavian girls who seem to speak every known human tongue. The guard at the passport control is not especially friendly, and when he takes my passport he mutters something about, "French O.K. Americans not O.K." After several minutes the passport is returned duly stamped. Next we buy gasoline coupons. We want enough gasoline to get us through Yugoslavia and Greece, some 350 liters, which cost $45. We head off through the pleasant forest and farmland that leads from the border to Zagreb. The road is excellent and the machine spins happily along to the city. We make for the Hotel Intercontinental. My theory, endorsed by the Jaccoux, is that when we can we should make the stopovers as pleasant as possible. We will have plenty of opportunity to rough it later. The hotel is an immense monolithic structure with a superb and incredibly elegant restaurant called, somewhat oddly, Rubin's. We retire for the night with the feeling that, at long last, we are really under way.

Zagreb is as far as I have been before on our route so that all that is to follow will be *terra incognita* for all of us. We head for Belgrade on the central highway. At a gasoline station we encounter a group of eight French medical students in two battered Deux Chevaux. They are returning from India looking fit and tanned. They tell us that there are three routes through Turkey, and one or another of them has taken all three. They categorically recommend the northern route by the Black Sea both for its beauty and for the roads which, while bad, are better than the other two. After lunch in Belgrade (I have initiated the Jaccoux into the delights of *Palat Schinken*—that ubiquitous Middle European dessert, a sort of light pancake stuffed, in this case with sugared nuts), we head southeast to Skopje in Macedonia. We can already begin to sense that we have left Western Europe. The people have a swarthy Mediterranean look. For some reason I am reminded of the paradox of the grains of straw. Each grain adds, of itself, nothing to the accumulation of straw, but by piling grain upon grain one soon fills the barn. Each change of racial type, mile by mile as we proceed east, is hardly noticeable, but somehow, by the time we will have reached Asia, almost all of the racial characteristics will have altered beyond recognition. It has begun to rain, and Jaccoux has taken the helm. Night has fallen but by a virtuoso feat of mountain driving Jaccoux lands us in Skopje by nine.

Skopje was the scene of a terrible earthquake a few years ago and the scars are everywhere; new buildings among the mounds of twisted earth. Michèle has written in her *carnet*— "*triste ville.*" After a somewhat dismal dinner we are asleep by 10:30.

September 8 and 9: Greece

It is a bright, sun-filled day. We make rapid progress through the barren hills of southern Yugoslavia to the Greek border town of Efzonoi, thirty or so miles from Salonika, on the sea. The Greek-Yugoslav border is an easy one to cross. No one asks any questions, and no one looks into the Land Rover, which is just as well. At the border we catch a glimpse of a Greek soldier dressed in the traditional white skirt with a hat with a red pom-pom on top like a maraschino cherry. Michèle's first glimpse of her *pays natal* is a bit disillusioning—the road is a chaos of trucks, and it wanders through a tangle of dismal-looking towns to the industrial suburbs of Salonika. We make for the sea and treat ourselves to a fine lunch in an outdoor restaurant. Michèle is a striking blonde and is clearly much admired by the local male population. "*Ici, j'aurais beaucoup de succès,*" she allows. After lunch we head eastward. Sometimes we can see the sea, and sometimes the road follows the inland hills. We have no special destination in mind and are quite prepared to sleep in the machine if nothing else comes along by nightfall. Just as the sun is setting the road has, once again, found the sea, and we are confronted with the all but incredibly beautiful sight of the fishing port of Kavalla. I must confess that I had never heard of Kavalla—this is one of the delights of being a not overly well-informed traveler—and its white stone buildings now glowing pink in the setting sun and offset by the blue of the sea all but take our breath away. Boats are everywhere. We find an excellent hotel on the water and make our way into the shops to try to locate a plastic funnel which we intend to make use of in order to pour the contents of our jerrycans of Yugoslavian gasoline into the machine. The Jaccoux have, somehow, come upon a French-speaking Greek who has translated "*etonoir*"—"funnel"—into Greek. He is an elderly gentleman whose son has migrated to Paris, and he offers to accompany us to various hardware stores in which a plastic funnel might be located. We have, in fact, located a bright yellow funnel, and our companion has guided us to an outdoor restaurant-cafe. We have tender fish and sweet white wine. The stars have come out to take up their ancient posts overlooking the black and gentle sea. The warm night is alive with music and laughter. Whatever Greece may be on other nights in other places, it is here, tonight, in Kavalla, a happy, tranquil place.

We are still in this euphoric state when we leave Kavalla early the next morning. Tonight we will be in Istanbul, overlooking Asia. According to the map, our route heads, at one point, into the sea. I have always been fascinated by trails and roads. When one studies them on maps, they seem to be confronted with insolvable problems. They lead into mountains or lakes or across national boundaries. But one knows that somehow these problems will resolve themselves in some way. In this case there is a giant causeway—a bridge—into the sea. The road is at the level of the water, and one almost has the feeling of being on a boat. Sea birds glide across the bow of the machine. I am driving and going very slowly, partly because the road is narrow, and partly because I am reluctant to see it end. I glance vaguely out of the corner of my eye. There is a truck just entering the causeway. It is on our side of the road but we are still separated by several hundred yards. I slow down still more. The truck is still on our side of the road. I have now stopped and am desperately blowing the horn. Just before it hits us I catch a glimpse of the driver in animated conversation with a woman—no doubt his wife. He is looking intently at her and simply has not seen us. There is a horrible thud and then the crash and tinkle of broken glass. At first, I simply cannot believe it has happened. We are all right. We were stopped, and fortunately the truck was going very slowly. I get out and look at the machine. It is so sad. The bright blue fender has been crushed into a tire and hangs like a broken wing. The lights on the left side, the fog light as well, have been smashed. The driver of the truck shows no special interest in us. He is concerned with his truck. After verifying that one of his lights is broken, he appears to be ready to drive off. I go to his truck and am prepared to pull him bodily out of it if he moves it a millimeter. Jaccoux makes a significant point of photographing the truck, the driver, and the license plate of the truck. He has also traced the position of the truck's wheels with a piece of red sketching crayon, part of Michèle's drawing equipment, on the road. The driver has gotten the message and has apparently given up the idea of flight. He is an elderly man, obviously poor, and obviously as miserable as we are about the accident. I am no longer angry and would move on, but the machine is stuck—the fender is blocking the tire. We are a long way from anywhere and we have no choice but to wait for someone to come along. For half an hour we are passed by an incessant flow of military caravans; jeeps and army trucks by the dozens. They do not stop and their only concern is that there is enough room for them to pass as quickly as possible. Finally a British car comes along, and one of the occupants, a young man, hearing us talking in French, says, looking at our British plate, "*Mais vous êtes Anglais comme moi.*" He turns out to be a Swiss from the Valais, and he says he will alert the police in the nearest town. Another hour goes by—more caravans of soldiers. A truck stops. It is a friend of our truck driver. The friend, who speaks some English, offers us some sum of drachmas if we do not involve the police. He does not offer a method for getting the machine going again, and all the drachmas in Christendom will not do that without help. Finally, we spot a smart-looking white jeep with three uniformed men in it—the police. At first they do not show any interest in us at all, and the truck driver tells them his tale—whatever that is. However they begin to take measurements of the scene and, more important, two of them succeed in freeing the fender from the tire. Jaccoux starts the machine, and much to our delight all its vital parts appear to be intact. We are ordered to follow the jeep eastward, towards Istanbul, and the truck driver follows as well. After a half hour or so we are in some town and are led to the police station and taken into the captain's office, which oddly enough is decorated with a photograph of the king. There are some mysterious telephone calls, and soon after a man appears who will act as the official interpreter. The room begins to take on the atmoshere of an official inquest—we each tell our tale of woe in our native tongue and it is all taken down very gravely. It turns out that the driver is insured and that he is quite willing to dictate a statement to his insurance company indicating his responsibility for the accident. The insurance company is phoned in Kavalla, and they insist on coming to our town and photographing the Land Rover. This will take until three in the afternoon, but it seems like the best solution to everyone. I explain that I do not want to cause the truck driver any difficulties, I just want the statement from the insurance company and to get on to Istanbul. There appears to be general good feeling on the part of everyone, and we, on our part, begin to explore the town, looking for a place to have lunch. We find an outdoor cafe, and while we are eating a tank makes it ugly way down the middle of the main street. It does not stop. It does not seem to have any special place to go—it just cruises with an angry whirring crunching sound on the pavement. It seems to be making, by its presence, some sort of statement. The people in the cafe look at it sullenly, but without any special surprise, as if this were an occurrence that took place every noon. After lunch I look for the post office. I want to phone the insurance company's—our insurance company's—representative in Istanbul to explain what has happened and to see if he will contact the Land Rover people in Istanbul. When I find it, it is filled with people also making phone calls, and I put my name on the list. (Fortunately my insurance policy has the Istanbul telephone number.) The wall of the post office is decorated with a poster showing a soldier with a bayonet apparently rising from a flame. There appears to be some kind of phoenix behind him, and I can make out the words April 27—the date of the glorious revolution of the colonels. An hour goes by, and finally I fall asleep on the hard bench. I am awakened by the sound of my name, and when I pick up the phone I am greeted by a cultured British voice. I explain as briefly as I can where we are and why and ask if he could be so good as to phone the Rover garage and perhaps a hotel since we will be getting to Istanbul very late. "I am not a travel bureau. I am an insurance agent," he replies testily, "and besides there is a Red Cross convention in Istanbul and all the hotels are full." Armed with this happy news, I return to the Jaccoux and the machine. It is by now well past three, and there is no sign of the insurance agent from Kavalla. I have discovered the location of our "interpreter" of the morning, and when I mention how far we have to go that day, he says that he is sure the man will be there any moment. Another half hour goes by and it begins to dawn on me that no insurance man is coming, or perhaps was even intended to come, from Kavalla. Again I speak to the interpreter and tell him that we can only wait a few minutes. "A few minutes will not be enough," he says. Now really furious I find my way back to the police station. Everyone is asleep, but by making enough noise I manage to awake the captain. I tell him that we are leaving for Istanbul, and we want a signed statement from him about the accident for the insurance company. He reassembles the entire cast of the morning, the truck driver, the interpreter, and everyone. In ten minutes or so we have our statement and are off for Istanbul.

September 9 to September 13: Istanbul

The eastern part of Greece, as one approaches the Turkish border, resembles nothing so much as an armed camp. Military bases seem to be everywhere. Each town appears to have its local garrison, and the poster showing the soldier emerging from the flames decorates the highway every few miles. The last large city before the border is Alexandroupolis. From this point we will be following, more or less, the route of Alexander the Great, through Asia Minor into Pakistan. Alexander, who was not a Hellenic Greek but a Macedonian, crossed the Dardenelles in 333 B.C. with an expedition that included poets and scholars, as well as an army of several thousand men, and a small navy. His goal was to restore the Panhellenic empire that the Persians under Darius, the King of Kings, had taken from his father Philip. His "crusade," if that is the right word, lasted some eight years, and took him, finally, across the Hindu Kush, into what is now the northwest frontier of Pakistan, to Taxila, not far from the present capital of Pakistan, Islamabad, down the Indus, to a place near what is now Karachi, where in 325 B.C. his troops, by now exhausted and rebellious, embarked by sea for Greece. He founded Alexandrias throughout Asia Minor, which inspired Voltaire to remark that Alexander had founded more cities in Asia than most of his predecessors had destroyed. We will pass through many of them if we can restore the wounded machine to something like its original condition. Alexander's army walked, of course—a sobering thought.

At sunset we reach the Turkish border post. We find a substantial assembly of automobiles of various nationalities, with their drivers industriously filling out assorted long forms. It is the dinner hour, and the Turkish border police appear, quite understandably, to be much more concerned with their kebabs than with us. I am spared filling out a particularly tedious-looking green form—some sort of insurance document for the machine—by being in possession of the *carnet*. At least it is good for something. Finally one of the officials, an attractive lady, rises from her dinner and emerges from the police post long enough to give the machine a perfunctory external look. Its contents do not seem to interest her. And we are free to leave.

The sun has set and we do not have very much left in the way of automobile lights when we head across the semidesert from the frontier to Istanbul. We had vowed not to drive at night here, but we have no choice as there do not seem to be any real towns between the frontier and Istanbul. We have not eaten, but we have decided to get on as fast as possible and to worry about food later. (To add to the general ambience the amber warning light on the dash has started to glow like the Kohinoor diamond and we have finally throttled it with some adhesive tape.) We pass some caravans with camels—the first we have seen. The road is very good and when we are within hailing distance of Istanbul at about ten we stop in a roadside restaurant to try to phone ahead for a hotel. I phone the Hilton with the thought that, because of its size, there might be some rooms. "Fully booked; A Red Cross conference, all the hotels in Istanbul are fully booked." About eleven we arrive in the center of Istanbul. Using a map from the *Guide Bleu*, Jaccoux succeeds in navigating, after innumerable trials, across one of the bridges that span the Golden Horn. (At one point we found ourselves in a sort of cul de sac—a series of one-way streets which took us nearly an hour to get clear of.) We make for one of the larger hotels on a hill overlooking the Bosporus. "Fully booked—the Red Cross." The Red Cross—*nom de Dieu*—if we do not get a place to sleep and something to eat soon we will need the Red Cross, and perhaps Blue Cross as well. The night clerk has kindly agreed to phone all of the hotels he can think of, both in Istanbul and environs. Nothing—"fully booked." After about three quarters of an hour—it is now nearly 1:00 A.M.—a mysterious figure comes into the lobby and, hearing of our plight, points out to the clerk that his father works in a hotel not far away and perhaps something might be arranged. Another phone call. We are offered a rather bizarre arrangement. Two rooms in this hotel—if that is what it is—are shortly to be liberated by people "who are about to take a plane," and we can have their rooms, but only for the rest of the night. It sounds pretty fishy, but we are in no position to hold out. We are led off to a neighboring street and soon find ourselves in the lobby of a rather delightful small hotel. So far, so good. However, the two rooms have now shrunk down to one room—the other will be liberated somewhat later—perhaps there is a second plane leaving Istanbul at three in the morning. My father has always lived by a simple axiom, "when in doubt—eat," and that is the very thing that I suggest we do at once. The night manager of our prospective domicile provides us with a guide—a night bellboy—who leads us to some sort of all-night bar and grill nearby. The food is not much good, but we have not had anything to eat since noon and we have no trouble in finishing it off with some Turkish wine. It is now two, and I propose that I will take the liberated room—rise at the crack of dawn and deal with the machine while the Jaccoux can rise when they will and find us a place to stay while the machine is undergoing surgery. At two-thirty I stagger into a quite comfortable small hotel room and go to sleep.

By eight the following morning I am up and have had breakfast. I have also confronted the day clerk at the hotel—a somewhat bizarre-looking gentleman, totally bald and apparently in possession of only one front tooth, which gives him the appearance of a comic wrestler. His name, I learn, is Ahmad. Ahmad seems to have a special weakness for the French language and for the French, in general, and after a long and feeling discourse in French, in which I tell him how we have struggled over the hills from France to Istanbul, he "discovers" that he can keep us on for an additional night, but after that he is "fully booked." So be it—and now the Land Rover garage. Ahmad helps me locate it in the Istanbul telephone directory and much to our mutual astonishment, and my delight, it turns out to be just in back of our hotel. I drive the machine to the garage and learn that, indeed, our insurance agent has called and we are expected. However, I am informed by the owner, a swarthy type who can barely keep himself awake, that there does not exist a spare fender in all of Istanbul for a Land Rover. However, he has a friend, a genius at working in aluminum—apparently the Land Rover fenders are made of aluminum—who, he is sure, can make us a fender in his shop. As he is telling me this a man drives up in some sort of British car and informs the garage owner that both of his back lights were clipped off his car while he was watching a film in downtown Istanbul. He also regales me with a number of tales of how cars have been completely stripped while undergoing repairs in various garages and their contents never seen again. My naturally suspicious nature is further aroused when the garage owner does not seem to be able to tell me his friend's prices. "We can talk about those things later." Later, when later? We have thousands of miles to drive and we must get the machine fixed *now*. I decide to phone our insurance agent, figuring that since the company that he represents is on our side he can tell me what to do. "I have dispatched the 'Surveyor' to the Land Rover place and he will be along shortly to survey the damage." I so inform the garage owner, who announces that, in that case, he is going home and can be found there if we want the services of his friend the aluminum man. An hour goes by and there is no sign of the "Surveyor." Another phone call to the insurance agent. The "Surveyor" has gone to the Land Rover showroom by mistake apparently under the impression that I might have put the machine on sale. He is on his way. Another hour goes by.

Finally an incredibly dilapidated taxi pulls up and out steps a figure who might have emerged from Durrell's *Alexandria Quartet*; a man with a look of infinite shrewdness, ageless, with a dark, withered complexion that could be of any race or nationality—the eternal "fixer" of the Middle East. He unloads himself carefully from the taxi. His first words to me, said in an exceedingly confidential whisper, are, "The report, of course, will be in English." Puzzled by my blank and incredulous look, he repeats the same thing in French. He is about to repeat it in German and God knows what other languages, when I blurt out, "What report? I am not interested in a report. I just want to get the machine fixed!" It has become clear to me that unless I can divert his attentions from the "report," whatever that is, to the Land Rover itself we will be there all day. He insists on giving me his card. It reads in part "E. L. Kissa Surveyor, VITSAN llac Sanayii Mumessillik ve Ticaret A. S. Lloyd's Agents at the Port of Istanbul." This having been done, he proceeds to examine the stricken machine, emitting soft cooing sounds of sympathy as he runs his hand over the gnarled and useless fender. "We shall speak in French," he whispers to me. "*Nous, nous parlerons en Français*," he repeats somewhat louder. "We shall go to the Rambler's garage," he says in French. The "Rambler's garage" is, it seems to me, a new and wholly undesirable element in the discussion. I point out to him that I have had a firm offer, at least I think it is a firm offer, of a newly made fender *chez* Rover. He says, now in English and in an incredibly conspiratorial whisper, "What if the Rambler's can do the job more quickly?" I have no very good answer, and allow myself to be led to the machine and guided through a maze of streets to a back alley. A large metal gate is swung open, and I drive the machine into an open courtyard. The sight that confronts me is not reassuring. It looks like a workshop out of *Oliver Twist*. Dozens of small boys appear to be pounding various metal plates more or less at random. Over the general tintinnabulation there is a radio playing the keening music of the Middle East. The proprietor, a short, strikingly handsome man with a bushy mustache emerges from his office. I am ushered inside. "We shall take some coffee," says the Surveyor.

After a few minutes, a factotum appears with a tray bearing three cups of sweet Turkish coffee. It is so sweet that it makes my mouth pucker, and I make the mistake of trying to drink it to the bottom of the tiny cup and encounter a miasma of extremely bitter dregs which stick in my teeth. "I will go to the Rover garage and see if they have a fender," the proprietor says. This seems to me like a losing move since we have just come from the Rover garage, where there is, as far as I can make out, no fender to be found. "We will try," he says and leaves. An hour goes by and just as I am ready to take the machine and depart, the proprietor returns to announce that he has turned up a new Land Rover fender of just the right size. "The last one in Istanbul," he assures me. He and the Surveyor discuss the price, and it seems very reasonable to me. They are even willing to toss in a free lubrication. Moreover, the proprietor suggests making a list of the contents of the car which we will both sign. It takes me about fifteen minutes to recall its multifoliate contents. Meanwhile the Surveyor stands over me beaming like a proud parent. "They are Greeks," he says to me in French referring to the patron, "and I too am a Greek from Rhodes." I am rapidly growing fonder of the Surveyor and am emboldened to show him the note which has been written by the Greek police in reference to our encounter with the truck. We have been had. The note, when translated, says nothing about the accident. It only gives the name of the truck driver and the address of his insurance company in Kavalla.

The machine will be ready in four days. When I return to the hotel the Jaccoux have gone out and Ahmad tells me some sort of story about Jaccoux having gotten us a room somewhere else. It seems to me that there is a misunderstanding so I go through my routine with the mountains and France once again, and this time I manage to ply a commitment out of Ahmad for four days. When Jaccoux comes back (it was five in the morning before their room was finally liberated) he is dumbfounded, since Ahmad has told him earlier in the morning that the hotel is "fully booked." "*Quel pays*," mutters Jaccoux. Four days in Istanbul—would that it had been forty! We revel in the wonders of the city. We ride boats—on one trip we cross between Europe and Asia (Asia begins on the other side of the Bosporus across from Istanbul) seven times. We eat by the sea (the proprietor of the garage has given us the name of his favorite restaurant in Tarabya, some fifteen miles from Istanbul on the shores of the Bosporus). The food is simply marvelous. There are deliciously spiced hot and cold hors d'oeuvres, meats and fish, and the wonderful sweet honey-flavored Turkish pastries. The city is so beautiful, especially by night, when from the high hills one can look out and see boats moving in all directions under the soft lights that play over the mosques. We swim. We loaf. We let the marvels of the city flow beneath our feet.

The four days are over, and it is almost with reluctance that we reclaim the machine. It looks even better than before. Everything has been restored, and it has been washed and polished a spotless blue. The Surveyor is there with his "report" which, indeed, is in English. We have paid the rather modest bill and are, once again, ready to turn East to Anatolia and Pakistan.

Anatolia

All of Turkey is on one time, that of Istanbul. (According to the *Guide Bleu* it becomes an hour and a half later the instant one crosses the Turko-Iranian border.) As we move east, we are going to be racing the setting sun both because of the lack of change of time in Turkey, and also because the days are getting shorter anyway. At the crack of dawn we head for one of the ferry boats that transports cars and people from Istanbul to Uskudar, the first town in Asian Turkey across the Bosporus. As it is Saturday, there appears to be a mob of automobiles full of picnicking Turkish families awaiting their turn to get a place on one of the boats. After about a half an hour, Jaccoux, by one of those incredibly audacious driving maneuvers for which the French are noted, has succeeded in mounting a boat just before the gangway is lifted. We head due east for Ankara. Even if we had not been informed by the map there would be no doubt that we are now in the Middle East—the car license plates. There are cars from among other places Kuwait, Iran, Syria, and Pakistan. We pass a Lebanese car driven by a very pretty girl. The car appears to contain her entire family—two other very pretty girls, and a somewhat dour-looking set of parents. We stop for gasoline and they stop for gasoline and we have a very lively and giggly (on their part) talk in French. Just before Ankara the route branches south into the Arab world, and we lose the girls and their parents and the cars from Kuwait and Syria.

By a scrupulous reading of the fine print in the *Guide Bleu* Jaccoux has managed to unearth the whereabouts of a restaurant in Ankara noted for *doner kebab*, that ubiquitous and splendid Turkish dish consisting of thin slices of mutton roasted and served, most often, with a yoghurt sauce. Not having the slightest idea of how to make our way through Ankara, we leave the machine at its outer edge, just at the junction of the route to the Black Sea, and take a taxi. Ankara is a stocky solid-looking fortresslike city carved out of the desert by Ataturk in 1923 and made by him the national capital. It seems to have everything but water, and there is a dusty desert pall that hangs in the hot afternoon air. After a feast of *doner kebab*, wine, and baklava, we regain the thoroughly heated machine and head north. The roads are good if slightly mountainous and by sunset we arrive in a small town called Corum. After some exploration we locate one of the *Guide Bleu*'s flagged (that is, recommended) hotels, which is simple but comfortable. Corum seems to be noted for the manufacture of caps, and after dinner I purchase a rakish purple affair that, I hope, will keep the dust and sand out of my hair.

At sunrise we are awakened by the cry of the muezzin, electronically amplified from a neighboring mosque, and are off for the sea. This is not one of our better days. Jaccoux and I are having driver incompatibility problems. Jaccoux belongs to, and in fact is a leading exponent of, the French school of driving. Their motto is *"attaque."* I believe in defensive driving and drive under the general assumption that all oncoming cars are driven either by potential or actual maniacs or by people who are about to suffer fatal coronaries while at the wheel. The Land Rover is not ideally suited for attacks on slower cars since there are few cars that are much slower than a fully loaded Land Rover. But Jaccoux, who has the reflexes and temperament of a racing car driver, manages to get the machine to perform prodigious feats of which I thought it was incapable in principle. To add to that general atmosphere we are more or less obliged to navigate the machine in pairs since it is equipped with British drive and the driver simply cannot see what is coming without help from the passenger to his left, especially if he wants to pass something like a truck or bus. Hence, each time we pass there is a constant relay of signals like "*ça ne vas pas*" or "*vas y, mais vite nomme de Dieu!*" and the like. This might be entertaining on a short trip but we have now been in the machine for over a week and our nerves, at least mine, are beginning to show some wear. To boot, Jaccoux has come within an ace of demolishing an ancient and evidently somewhat cracked Turkish peasant woman who insisted on chasing her cow in front of the machine. By braking and sliding the machine like a slaloming skier he has avoided both the lady and her cow—but by millimeters. We all feel it is time for a swim, and finally we locate something of a Black Sea beach. The waves are extremely high and, idiotically, I have forgotten to remove my sunglasses before assailing the brine. The sunglasses are a specially made pair, designed for the French alpine school, and they are marvelous for both driving and glaciers. I dive under a wave and the glasses are gone. We search the sea and the beach, but they are definitively gone. There is nothing to be done about them, but I have decided that when Jaccoux drives I will plant myself horizontally, in the back seat—Michèle can act as navigator—and hope for the best.

At sundown we arrive in Trabzon in Turkish Armenia on the sea. Trabzon was founded by Greeks in the first century b.c.—post-Alexandrian Greeks. (Alexander headed south, after crossing the Dardanelles into Syria, Palestine and Egypt, where, of course, he founded Alexandria. Our path will not again cross his until we reach Iran.) By the time we locate the *Guide Bleu* hotel—it is on the highest hill in town—night has fallen and among other things we have been stoned by a band of young Turks who apparently think it is funny to see how many rocks they can bounce off of the machine. One of the little monsters has in fact attempted to attach himself to the wheel mounted on the rear door but has been shaken loose at the first bump in the road. Despite this rather inauspicious introduction, Trabzon turns out to be a colorful, amiable seaside resort town, with its shop windows crammed with magnificent-looking Turkish pastries, apparently a local specialty.

The next morning, at the muezzin's cry, we head south and east. This part of Turkey, which is close to the Russian border, is both mountainous and military. The narrow roads wind up and down steep hills. At one point, on top of a pass, we come upon two French ladies heading for Teheran in a Peugeot. Their car has overheated, and they are watering it down and seem to be all right. Eventually, after a spate of dirt roads, we descend on the central Turkish plateau where the northern route through Turkey rejoins the central route. It is a wild and incredibly beautiful country, like the Russian steppes, with great vistas of fields and mountains. And it is swarming with soldiers. Caravans of tanks and jeeps dot the fields and to add to the general effect the sky is dark, the wind is strong and chill, and rain, mixed with snow, falls from time to time. We pass through Erzurum, the largest city in eastern Turkey and head eastward for Agri, the last substantial town before the Iranian border. The road has become dirt and the dirt a dark reddish mud in the rain. At one point we are stopped by a landslide which has blocked a line of cars and trucks on both sides of it. Fortunately, by the time we have arrived a bulldozer is clearing off the last of the mud. By the time we reach Agri it is pitch dark and we grope around the dimly lit streets trying to locate the Acar Palas Hotel, the only one mentioned in the *Guide*. It is a ghastly, filthy dump teaming with unkempt-looking men who eye Michèle lasciviously. We park Michèle in what we assume is a carefully locked room, and Jaccoux and I descend into the street to secure the machine. (We have evolved a procedure for removing the contents of the roof rack and storing them inside the Land Rover, covered by a white tarpaulin so that they will attract as little attention as possible.) When we return, armed with two cans of insecticide, Michèle informs us that a Turkish gentleman has, somehow, gotten into her room but having decided, correctly, that Michèle is not someone whom it pays to annoy, has left. The rooms are in a total state of filth; the beds have clearly been slept in (forewarned by the *Guide* that the custom in Turkish provincial hotels is to hire out, individually, all the beds in a room, we have made sure that we have hired all of them in our respective rooms). A good spraying eliminates most of the visible fauna, and I succeed in making some sort of sleeping arrangement between two blankets, these being, at least super- ficially, cleaner looking than the sheets. We spend an almost sleepless night, and it is with the greatest sense of relief that the muezzin's cry tells us that it is sunrise and time to head eastward to Iran.

Iran

The route from Agri to the Iranian border is all dirt, but the scenery is magnificent. On our left, Mount Ararat looms over us. (For a fleeting moment we thought of trying to climb it, but the *Guide Bleu* informs us that the route leading to its base is a military road and can only be used with special permission of the military authorities who, presumably, were not around in the time of Noah.) Ararat is a squat, massive, snow-covered volcanic peak, not very elegant, but a good port in a flood. By midmorning we arrive, bleary eyed from our sleepless night at the Turkish border post of Gurbulak. Dozens of cars and trucks are already there, some going into Turkey and some out. The Turkish customs officials are not very pleasant. "Iran visa?" one asks, "not visa-finished" referring presumably to our trip. The Jaccoux did not need a visa for Iran and mine was in order so he lets us go, saying in French, "*Allez et dépêchez-vous.*" Be- tween Turkey and Iran stands a large and solid-looking iron gate presided over by an aged uniformed individual who gives every impression of having his brain thoroughly addled by overexposure to the sun. "Iran visa," he commands. I hand over my passport, and he studies it, upsidedown, leafing through its innumerable pages until he comes to my Afghan visa. It is a rather handsome visa, as they go, and he spends several minutes admiring it. I don't know what he thinks he is looking at, but it seems to make him happy and he lets us through the gate. We now have to repeat the formalities on the other side. At this point Jaccoux runs afoul of a health inspector. For some reason, comprehensible only to the French, his doctor had stamped his revaccination for smallpox *above* his original vaccination. The health inspector decides that since his original vaccination had expired he had not met the requirements for entry into Iran. A spirited discussion ensues, and just when I think Jaccoux is about to lift the health inspector off of the floor and bounce him a few times from his desk, another one of those mysterious, soft-voiced strangers materializes from nowhere and with great tact explains to our man what the word "revaccination" means. By this time we have spent over an hour in various custom's sheds—oddly enough, no one looked into the machine—and to boot, we have lost an hour and a half with the time change at the border. It is now late morning, and the day is sparkling and warm and when we emerge from the border post the scene that greets us is a sort of paradise. A marvelous asphalted road leads off through fields and mountains giving way to an ochre mountainous desert. Every several miles the vista is interrupted by a gleaming new gasoline station replete with motorized gasoline pumps. (In eastern Turkey most of the pumps are operated by hand and it requires the persuasiveness of Genghis Khan to convince their owners to squeeze out all of the necessary fluid.) All of this comes as a pleasant surprise since the *Guide Bleu* for the Moyen-Orient, written in 1965 and by which we are now navigating, gives a description of this part of the route which makes it sound like a Calvary of the first water. Happily for us, the Iranians have been engaged in a vast program of road building and the route from the border to Tabriz, the first major city before Teheran, is nothing short of superb.

Tabriz is a large city of at least 300,000 inhabitants which traces its origins to the eighth century A.D. It is a frequent locale for sizeable earthquakes, and it has, as is common in Iran, an open sewage system of canals that run in lively streams between the sidewalks and the streets, giving the town a vaguely Venetian appearance. I am, indeed, straddling the three or four feet of running drainage between the machine and the sidewalk and attempting, without falling into the canal, to unload a certain amount of vital baggage which is being handed to me from the depths of the machine by one or another of the Jaccoux, when I am interrupted by the sound of a dulcet English voice—female. "I say, it's jolly good to see some English faces," she says, apparently taking our British license plate and the Land Rover as firm evidence of our nationality. When I am able to readjust my equilibrium so that I can turn to look at the owner of the voice I discover that she is a delightful-looking elfin blond dressed in black slacks that appear to have accumulated a good deal of dust. I explain, in general terms, who we are and where we are going, and she informs me that she is an art student from London and that, having departed from the British isles some two months prior with just the then legal limit of fifty pounds, she has been spending the subsequent time *hitchhiking* by herself throughout Iran. She is in fact on her way back to England, also hitchhiking, and she figures that it will take her six and one half days; three and a half days to get through Turkey, where, she says, it is too dangerous for her, alone, to hitch at night, and three days in Europe where, she says, it is not. I inquire as to where she plans to board during her stay in Turkey, having a fresh memory of the Accar Palas in Agri, and she informs us that this is, usually, no trouble, since the minute the police find out that she in town, alone, they usually put her up in the station house. Since it is still early I suggest that she might join us in exploring the town which, according to the *Guide Bleu*, has a celebrated blue mosque—a mosque with the domes done in blue inlay, very lovely and very common in Iran—and a museum. "I hope there are no pots," she says, referring to the museum; "I've had pots to here," pointing to her forehead. After a brief visit to the mosque, it is largely in ruins due to various earthquakes, we make for the museum. "Pots—more pots," she groans. Then, coming to a particularly fetching piece of statuary, she suggests, "Let's nick it, it would look lovely on Mum's mantle." The presence of an armed guard inhibits the felony, and we ascend to the second floor of the museum which houses a photographic exhibit. Most of the photographs appear to be of the Shah, and at the sight of the first one, almost life-size, she says, "It's 'ihm again! I'm sick of 'ihm too." After a bit of tea and a cookie she is off in the direction of Turkey.

After a good night's sleep we are off in the direction of Teheran, at which we arrive in the late afternoon. Seen from the road, Teheran presents the appearance of a swarming, dusty concrete warren, sweltering in the September desert heat. Lured by the prospect of a swimming pool, we head for the Teheran Hilton through an almost solid mass of automobiles moving with the apparently random motion which physicists attribute to the large gas molecules in a heated vapor. Jaccoux, steeled by years of driving in Parisian traffic, has taken the helm, and aided by the fact that the Land Rover is about twice the size and mass of the minicars that glut Teheranian traffic, he manages to force a passage to the fringe of town where the Hilton is located on the crest of a hill. There is, to be sure, a magnificent pool, *chez* Hilton, but there is also a congress of Iranian dentists, and the place is "fully booked." In fact every place appears to be "fully booked," but we finally land in a hotel so new that it is not even officially open. We have decided to spend two or three days in Teheran, partly to catch our breath. We are by this time, after two weeks on the road, a little shopworn. But we also want to give the machine a thorough servicing. We take, by air, a brief side trip to Isfahan, which contains some of the most beautiful blue mosques in the world. by September 20 we, and the machine, have recuperated sufficiently to head north to the Caspian.

Our route, past Mount Damavand, the highest mountain in Iran (it is over 19,000 feet) is probably, more or less, the same as Alexander's. After conquering Persepolis, the capital of Darius, early in the year 330 and apparently burning it, (some historians think it was an act of revenge for the sacking of Athens by Xerxes, and some feel, given Alexander's propensity for *building* cities, that the fire was accidental) Alexander set himself up as the king of the Persians. He had spent three years in Asia, and although his original intentions had been to hellenize Asia Minor, he had himself begun to take on the characteristics of an Oriental potentate and, indeed, when he left the same year on his march east, it is estimated that about two-thirds of his army were Persian, the rest being his original Macedonians. He, like we, headed north to the Caspian.

It is unlikely that skiing was much in vogue in 330 B.C., but it is now in Iran, and we passed (near Damavand) a new ski resort replete with a couple of small tows. It was too early in the year for snow, but the Jaccoux gave the plant a professional examination and found the slopes practically flat compared to what they are used to in Chamonix. The mountain air, light and fresh, was a relief after the desert lowlands. We make rapid progress to the Caspian, but the road follows a route somewhat removed from the sea so that we cannot find a place to swim. We have decided to spend the night in a town that, at least from the map, appears to be on the sea, a few miles from the Russian frontier. However, when we arrive there we discover that it has neither a beach nor a hotel, so we head south to Gorgan, on the fringe of the desert. While Gorgan is a town of only some 20,000, it is on the main route to Afghanistan, and it is also on the route from Teheran to Mechhed, one of the holiest cities in Islam and a scene of frequent pilgrimages, and hence has a surprisingly modern and comfortable hotel with the curious name Hotel Miami.

By five the next morning we are again heading east. In the nearly four thousand miles we have traveled we have, up until now, encountered surprisingly few really bad roads. To be sure, the roads through eastern Turkey are narrow and mountainous, but, except for perhaps two or three hundred miles, they are at least well paved. However, no sooner have we left Gorgon and headed into the desert than we hit a stretch of road, nearly six hundred miles long, which has to be seen to be believed. It consists entirely of dirt, sand, and small rocks. The passage of innumerable cars, trucks, and buses has corrugated it into a sort of washboard. This has the interesting property, typical of such roads, that there are only two speeds at which one can drive without being shaken, literally, to pieces—ten miles an hour at which speed the machine creaks over each bump, or sixty, at which speed the machine sort of flies from bump to bump occasionally landing with a sickening crack on one of the larger rocks. To add to the general discomfort of the road the temperature outside is well over a hundred and indeed the thermometer which we have mounted over the dashboard is in the shade and well ventilated by the open front grilles (one of the nice features of the Land Rover is that there are two grilles below the front windshields that can be opened to various apertures to let in a stream of fresh air) and reads, during most of the day, about 104°. Within a half an hour we are covered with a thick layer of dust, and Michèle notes that both Jaccoux's hair and mine have now turned white. Passing anything is a nightmare. All moving vehicles are followed by a thick, impenetrable cloud of sand. Once inside it one can see nothing until one gets to a point of a few feet behind the rear wheels of the conveyance one is trying to pass—often a bus or a truck. At this point one often finds oneself confronted by an oncoming vehicle also trailing a cloud of dust and one is forced to retreat back into the cloud of the car in front. The standard operating procedure appears to be for everyone to travel with their lights on in high beam on the theory that this will give other cars an additional warning as to where one is in the dust. However, the lights soon become buried in dirt and are not of much help. Sometime in mid-morning, with Jaccoux at the wheel, the machine begins to lurch violently. We have blown a tire. We manage to get the Land Rover off of the main track and set about the change the tire. A car pulls up—a small French car obviously worse for the wear. Its occupants, also covered with dust, emerge and ask if they can be of help. There is not much for them to do and as they set off they remark, with a somewhat envious reference to the spaciousness of the machine, "*Ici il y'a l'avion et ça.*" This is the first time we have had to change a tire, and we attempt to get some guidance from the Land Rover manual. While it is full of erudite advice on how to adjust "carburetters" and "air cleaners," nowhere does it say at what point on the machine's chassis one should place the lifting jack. While we are pondering this question Michèle brings out our transistor radio and tunes to a Russian station which is playing, in Russian, "Has Anybody Seen My Gal?" Our first tentative attempt with the jack is a failure and after lifting a few feet, the machine once again buries itself in the sand. (Visions of Alexander marching, day after day, week after week, along this same route flit through my mind.) Finally we locate a vital spot near the wheel and proceed to change the tire. The broken one has a gash in it several inches long, evidently made by a sharp rock. We stop for lunch in a small desert town built around an oasis. The machine is at once surrounded by curious schoolchildren who want, apart from staring at us, matches and foreign coins and postage stamps. Fortunately we have some French centimes and a few French and American stamps and we are led off to a place to eat. As it is the fall harvest time, Persian melons are plentiful. A good Persian melon tastes like ambrosia; it is full of delightful sugary water, just right for a desert thirst, and its thick skin protects it, presumably, from the invasions of amoeba that make fresh vegetables in Asia Minor a positive menace. Since leaving Turkey, our diet, purchased in local restaurants (we are still hanging on to the provisions in the Land Rover) has degenerated into endless mounds of rice, usually cooked in mutton fat which gives it somewhat unappetizing greasy consistency, tea, available everywhere, and, occasionally, goat's meat. From time to time we have been able to find fresh eggs served with unleavened bread—but the melons are keeping us, we hope, from beriberi or worse. We never have less than two melons in the machine. We have filled two plastic jerrycans with water from the hotel in Teheran which has, allegedly, been chlorinated. We have several small canteens with us, and Michèle has laced their contents with a good dousing of pernod. We are losing weight hand over fist, but after our excesses in the Turkish restaurants in western Turkey, this is not a catastrophe. We have been taking mexaform tablets three times a day as protection against dysentery, and so far, fingers crossed, we seem to have escaped.

After lunch we head back into the desert. We come upon a truck in a state of complete collapse. We give the driver a lift to the next oasis, and as we jounce along he says "asphalt, asphalt," apparently the only English word he knows, over and over again, as in prayer. Everywhere there is evidence of crews building a new road that, in a few years, will stretch through this part of Iran and will make the east-west traverse of the country a scenic pleasure. By nightfall we arrive in Mechhed too exhausted to do much else than look for the nearest large hotel. It is an elegant one with an underground garage, and the manager insists that we put the machine inside. This would be an excellent idea except that it doesn't fit through the door and, in fact, Jaccoux nearly takes the top off of it before he can extricate himself by applying fourwheel drive in reverse. Our last act, before passing out for the night, is to clean the air filter of the engine with gasoline. The Land Rover manual has assured us that the most dire consequences will follow, when operating under desert conditions, if the filter is not kept immaculate, and indeed, when we open it, it is practically a solid mass of oily mud.

Afghanistan

The route from Mechhed to the Afghan border post at Islam Qala is the worst yet—about a hundred miles worth. The heat, even in the early morning, is almost unbearable. By the time we arrive at the Iranian border post of Saadabad we have just about had it. We see a kiosk advertising Pepsi-Cola, and throwing hygienic caution to the winds we consume several bottles apiece. Getting out of Iran involves several stages—visits to diverse offices for examinations of passports and, of course, the *carnet*. Fortunately, the Iranian border police, also suffering from the heat, are in no mood to prolong the formalities and, in a half hour or so we proceed towards the border. We pass a quarantine camp, army tents filled with people sunning themselves, that houses all travelers coming *from* Afghanistan. They must sit for a few days to make sure they are not carrying cholera. Cholera epidemics are common here in the summer and, unfortunately, the existing cholera vaccination is no firm guarantee that one will not come down with the disease. (Someone has remarked that the severity of the case one acquires *after* the vaccination is about the difference between the case one would have acquired with no vaccination and one's reaction to the vaccination.) The Iranians simply do not take any chances, and the camp appeared to be packed with idle motorists taking a brief, enforced, vacation in the desert.

We had been counseled by innumerable travelers that crossing the Iran-Aghan frontier required the patience of Job and the fortitude of James Bond (it is also closed after 6:00 P.M.) and, therefore, were pleasantly surprised that the first obstacle—a sort of wooden gate—was easily crossed by showing a pleasant, if somnolent, Afghan soldier our visas and entry permits. We were next ushered to a small building where an Afghan customs official asked us to fill out several forms pertaining to our personal belongings and the machine. Thinking, naively, that we were now free to enter Afghanistan we made for a second wooden gate, but were turned back and told to enter another set of buildings in front of which could be seen a sizable array of automobiles including a newish looking small blue Land Rover. Its occupants turned out to be middle-aged American couple who had taken the same route that we had although, wisely, they had allowed themselves about two months for the trip. We made for an interior office and were greeted by a scene that looked like something from an Ionesco play. As nearly as I could make out the cast of characters included three official people, two of them dressed in white uniforms and the third in a dark suit. The bench along one of the walls was crammed with individuals of all sorts who looked as if they had been there since the beginning of time and were destined to remain forever. The rest of the room was crowded with people coming and going at random. Someone, a servant perhaps, kept appearing and disappearing with tea for the official people. Money seemed to be changing hands but to what end one could only imagine. The desk of the official person in civilian clothes was piled high with passports of every hue. Thinking that it was probably the thing to do I placed our three passports on the pile, but they were soon lost under a mound of passports freshly deposited on top of ours. After a half an hour in which absolutely nothing happened with the growing heap of passports I decided that some action might be desirable and left the room to see if there were not some other official person somewhere in the building who might know what was supposed to happen. I found an open door and when I went inside another official person in a uniform indicated, with vigorous gestures, that I was to get out of his room and back into the other one. When I returned two of the official people had left and the third, when I approached him, indicated that he was only concerned with people who were *leaving* Afghanistan and that our problem, namely *entering* the country, lay outside his specialty. Another half hour went by. The man in the suit returned and proceeded to open up a huge ledger very slowly and with great care lest its pages disintegrate on the spot. By now our passports had receded to the bottom of the pile and it was another half an hour before they once again surfaced. They were examined from every possible angle—even upside down—and finally, with a pen that constantly ran out of ink and had to be refilled, variously presumably relevant notations were entered into the great book. I was asked for the license number of the machine and when I said HXC 146 H it was duly entered as HXC 146 8. Anticipating all sorts of complications if the number were incorrectly given I tried to correct the 8 to an H, but to no avail. Each pronunciation of "H" seemed only to deepen the confusion. In fact, just before he was about to put our passports back under the pile one of the people on the bench against the wall said "Ach, ach" several times in a loud voice, making a sound which, under other circumstances I would have interpreted as a sneeze. Whatever it was, it seemed to do the trick and before long we were able to show our passports to the soldier at the gate and were officially admitted to Afghanistan.

We had been told that the main roads in Afghanistan were excellent, thanks to a spate of competitive road building by the Americans and Russians, each of whom had built part of the route that leads from the border to Kabul, the capital city. In fact, that first stretch, to Herat, built by the Russians, was absolutely incredible: a broad stretch of wide, two-lane highway, apparently in concrete, over which the machine floated like a bird. The Afghans had recently become aware of the potential economic importance of tourism, and beside the road, about every fifty miles or so, one could find clearly indicated gasoline stations. These were in general the hand-operated variety, and once again, one had to persuade their owners or attendants to keep manning the pump until the tank was full. We had also filled our jerrycans in Iran, just in case. Payment for the vital fluid was something of a problem. The only word of "farsi," the language of western Afghanistan, that we had managed to acquire was *"harbutza"*—if that is the transliteration—the word for "melon." The Afghan melons, in season, are, if anything, even better than the Persian melons. This was hardly the basis for an intricate commercial transaction involving gasoline. There seemed to be some tendency for the gasoline pumper to return change for any bill in what appeared to be arbitrary quantities, more, I think, out of a sense of reluctance to engage in the necessary arithmetical computation than anything else. Since our tourist booklet indicated that the essence should cost 25 Afghanis per gallon we would give the attendant something like what we thought was the exact amount and hope for the best.

The scenery was magnificent; a wild desert land broken by the occasional outcropping of severe-looking mountains in reddish rock. The route was lined with enormous camel caravans of nomads, the Kochi's who move seasonally from the highlands of central Afghanistan to the lowlands in the south to find new grazing for their flocks of sheep. The men, looking for all the world like characters out of the Bible, often wore flowing beards and magnificent brightly colored Afghan coats lined with sheep wool, and the women, brightly dressed, covered in silver jewelry, had the wild beauty of gypsy princesses. (There is a theory—the "Bani Israeli" theory—of the origin of the Afghan people, or at least some of them, which seeks to connect them with the lost Ten Tribes of Israel. The proponents of this view cite as evidence the facial characteristics of the people and their biblical names, while the opponents, and I think they include most modern authorities on the subject, point out that the dominant Afghan language, Pashto, which is Indo-Aryan, has no trace of a Hebrew origin, and moreover, essentially all Afghans are Moslems, while Jews, whatever else, tend to cling, in the face of most imaginable obstacles, to Judaism. Afghanistan has been the scene of so much racial mixing, due to an almost unbroken history of foreign invasions from all quarters, that it is hard to imagine how any racial characteristic could have been preserved undiluted for very long.)

Late in the afternoon the road becomes bordered with trees, a sure sign of an oasis, and soon afterwards we can make out the ancient city of Herat. It was conquered and rebuilt by Alexander in 330. One of the fixed natural laws of the deserts of Asia Minor is that civilization follows the water. Toynbee has estimated that there are cycles of drought in Asia Minor about every six hundred years. When drought moves over the land, people migrate and, in the past, fresh waves of conquest began. It is believed by some scientists that our planet is gradually heating up—even the polar ice caps appear to be slowly melting. Perhaps in the days of Alexander this part of Asia Minor was cooler, wetter, and more benign, otherwise his march from Greece through these deserts seems incredible. We make for a new, modern hotel built a few years ago by the Russians. It has a somewhat bilious-looking swimming pool attached and, indeed, we are joined alongside it by a team of Russians, very young and athletic looking, who turn out to be vehicle engineers who have driven some new Russian trucks down from the Pamirs in order to test how they perform on the desert roads. Their trip, which has just begun, will last for several months. They are all dressed in identical blue gym suits and, later, we exchange some views on the roads and they accept a pint of our British motor oil, which we have brought along as a reserve supply, to see how it works in their trucks.

After a brief swim we set out to explore Herat. Herat must be one of the loveliest places on earth. In the setting sun the houses and minarets—there are only six still standing, built in the fifteenth century, the rest having been partly destroyed by earthquakes and partly, deliberately, by the British in 1885, when they thought that their presence would make defense of the city against the Russians more difficult—all made of red sandstone or earth—glow with a gentle inner fire. Horse-drawn carriages with little jingling bells punctuate the peaceful silence of the city. The people are extremely friendly, and we are surrounded wherever we go by children whose parents ask us to take their pictures. We visit an old mosque, and when we greet its ancient guardian with *"Salam Aleichim"*—"Peace Be With You"—he puts his hand over his heart in the traditional Afghan salute. The bazaar is full of wonderful Afghan clothing; karakul hats and Afghan coats lined with karakul, cloth decorated with tiny mirrors, and light Afghan shirts in many colors and decorated with fine embroidery. Everything and everyone appears to be in harmony with the simplicity and beauty of an oasis in a red and tranquil desert.

The next morning, early, we head for Kandahar, now the second largest city in Afghanistan, also founded by Alexander. This promises to be the hottest day of the trip. We are heading almost due south and Kandahar, which is not far from Afghanistan's southern border with Pakistan, is approximately situated on the latitude of the Sahara Desert. The route from Herat to Kandahar, Alexander's route, is straight through the desert. But since 1966 it has been paved courtesy of U.S. AID. The heat is unbelievable. It appears to invade the machine like a menacing active force embracing everything in a dry, infernal grip. Every few miles on the route we see fantastic mirages in the desert— lakes and forests—which, of course, evanesce when we approach. The engine temperature of the machine, judging from the gauge on the dashboard, is hovering close to the danger point, but miraculously nothing boils over. About noon we find an oasis village on a river. Most of its inhabitants appear to be prone under various trees. There are a few dilapidated trucks, their engines uncovered like skeletons, loaded with all but prostrate people heading in one direction or another. We stop in a small, dirty tea shop and restaurant. The density of flies is such that we decide not to risk a meal, but we do take a glass of warm, in fact, boiling hot tea. We also purchase our daily ration of melons and find a spot under a bridge where there is a beach to eat the melons and swim. Michèle arouses a curious stare or two by appearing in a late model black French bikini. But we are too hot to care. The water is delicious—God knows what's in it. We are too hot to care about that either. After a blissful bath, we gorge on our melons and continue south. The rest of the afternoon passes as in a fevered dream and by sunset we pull up at the government hotel, a slightly more rundown version of the one in Herat, in Kandahar. A cluster of vehicles is drawn up in front of it, their occupants, it turns out, sleeping through the afternoon before setting off to Herat by night. (We are told that most people try to do this stretch at night and that we have been lucky to get through without a breakdown.) There is an English family who have been stranded in Kandahar for several days when a part in their Land Rover gave out and no replacement could be found in all of Afghanistan. They were calmly waiting for a new part to be flown from England.

Kandahar was an important way station on the great Silk Route that went from India and China to Europe and which, more or less, disappeared after Vasco da Gama opened up the sea route around the Cape of Good Hope in 1498. It still has the aspects of a bazaar. Almost everything imaginable can be purchased in Kandahar, from hashish to guns, both modern and ancient. Indeed, Jaccoux added a second *"flingue"*—a wicked-looking automatic—to our unused arsenal. While this delicate purchase was being negotiated I sat on a curbstone watching the local baker making hot *"chapatis"*—unleavened bread—in an open stone hearth. The dough was spun into a large flat pancake and then dumped into the hearth, and after a half a minute or so a large, warm, tasty-looking circle of bread was extracted. Both Jaccoux purchased beautiful karakul-lined coats to keep themselves warm during the skiing season in the Alps (the only disadvantage of these coats, I am told by the experts, is that it is all but impossible to remove the smell of live sheep from them), thence we retired to the government hotel.

The following morning we headed off, again on the U.S. AID highway, which, incidentally, is being maintained (in some places there were sweepers, men with brooms, sweeping away offending stones and pebbles) by a system of highway tolls not unlike that of the New Jersey Turnpike. (One difference, perhaps, is that the Afghan toll collectors are not averse to offering to exchange dollars, and in one instance, one of them also wanted to sell us lunch.) About midafternoon, after a day of desert driving, we enter the Kabul Valley. Again there is a sense of an oasis in a desert, but an oasis hemmed in by

A street scene in Kandahar, Afghanistan

mountains. Once reaching Kabul, we head in a straight line for the brand new Intercontinental Hotel, which is easy to locate since it is on top of a high hill overlooking the city. Our motivation is also straightforward. We are hungry. We have been living for something like a week on a diet consisting, in first approximation, of rice, eggs, *chapatis*, tea, and melon. The prospect of a Western meal beckons us like the Sirens of the ancient mariners. In fact the Intercontinental offers a splendid array of international food flown into Kabul from all corners of the globe. Apart from exploring Kabul, we have at least two plans in mind. In the first place I must go to the Pakistan Embassy in Kabul and settle, once and for all, the question of the road permit into Pakistan. A brief visit to the Embassy confirms our suspicion that the permit is irrelevant if we do not intend to take the car across the Indian border. Why the consul in New York could not have informed us of this elementary fact to begin with remains one of the numerous mysteries of the East.

Our second plan requires a brief historical discourse to explain. After his march through Persia, Alexander headed north into what was then Bactria, now essentially northern Afghanistan. (In fact Alexander appears to have followed, more or less, the modern road from Kabul towards the Pakistan border and then headed north at some point near the present city of Jalalabad in Afghanistan.) Consolidating his conquests in Bactria took him from 330 to 327 B.C. As Fosco Maraini notes in his book *Where Four Worlds Meet*, when he did set out for India in 327, "His army of forty thousand fighting men was accompanied by at least as many non-combatant auxiliaries and campfollowers of either sex; wives and children, concubines, slaves, artisans of every description, seamen and ship's carpenters to facilitate the exploration of Ocean, poets (the ambassadors extraordinaire of those times) and philosophers, technicians and traders, merchants and seers." Another brilliant book on the history and peoples of this region—the eastern border of Afghanistan and the northwest frontier of Pakistan—*The Pathans* ("Pathan" is a generic term for the tribes that did and still do inhabit the area. Loosely speaking, these are the peoples, now Moslem, who speak the closely related languages of Pashtu and Pahktu), by Sir Olaf Caroe, who spent a lifetime in the area and was the last British governor of the northwest frontier before the 1947 partition of Pakistan, characterizes Alexander's expedition as really a "raid." Caroe's point is that Alexander's whole voyage to India (which ultimately ended in failure since, on the one hand he could not subdue the powers of the subcontinent, and on the other, he could not convince his rebellious troops to march further east) lasted only twelve months. As Caroe puts it, "his was a oneway passage." Shortly afterward Alexander died in Babylon. For a century or so Bactria was ruled over by the generals, or the descendents of the generals, of his original army. Soon after, the country was invaded from all sides, and the next century was a jumbled history of conquests from Persia and India and the transplantation into the region of Zoroastrianism from Persia and Hinduism from India. There was also a relatively brief, but very significant, import of Buddhism into Afghanistan from Nepal and India. Buddha was born in what is now southern Nepal in 563 B.C. In its original form the Hinayana, or Lesser Vehicle version, Buddhism was not really a religion with a deity, but rather a philosophy of life with Buddha as its teacher and founder. However, as Buddhism evolved, it became transmuted into the Mahayana, or the Buddhism of the Greater Vehicle, in which Buddha became deified. In its original form the doctrine was iconoclastic and no images of Buddha were made or drawn. But with the Greater Vehicle Buddha began to be represented in the now familiar form. The fascinating thing is that the first representations of Buddha, perhaps in the first or second centuries A.D., were done by Greek or Greco-Roman artists and were based on the model of the statues of Apollo. This gave rise to an entire art form that goes under the general name of Ghandaric art. (Ghandara was the ancient name of the Pathan country, which had, for most of its history, its center of gravity in the plains around the present city of Peshawar in Pakistan.) Buddhism did not make lasting inroads into Ghandara. Caroe notes, "In some strange manner the atmosphere was too rarified for the people of these parts; that age passed like a vision and left no memory."

What it *did* leave was a magnificent art form mainly in stone (at least what is preserved is in stone), consisting of thousands upon thousands of carvings on walls, on the sides of rocks, and as statues pure and simple of Buddha and his disciples. These carvings combine the exotic mysteriousness of the East with the cultural skills of Greece and Rome. (I saw one head of Buddha with those narrow, somnolent oriental eyes but with a perfect

Roman nose.) Often the faces are of the Orient, but the clothes are the flowing robes of Greece. The most extraordinary example of Ghandaric art is found in Bamiyan in Afghanistan, about 150 miles northwest of Kabul in a valley that nestles between the snow-covered ranges of the Hindu Kush and the Kohi-Baba. This valley is tucked away in the mountains and was probably one of the last strongholds of the Buddhists before they were overrun by invaders from the east and west. There, on the side of a cliff, in red sandstone, artists—how many and how long it took them no one can say—carved two enormous statues of the Buddha, the smaller being 115 feet high and the larger being 175 feet high. These statues have been partly destroyed— the tops of the faces have been cut away, one would almost say deliberately, but enough remains so that one can get a good idea of how magnificent they must have been. In any event, after settling our affairs with the Pakistan Embassy we headed northwest to Bamiyan.

The route to Bamiyan begins with the best of intentions. It follows the Russian-built main road from Kabul north to the Russian frontier. The Russians completed the northern highway in 1964 and by building a tunnel under what used to be the track over the Salang Pass in the high country they shortened the distance to the Russian border, by road, to one third of what it was. The road is well built but suffers, as do all roads in this part of the world, from being too narrow to comfortably contain the flow of machines, people, and animals that use it. Caravans of people and animals are everywhere and driving becomes a constant obstacle course. We follow the road for some thirty miles to Charikar, where we are obliged to leave it and turn west to get to Bamiyan. A minuscule sign points the way to Bamiyan, and after a few hundred yards the road, dirt, and rocks become so bad that I assume that we have made a mistake and go back to make sure that we have not taken the wrong turn. Alas, there is no mistake, and we spend the next five hours, at speeds of something like twenty miles an hour, bouncing over what is surely the worst road that we have yet come upon. The scenery is, on the other hand, magnificent. There are deep gorges, mountain passes, and places where the river valley opens up enough to reveal well-tended fields of grain. There are also tribes of Kochis on the march south, magnificent-looking people, but when Jaccoux stops to take some pictures they make it clear that unless we put away our cameras they are going to attack us and our machine with rocks, and perhaps worse. They do not appear overtly hostile, but they are not interested in being regarded as curiosities by tourists. Just before Bamiyan, the valley opens up into a wide basin set in among the surrounding mountains, an ideal place for a retreat both from the world as a whole and from hostile invaders. Our gasoline supply, even including the two full jerrycans, is dangerously low, and it has become clear that if we do not find a gasoline pump we will be in difficulties as far as getting back, since there are none before one returns to the main route. Happily, there is a gasoline station just before Bamiyan and we feed the machine. It is now about two in the afternoon, and we decide to feed ourselves at the large, and somewhat rundown, government hotel outside the town. It is set on a high hill and from it we can survey the valley including the cliff with the two Buddhas which is just in front of it. Although we are too far away to get a feeling for the details of the carvings, we are awed by their massive power. They are set back from the face of the cliff in caves which have clearly been hacked out of the mountain before the carving began. It is our plan, now that we have the necessary fuel, to push on before sunset about forty miles to Band-I-Amir, where there is a string of celebrated deep mountain lakes. We will camp by one of the lakes and then return the next day to explore the Buddhas.

The drive to the lakes is even more rugged than the drive to Bamiyan, and half the time one has the impression that one is more or less making one's road. The country is wild and mountainous and incredibly beautiful. After a few hours we come out on a high cliff, and down below is the first of the lakes, a circle of cobalt blue, surrounded by massive red cliffs. By a dexterous use of four-wheel drive Jaccoux succeeds in maneuvering us down the side of the valley, and we set up camp just *under* one of the lakes. This lake is, in fact, contained in a sort of lunar crater whose sides are well above the floor of the valley. The top of the crater constantly spills water over—the lake is, no doubt, being fed by a river somewhere—and this runs down into the valley in a series of small falls and streams. Band-I-Amir must be about ten thousand feet up and we can tell by the rapidly falling temperature in the late afternoon that we are going to be in for a cold night. We have decided to try out our high-altitude camping equipment—the doubly lined tents and the down sleeping bags. The tents appear to require at least a master's degree in engineering to set up, but aided by Michèle's experience as a one-time member of the French Girl Scouts, we arrive. Jaccoux enters one of the small tents and after a few moments emerges to announce that it was not a tent "but a coffin." The tents having been set up, we proceed to make our first meal *chez* the Land Rover. We turn up a can of Italian canneloni, some paté, and a Swiss vegetable soup and set to work cooking and spreading. The result is excellent and to the tune of shepherd's flutes—our camp is not far from a pastoral village—we retire for a good, if somewhat chilly, night's sleep. Indeed, when we arise the following morning, the tents are covered in frost, and many of the smaller streams leading down from our elevated lake have frozen over. After a brief scramble around the lake, and a breakfast of coffee, bread, and jam, we reassemble all of the gear in the machine and prepare to head off. Jaccoux tries to start it. Nothing; not a sound nor flicker, no lights and no horn. Clearly the battery is dead. This seems incredible since we had just had the car thoroughly serviced—we even had our roof-rack rewelded—in a Kabul garage that is used primarily for the local buses. Despite our, we thought, careful instructions, no one had bothered to check the water level in the battery which, indeed, when we opened it, turned out to be nonexistent. I do not think that anything short of a tank could have towed the machine out of the sandy floor of the valley. However, Jaccoux remembered that among our effects were two plastic vials of sterilized water which were hidden away to be used in extremis in the desert. The vials were dug out and opened and their contents emptied into the parched battery which miraculously blossomed sufficiently so that the machine started. I do not think that I have heard such a pleasant sound as the whirring of that engine on the morning in Band-I-Amir.

The trip back to Kabul is uneventful. We stop and clamber around the Buddhas. They seem to be undergoing some kind of restoration and are surrounded by scaffolding and equipment. It is possible, at least in principle, to climb up the interior of the carvings by a series of tunnels and passageways, some of which were closed because of the repairs. When seen from close up, the cliff turns out to be full of small caves in which the monks no doubt lived. On the walls and roofs of some of the caves one can make out faint remains of wall paintings, rather like the Tibetan *thankas*, that must have decorated the caves throughout. By dint of some jarring high-speed driving by Jaccoux on the dirt roads, we manage to get back to the main highway by nightfall and by eight we are in Kabul. We spend a day exploring the bazaars. (Kabul is a paradise for souvenir hunters. Never have I seen such an assortment of carvings, painted cloth, ancient and modern guns, and clothing of every variety. Two items struck me. The first was the fascinating local work in marble and onyx. The Afghans specialize in making sculptures of fruit—pears done in white marble and apples done in a variety of colors. The second was a variety of exceedingly weird, totemistic statues in wood and stone from Nuristan. Nuristan is a section of Afghanistan near Pakistan in the Hindu-Kush mountains. It is probable that it may have been through this territory that Alexander's army entered the subcontinent. Until the Moslem conquests of Afghanistan, the people of these valleys practiced a pagan religion with a good deal of totemistic nature imagery. Those who did not flee or convert were killed. (Nuristan means the Land of Light—presumably the light of the Prophet.) The survivors made their way across the passes into the mountainous region near Tirich Mir in Chitral, where, according to Maraini, they still practice something like their original religion. They are known as Kafirs—meaning "unclean" or "pagan," and the country they inhabit, a few small valleys in Chitral, is known as Kafiristan. We also intend to visit Kafiristan once we get into Pakistan. However, the present-day Nuristanis produce statuary, large wooden statues containing innumerable glowering faces, that must be the remnant of their original pagan religious tradition. The statues have something of the air of watchful primitive gods. (Moslems are, of course, iconoclastic, and there is no Moslem plastic art that is, properly speaking, religious.) We also decide to chance a meal in one of the restaurants in town. Apart from the presence of innumerable hippies who then crowded the country, in large part because of the easy access to drugs, the place looks pretty dreary and rather filthy, and, in fact, after one look at the "buffet table" we flee back to the fleshpots of the Intercontinental. Afghanistan is notorious for hepatitis and even Dr. de Haynin, our kindly medical genie, had acquired a mild case here.

The next day we head east. It is our intention to visit Nuristan, a substantial detour from our route, but shortly after traversing the Kabul Gorge—just after Kabul the road follows the Kabul River through an extremely deep and impressive rock gorge—the machine begins to develop symptoms of a major intestinal disorder. Each time we accelerate there is a horrible rattling sound. At one point we stop and, for about an hour, Jaccoux cleans and adjusts the carburetor, but to no avail. We think seriously of returning to Kabul, but as it seems to run so long as we are on level ground and do not have to accelerate too much, we decide to risk it and to head straight for the Pakistan border. The route to the border is flat and the road is excellent. The Afghan border station at Torkham, at which we arrive in the early afternoon, is modern and well organized. So it is on the twenty-ninth of September, chugging and snorting, but still going strong, we enter Pakistan, at the foot of the Khyber Pass, to begin the third part of our trip to Chitral and Tirich Mir.

9 A Passage to Pakistan, Part II: Pakistan

On August 14, 1947, Pakistan became a sovereign country. The word "Pakistan" was coined in 1933 by a young Moslem student in Cambridge named Choudhri Rahmat Ali. As he explained it in a pamphlet entitled "Now or Never," "Pakistan" is both a Persian and an Urdu word, composed of letters taken from the names of their homelands: that is, Punjab, Afghania (North-West Frontier Province), Kashmir, Iran, Sindh, Tukharistan, and Balochistan. ("Tukharistan" is presumably "Turkistan," the northern region of Afghanistan, and the "stan" in Pakistan comes from "Balochistan" more usually spelled "Baluchistan," a district of what is now Pakistan that borders Iran and Afghanistan in the south.) Some of the areas named in the acronymn—Sindh, the Punjab, and parts of Kashmir—are, of course, part of the present country of Pakistan. What was East Pakistan, (now the independent state of Bangladesh), was bordered by India, Burma, and the Bay of Bengal, was not included in the list; and, very likely, Iran was included to give a sense of the community of kindred nations that would be allied with each other rather than out of any sense of territorial ambition. The "Pakistan idea," the idea that Moslems of the subcontinent should have a homeland of their own, goes back at least a century. As many Pakistanis view it, at least now, the impetus towards forming a Moslem state arose because the Moslems of the subcontinent felt that they could not lead a full religious life in a predominantly Hindu country. (In this, the attitudes of the Pakistanis strongly resemble those of the Jews in forming Israel, and it is one of the sad ironies of the times that the two countries whose origins have so much in common spiritually are so violently antagonistic to each other.) In addi-

213

tion, men like Muhammed Ali Jinnah, the charismatic lawyer who was Pakistan's first governor general after partition (he died of tuberculosis at the age of seventy in September of 1948 only a short time after he had taken office), were as much, if not more concerned, about the possibility that Moslems would simply become an ineffectual political minority in a vast Hindu state. Jinnah, known simply as Quaid-i-Azam—The Great Leader—in Pakistan, was one of the prime movers of the Moslem League, an organization founded in 1906 to promote the interests of the Moslem minority in the subcontinent. For much of his lifetime, and that of the league, his major concern was the elimination of the British Raj and, in this, he had common interests with the Indian Congress party with whom he worked closely almost to the time of partition.

The partition of the subcontinent was an extremely bloody and traumatic affair, and the scars are still everywhere to be seen in Pakistan. During the civil rioting, looting, and outright massacres that occurred, involving both Hindus and Moslems; at least a half million people were killed and thirteen million refugees crossed from one side of the partition boundary to the other. Whole populations like the Sikhs in the Punjab, the fertile area that stretches from Lahore in Pakistan towards New Delhi, changed countries. People arrived by the hundreds of thousands in the major cities like Karachi with nothing but what they could carry in their arms. As a country Pakistan began with almost nothing. There was no civil service, no industry, no airline, horribly inadequate housing, and very little in the way of medical facilities. It is against this background that a visitor to modern Pakistan must view the often baffling and sometimes frustrating phenomena that he encounters, and, whatever else, every visitor to Pakistan who knows something of the conditions out of which it has evolved cannot help but be impressed by the enormous progress the country has made in just thirty years.

After leaving Chamonix on the fifth of September and following, as closely as we could the route of Alexander the Great through Asia Minor, we managed to arrive at the Pak-Afghan border town of Torkham, at the foot of the Khyber Pass, early in the afternoon of September 29. The Land Rover appeared to be basically sound although it had developed a severe engine knock in Afghanistan, and we were anxious to get it to some suitable garage before things got any worse. However, before doing so we had the frontier to cross as well as the Khyber Pass. I was not quite sure of what to expect at the frontier. Our trip took place just after the fire in the Aqsa Mosque in Jerusalem and, from reading various English-language newspapers during the overland trip it was clear that there was a good deal of anti-American feeling in the Moslem countries, although we had not encountered any during our trip. On the other hand, many French people who had recently been in Pakistan had remarked on the evident cordiality that the citizenry felt towards the French and especially, and above all, towards de Gaulle. In any event, we presented our various national credentials to a sweltering, and extremely friendly, Pakistani customs official. (The temperature was well over a hundred and the humidity was all but unbearable.) After studying them for some time he pointed to me and asked "U.S.?" I said yes, and then he pointed to the Jaccoux and said "French," to which they nodded. "The same car?" he asked, as if he were surprised. When I explained that we had been in the same car for nearly a month, he smiled kindly as if this were a splendidly funny joke, and soon after we were dismissed and allowed to proceed to the Khyber.

Historians seem to be agreed that when he crossed the mountains from what is now Afghanistan to what is now Pakistan in 327 B.C. Alexander did not use the Khyber Pass. He probably crossed a hundred miles or so to the north. Why this was one can only speculate. Perhaps he was aware of the geographical fact that upon negotiating the Khyber it is then necessary to cross the Kabul and the Indus rivers, no simple feat without bridges, before really setting foot on the subcontinent. Or perhaps he had been forewarned of the innumerable possibilities for ambush in the rugged terrain surrounding the pass. He does seem to have sent an auxiliary force under his general Hephaestion to follow the Kunar with the idea of building some kind of bridge across it. However the Khyber has been the invasion route of most of the armies from the west, and certainly the Mogul armies that followed his footsteps into India in the subsequent centuries. Since the creation of Pakistan in 1947, Pak-Afghan relations have not been especially cordial (Afghanistan was the only country to vote against Pakistan's admission to the United Nations) and probably for that reason, as well as the difficulties of the terrain, none of the passes to the north of the Khyber have motorable roads. As passes go, the Khyber is a bit of a disappointment scenically. The terrain is incredibly rugged and barren, but the road is so hemmed in by the cliffs on either side, which is why it *is* such an ideal spot for ambush, that one does not get to see much of the countryside. It is, at least now, a tremendously active route, with caravans of trucks and busses, and the biggest danger for a western driver is forgetting that in Pakistan traffic, *à l'Anglaise*, is to the left. The first and most striking feature about the visible populace is that it is almost entirely male and that all men above the age of puberty are heavily armed. Never have I seen such a concentration of weapons. They range from submachine guns and even small field pieces to daggers. Nearly every man wears at least one cartridge belt, and one simply must get used to the fact that everywhere one goes in the frontier one is surrounded by people carrying guns. There are, in fact, several local gun factories that manufacture weapons copied identically from European and American models. Part of the reason for so much armament are the blood feuds for which the frontier is celebrated. These go back generations and often result in the massacre of entire families. In an extraordinary book on these tribesmen, *The Pathans*, Sir Olaf Caroe, who spent a lifetime among them and who was the last governor of the North-West Frontier Province before partition, writes, "Only a generation back a certain Mohmand malik [the Mohmands are one of the frontier tribes and a *malik* is a tribal chief or elder] whom I knew called a banquet in Gandab to signalize a reconciliation with fellow-tribesmen who had killed his father and all his relatives, leaving only himself, a child they pitied and found too young to kill. When he grew to man's estate, with a fine show of *bonhomie* he invited them all beneath his roof and when they were inside, he and his retainers shot them, everyone. Even the laws of hospitality will go down before the calculated enmity bequeathed by a blood-feud."

And he goes on, "It is for reasons of this kind that once, in 1947, sitting down to a feast in this same Gandab with some two hundred tribesmen, I found myself the only man unarmed. Every malik, as he sat at meat, carried his rifle slung on his shoulder, and on asking to see the magazines, I found every weapon loaded. This did not spoil the jokes and jollity; indeed it was then I heard the story of the massacre in Gandab a generation back and afterwards confirmed it."

On a heavily traveled route, like the Khyber, the visitor is quite safe. However, in much of the frontier country, especially at night, one is not safe and the goverment of Pakistan does not guarantee the safety of travelers in the tribal areas if they wander off of the main routes. (There is, among other things, a good deal of smuggling from Afghanistan in an attempt to escape the extremely heavy import duties the government imposes on foreign goods, and most of this is done at night.) As we had an ailing Land Rover and as I had a commitment to be in Rawalpindi, we headed directly to Peshawar, the first large city after the frontier, and, in many ways the spiritual locus of the Pathan country.

The summer climate in Peshawar is noted as being among the most uncomfortable in the world. Temperatures reach 120 or so and are accompanied by a heavy monsoon humidity. Even in late September it was pretty awful, and we had all we could do to drag ourselves to the Dean's Hotel, a celebrated Victorian establishment featuring small cottages that surround the main building. This hotel was part of the Oberoi chain, an Indian chain, since taken over and run by the government of Pakistan. The hotel is simple, but comfortable, and I was especially pleased to find that it served a local beer. Pakistan, as a Moslem country, is notably dry, but a good beer is made in Muree, a hill station near Rawalpindi, and Muree Beer is readily available in the larger cities. Between the three of us we consumed several pints, barely enough to replace the fluids that had been seeping out of every pore, but enough to put us to sleep despite the murderous heat.

Early the next morning we headed off on the road that, before partition, was the celebrated trunk route from the frontier to Calcutta in the east. The countryside was lush and tropical—banana and tobacco plantations—and the contrast with the stark Afghan desert land striking. There is little wonder that so many of the Mogul emperors were tempted by the Vale of Peshawar and, indeed, many of them, like Babur and Akbar, had summer capitals in Kabul and wintered in Peshawar where the winter climate is marvelous. This historical association helps to explain why many Afghans feel a proprietary interest in this part of Pakistan and why there is tension between the two countries. Some Afghans would like to see this area made into an independent nation which they call Pahktunistan or Pushtunistan. The present boundary, called the Durand line, was laid out in 1893 by a British mission under the direction of Sir Mortimer Durand. In general the boundary follows the mountain ranges that separate the two countries, although in some instances it does divide some of the Pathan tribes who, in any event, migrate back and forth across it seasonally. One has the impression that most of the tribesmen, who, in fact, had at the time of partition, some option as to their status (they could have remained as independent princely states) and who opted for association with Pakistan, are loyal to it and, indeed constitute an important element in the armed forces of the country. Historically the tribes have had much closer associations within themselves and with each other than with any national entity, but this may be changing. (As an illustration, I met a young boy, perhaps nine or ten years old, in Islamabad who was bilingual in Urdu, the national language, and Pahktu, the version of the tribal language that is spoken on the Pakistani side of the frontier—Pashtu, the softer dialect, is spoken on the Afghan side. He was teaching me the difference between the Urdu number system and the Pahktu numbers—in Urdu, for example "five" is *panch* whereas in Pahktu it is *panzai*. When I asked him if he was a Pathan he said "No—Pakistan.") So long as the tribes continue to find their economic situation improving, as it has been, it is unlikely that the notion of an independent Pahktunistan will have much appeal.

After about an hour's worth of driving we came to the Indus River. The course of the Indus as it wanders through Pakistan practically violates the laws of gravity. The Indus is born in the glaciers on the Pak-Chinese frontier, in China actually. It then flows almost due west into Pakistan. It first flows south for a few miles and then it turns northwest until it reaches Skardu in the high mountain country of Baltistan—a "political agency" administered by Pakistan. (Pakistan has maintained a certain number of these agencies that neighbor Kashmir on a special unincorporated basis, presumably as a protest and a symbol of the fact that the Pakistanis do not accept the present status of Kashmir as a settled matter. The Indians, on the other hand, do, and the status of Indian Kashmir—which the Pakistan press consistently refers to as "occupied Kashmir"—is taken to be that of any other Indian state.) It then continues northwest in a deep gorge past the town of Gilgit, the *chef lieu* of the Gilgit Agency, whence it turns south in the general direction of Peshawar. It continues south and slightly west until it finally comes out in the Arabian Sea near Karachi. This lower part of the Indus, at Mohenjo-Daro and Harappa, contains traces of perhaps the oldest civilization on the subcontinent. The artifacts and statuary from these Indus people have been dated back at least five thousand years when they were apparently overrun by a more aggressive, but less culturally developed warrior race from whom the Aryan population of the subcontinent has evolved. At the place where the Peshawar road meets the Indus there is the celebrated Attock Fort, a massive structure that was built by the Mogul emperor Akbar in the late sixteenth century. At this point the Indus is spanned by a somewhat rickety-looking but apparently solid bridge built by the British in the late nineteenth century.

Across the Indus, the countryside changes from one of humid fertility to the more arid, semimountainous terrain that is characteristic of the frontier. Just before coming to Rawalpindi—known everywhere in Pakistan as simply 'Pindi—we came to the Margalla Hills and the Margalla Pass with its celebrated monument to General John Nicholson—known as the "Lion of the Punjab"—who was killed during the Mutiny, or as Pakistanis prefer, the First War of Independence against the British in 1857. Many writers have remarked that it is the Margalla Hills that mark the real frontier between Europe and Asia. The peoples who live in Asia Minor have been historically and religiously oriented towards the Middle East and Persia. The Pathans are a sort of transition race and even their language has more Persian in it than anything else. (Urdu uses Persian script.) It is after Margalla that, beginning with the Punjab, the races, languages, and religions of the subcontinent take over. This appears to have been so even in the time of Alexander. His army first crossed the Hindu Kush, the mountain range that separates the northwest frontier of Pakistan from Afghanistan, and then moved south into what is now Swat. Swat was, and still is, one of the most beautiful and fertile valleys in all of Asia, and Alexander was sufficiently enchanted by it to conquer and garrison a city there, Ora, often known as Udegram, the ruins of which still stand. He then moved southeast to Taxila. Taxila was one of the great cities of Asia—it is located near the Margalla Hills—a center of trade which was for a long time one of the last strongholds of the Greco-Buddhist tradition, lasting until the fourth century A.D.—out of which came the magnificent school of Ghandaric art with its thousands of representations of Buddha and his disciples as depicted by artists in whom the influence of the Greek religious art is evident.

Maraini describes Alexander's cultural shock at his first real encounter with the subcontinent. Maraini writes:

Having invaded India, the Greeks spent some while at Taxila; and it is here that Alexander must have first become aware that he set foot in a new, alien, incomprehensible world which could not be translated into any terms he knew. Persia might, at a pinch, be viewed through Greek eyes, a blown-up exaggerated version of Greek notions taken to the ultimate extreme; but India was at once elusive, shattering, and monstrous, a constant challenge to every intellectual assumption and familiar emotional attitude. Yet Alexander's overriding desire was to search for traces of Dionysus's mythical journey through these far-off lands! The Indian gods, Brahmanic philosophy and ritual, the naked ascetics who despised all civilized refinement, the weird costumes, the social stratifications of the caste system—all these things disturbed and disgusted him. What he finally came to feel was not fear, exactly, but an obscure sort of repulsion. It is no accident that the battles of his Indian campaign were the most bloody of any in the whole Grand Adventure: a classic instance is the engagement he fought on the banks of the Hydaspes (the present day Jhelum) against the forces of King Porus (the king of the Punjab), at the height of the rainy season, a battle which ended as a horrible confused mess of men, horses and elephants, struggling between marsh and quagmire, with the jungle before them and the flooded river at their backs.

Maraini continues:

In India Alexander did not fight simply in order to win: his object was total annihilation. Perhaps that is why the Indian tradition, as though in revenge, has completely forgotten his name. Alexander survives in India only as the monster called "Skanda," with which mothers threaten their over-fractious children. Yet, odd though it may seem, it was his own men who finally put a stop to his ambitions. When the column had got some way beyond the present-day area of Lahore, and had reached a tributary of the Sultej—the last river of the Punjab—the troops threatened to mutiny. Alexander had the whole army paraded, and delivered a powerful oration on the theme of world empire, with glory for every individual soldier. He cited the examples of Hercules and Dionysus Achilles and Zeus, but all in vain. Finally he conceded defeat and let them turn about for the march home.

We headed for 'Pindi, which, at first sight, gave the impression of a sweltering, teeming bazaar. After collecting a month's worth of mail, we made for the new Hotel Intercontinental, which besides having a splendid swimming pool, is one of the principal social loci of 'Pindi. I at once contacted my confréres at the university which was then located on a temporary campus situated halfway between 'Pindi and Islamabad. It will move into its permanent quarters, an elegant array of modern buildings in Islamabad, in the next few years. My colleagues were pleased to hear from me, but they were a little surprised that I was there so soon. Because of the very serious student disturbances—some students were killed—during the events of the previous spring that led to the downfall of the regime of ex-president Ayub, the university schedule had been delayed a month, something that no one had bothered to tell me. It meant that I would have no lecturing obligations during the month of October. (On the other hand the winter recess had been cancelled so that we would all be able to make up for lost time.) They strongly encouraged me to spend the month traveling in Pakistan, and this fitted in excellently with our plan to see as much as possible of the mountain country before the snows came in November. The Land Rover was taken to the nearest garage, and its ailment was diagnosed as carbon deposits on the engine block due to excessive consumption of Afghan gas which must be of extremely low octane. In Pakistan a special high octane gasoline is sold under the general name "Aviation," and after a few treatments with "Aviation" the machine functioned normally. (Henceforth, wherever we traveled, we always kept a jerrycan of "Aviation" with us to spike the local brew.)

The next problem was how to organize the month. The geography of the frontier is extremely complicated. The Indus, as mentioned above, makes its erratic course through the mountains. There are, in fact, four principal mountain ranges in Pakistan. In the extreme northeast, on the Chinese frontier there is the Greater Karakoram. ("Karakoram" means "black gravel" in Turkestani.) The mountains in this range, which abut the Baltoro Glacier ("Baltoro" means "giver of life" in Baltistani) have both local names and surveyor's designations in terms of K-numbers. K-2, known also as Godwin Austen, is 28,250 feet high, and the second highest mountain in the world. (There is a K-1, the highest summit in the Masherbrum Range, at a mere 25,660 feet, not far away.) The Baltoro Glacier is, by all accounts, a formidable place, with very sudden temperature drops of fifty degrees at nightfall. K-2 is at least forty miles from the nearest village and lies in the Baltistan Agency in which all travel for non-Pakistanis is carefully regulated and restricted. In fact, we learned that if we had any intentions of wandering into the hinterlands this would require an application, in six copies, to the minister of Kashmir affairs, in Islamabad, with a detailed itinerary. Since we had almost no knowledge of the region except what we had been able to glean from a few mountaineering accounts (no one in either 'Pindi or Islamabad seemed to know much about it) we were not in a very favorable position to submit an itinerary. We were also told that it would take at least fifteen days before such a proposal could be studied and since we had only thirty altogether, a visit to the Baltoro was evidently out of the question. However, we learned, there would be no trouble to get to Skardu, the agency capital of Baltistan, from which we might be able to do some interesting jeeping. So we put Skardu at the top of the list.

To the south of the Greater Karakorams there are the Lesser Karakorams. These are nothing to sneeze at themselves. The highest mountain in this range is Rakaposhi, near Gilgit and Hunza, and it is the seventeenth highest mountain in the world at 25,500 feet. Gilgit is also a restricted area (among other things the Chinese, in collaboration with the Pakistan Army, were at that time building a road that would connect Sinkiang to the interior of Pakistan). But here again, so long as we were prepared to travel within a limited area we would be able to visit the agency—the Gilgit Agency but not Hunza near the Chinese frontier. Apart from Rakaposhi, the principal alpine attraction in Gilgit is Nanga Parbat which is the ninth highest mountain in the world at 26,660 feet. (In fact if one takes Gilgit as the center and draws a circle around it with a radius of about a hundred miles this area contains more high mountains than anywhere else on earth, including Nepal.) Nanga Parbat—which means "naked mountain"—is the western anchor point of the Himalayas. The Himalayas arise in some relatively obscure foothills in Pakistan when, suddenly, for no apparent reason, Nanga Parbat soars out of the earth in almost solitary isolation. The chain then gathers momentum and moves southward, and east, across northern India, Nepal, until on the eastern boundary of Nepal it makes one last leap with the isolated peak of Kanchenjunga, which is the third highest mountain in the world. (Kathmandu is, in fact, well south of Gilgit and 'Pindi.) Nanga Parbat has one of the most dramatic histories of any of the great mountains. It is a German mountain in the sense that Everest is an English mountain. In fact, before it was finally climbed in 1953 it claimed thirty-two lives, mostly German, which may be some sort of a national record in mountaineering. The 1953 expedition was also German, and it seems to have been marked by a good deal of internal friction and animosity. In any event, on the second of July the great German climber Hermann Buhl, who was later killed in the Himalayas of Nepal, set off for the summit with a teammate, Otto Kempter. Kempter gave out some three thousand feet below the summit, and Buhl, who was famous in the Alps for his solo climbing, simply went on alone. At seven at night, after sixteen hours of climbing, he was at the summit, where he took pictures and unfurled the flags of the Tyrol and Pakistan. He then calmly started down and when darkness came he found himself stranded at nearly 26,000 feet with no place even to sit down. Undaunted, Buhl spent the rest of the night standing and climbing slowly and steadily. The next day he managed to descend to the first camp below by sunset where he joined his surprised companions who never expected to see him alive. Nanga Parbat was high on our list of things to see.

To the west of Gilgit, on the northern frontier with Afghanistan, begins the Hindu Kush range which culminates with Tirich Mir at 25,260 feet in Chitral, a former princely state now simply a district of Pakistan. It was Maraini's ecstatic description of Tirich Mir that had inspired our trip to Pakistan in the first place. We also wanted to visit the Kafirs, a group of people, about a thousand, who live in three high valleys in Chitral, and who practice an ancient pagan religion and claim to be descendants of the soldiers of Alexander's army. This territory is open, no special permits are needed to travel there, and we hoped to do some modest climbing ourselves in either Swat, to the south of Chitral, or in the Himalayan foothills south of Gilgit. All of this was a fairly ambitious program for a month of activity following on a hard month of overland travel in the Land Rover, so we allowed ourselves a few days of rest in 'Pindi while we organized.

The first matter to be settled was how to get to the various places. The roads in the frontier are pretty awful. Nowhere are they paved, and they are often just wide enough for a single jeep to pass. Moreover, they are, in many instances, primarily military roads, and are open, if at all, to nonofficial traffic only sporadically and with special permission. On the other hand Pakistan International Airlines maintains a wide-ranging air service to the frontier, with flights to both Gilgit and Skardu.

We had spoken to several people who had made these flights and we had gathered the impression that they were among the most spectacular, and risky, mountain flights to be found anywhere. At the time of our visit, PIA used Fokker Friendships on these flights. The aircraft have a ceiling of something like 18,000 feet while a simple glance at the route shows that the mountain ranges through which they pass rarely get below 20,000. This means that the planes have to fly over passes with, at best, a few thousand feet to spare. Weather conditions must be perfect. As someone told us, "If there is a cloud in the sky anywhere along the route the pilots won't take off." And it often happens that hapless tourists are stuck in Gilgit or Skardu for days waiting for the plane from 'Pindi. The government maintains small rest houses in these areas that are used partly by tourists and partly by any official visitors who may have business on the frontier. It is almost impossible to get clear information about these establishments in 'Pindi, especially the ones in Baltistan, and so we decided on the general principle of *"on ne sais jamais"*—an invaluable maxim when traveling in the mountains—to carry enough equipment with us so that we would have a place to sleep no matter what. This meant lugging our two high-altitude tents and three down sleeping bags as well as a fair amount of food and clothing, including our down jackets and hiking shoes. Jaccoux, as a professional guide, is one of the world's experts at expeditionary packing, and I was constantly amazed by how much stuff he could cram into a canvas bag and a rucksack. We even managed to get a portable electric razor in, along with a medicine kit, without it spilling over. We decided to make Skardu our first port of call since at eight thousand feet it would get the coldest soonest. To this end we visited the Tourist Office in 'Pindi. They made out our Tourist Introduction Cards, official documents that state exactly where one is allowed to go in the restricted areas and without which one cannot even get airplane tickets. No one at the Tourist Office had ever visited Baltistan, but they had a list of the villages near Skardu that one could visit legally and agreed to write them all—*"on ne sais jamais"*—in our cards. The rest was up to us. There was no need, they happily assured us, to make any return reservations, since, as someone said, "The planes always come back nearly empty." This "advice" nearly did us in altogether as it was to turn out.

In the autumn the flights to the frontier leave at hours like five or six in the morning when the sky is clearest. Since they are subject to instant cancellation if the weather is not ideal one must phone PIA at four in the morning to see how the land lies. Since Jaccoux had done the packing I volunteered for this grim task. At four in the morning I was able to contact an alert-sounding PIA employee who said that everything looked "go." When we arrived at the airport, we found the waiting room— the frontier flights have their own terminal—filled with somnolent-looking frontiersmen. Skardu gets very little in the way of tourists, and there were none to be seen. The few women about were either veiled facially or totally covered in the tentlike *burkas* which envelop a woman like a shroud and from which she can peer out at the world through a cloth screenlike opening at the top. It looks like a cloth cage. The role of women in Pakistan is evolving. In the larger cities many go about unveiled and a few, a very few, even miniskirted. (Most wear a very attractive sort of pants suit with a long jacket.) In the frontier, however, *purdah* (the complete isolation of women) is common, and even in a city like 'Pindi women are almost invisible. Although there are exceptions, there appear to be no women secretaries, no women doctors, no waitresses, no maids, especially in private houses, and no receptionists. There are, of course, actresses, especially movie actresses. Indeed the films are among the most popular form of entertainment in the country— the Pakistanis make about 150 a year (men and women, by the way, are segregated in the movie theaters) as well as importing some, mostly terrible, from the West. There was at that time a very popular actress in Pakistan called Rozina. (Moslems, in general, have one name in Pakistan. If they have more than one the rest are usually titles like Khan, or Beg or Aayyid [a direct descendant from the Prophet]). Rozina was injured in an automobile accident that took place just outside of Islamabad. She was driving to Swat with her mother to work on a film. After the accident the newspapers pointed out that no less than eighteen films in which she was scheduled to act in the next few months were being held up during her recovery. There is evidence that the younger generation of women is beginning to defy the old traditions, especially in the large cities, and, indeed, in my class at the university there were a few girls, unveiled, who took part equally with the men. However, *purdah*, when it is not practiced literally, as it is in the countryside, is still deeply ingrained psychologically, and Pakistan is very much a male-oriented society.

The flight to Skardu, which lasts about an hour, is the most spectacularly beautiful mountain flight that I have ever made. The high mountains are not visible from 'Pindi, but as soon as the plane gathers a little altitude they begin to appear toward the north. The plane heads northwest over the Margalla Hills and into the Pathan country. It makes its way to the entrance of the Kaghan Valley, a beautiful place which we intended to visit, in the Land Rover, sometime later. It then flies along the Kunhar River, due north. The mountains now appear along both sides of the plane and at about the same altitude. (The highest mountain in the Kaghan is Malika Parbat, a Himalayan "foothill" at seventeen thousand feet.) One has the impression that with a slight downdraft the plane will land on top of one of them. (The PIA pilots, who are extremely friendly and obviously very competent, are happy to have visitors in the pilot's cabin on these flights. After learning this we spent most of our time in the cockpit, from which the mountain scenery is simply unbelievable. One can see the whole northern frontier all the way to K-2—a fantastic soaring isolated pyramid—and into the Himalayas of Indian Kashmir. As one PIA pilot told us, "We wouldn't trade this flight for any other in the world.") At the head of the valley is the Babusar Pass at 13,600 feet over which there is a small jeep road that leads into the Gilgit Agency and is closed by snow eight months of the year. The main road into Gilgit goes via Swat and will connect to the Chinese road from the north. After the pass, the plane moves across the face of Nanga Parbat. I do not imagine that it flies more than a mile or so from it, though the summit is some eight thousand feet above the flight path. Seen this way, Nanga Parbat looks like a tranquil fortress of snow and ice and it is difficult to imagine its murderous alpine history. One then reaches the Indus with Gilgit to the west and Skardu to the east. It is at this point that the Skardu flight becomes really difficult since the plane banks into the Indus gorge whose walls, on both sides, are disturbingly close, and considerably higher than the plane itself. It then descends into Skardu, which has a tiny, dirt air strip set on top of a mesa surrounded by mountains. There is little or no margin for error, and it is quite clear why the pilots won't go if the visibility is not absolutely perfect.

Our first impression of Skardu was of almost total desolation—a dry desert, covered with boulders, with sparse vegetation close to the banks of the Indus. We were met at the plane by a PIA official who seemed rather surprised to see us, but who found our tourist cards in order. He said that the PIA jeep had already gone to town, some fifteen miles away, but would be back in an hour or so, and would then take us to the government rest house, which, incidentally, he thought was filled up with various governmental officials. The day was bright and sunny, and we settled down in the sun where we could contemplate the magnificent mountain scenery to wait for the next development. A young European, a German alpinist it turned out, emerged from the PIA office and introduced himself. He was taking our flight back to 'Pindi, and he said that he had been stranded in Skardu for a few days as the weather had not been clear enough to fly. He told us that he had hitchhiked overland from Germany and was scouting the area for a German climbing group which was planning another attempt on Nanga Parbat. After a few minutes he boarded the plane which took off in a cloud of dust, just skimming over the mountains. Shortly afterwards we heard the sound of a plane and, at first, we thought that our pilot had, for some reason, turned back. However, when it landed it became clear that this was a freighter. (On clear days PIA flies relays of flights to the frontier to take advantage of the weather.) While a large crew of Baltistanis swarmed over the craft unloading it, the crew emerged and the pilot came over to talk to us. "This is the apple season," he said, "you should try the apples. They are marvelous." When we asked him from which point we could get the best view of the high mountains he answered, with a laugh, "From the aircraft, of course." After wishing us luck and inviting us to visit him in the pilot's cabin if we were ever on any of his flights, he too took off in another swirl of dust. After a half an hour a jeep bearing the green and white PIA trim drove up, and we loaded ourselves and our gear into it and bounced off on the dirt road that leads to the village of Skardu proper. A few trees lined the route, but the general feeling of the scenery was lunar. Skardu is a squat, dusty village with a resident population of, perhaps, a thousand people. There are a couple of main streets lined with open bazaars that sell essential items like food and clothing. Domestic animals, goats, and dogs wander here and there. We bounced through the village, past a large army camp—this part of the frontier has a substantial military presence—and pulled up in front of a trim-looking white bungalow—the government rest house. Several men were sitting in the dirt yard in front sunning themselves in chairs. They turned out to be government officials, most of whom were engaged in a water power project which, when completed, will supply Skardu with electric power. (There are a few generators in town which give some dim illumination between sunset and 9:00 P.M.) They had, indeed, filled up the place, but we were told that there would be no objection if we put up our tents in the front yard. In fact, the rest house would be glad to feed us if we could arrange our hours so as to eat in advance of the officials. After pitching camp we set out to explore the town. On one side of the rest house was the home of the political agent, who is the resident government representative in Skardu. As it was Sunday, we were informed that it was the agent's day off and that we would have to wait until the following morning before presenting our credentials. (While Friday is the traditional religious holy day of the Moslems in Pakistan—the mosques have special Friday services—Sunday, a legacy of the British, is in fact the day when the government offices close.) On the other side of the rest house were the police station and jail. We paid the gendarmarie a visit to see if we could arrange some sort of transportation, by jeep, into the hinterland. Despite some linguistic difficulties, we managed to communicate the essentials to a pair of tired guardians of law and order, who studied our tourist cards with some bewilderment. The town of Skardu apparently got few, if any, visitors and most travelers appear to get about as far as the air field.

Our first discovery was a large official residence, perched high on an embankment overlooking the Indus, belonging to the United Nations observers who supervise the uneasy truce line in Kashmir. They were apparently out supervising, and there was no sign of life from their quarters. Next we wandered by a large athletic field where a number of soldiers were playing soccer. They waved cheerfully and went on about their game. Jaccoux spotted an impressive-looking rock summit some distance away, and we set off for it thinking that it might afford a good view of the valley. We had gotten about halfway up when we caught sight of someone running in our direction and waving frantically. We stopped and when a young man, somewhat out of breath caught up to us, he explained in gestures, with a few English words tossed in for emphasis, that the hill was a military area and that we were not allowed on it. We then went into town escorted by our new guide who served as a translator in the shops. There wasn't much of anything to buy so we went back to the rest house and our guide disappeared.

At six, dinner was served—rice with curried mutton and tea— and we settled in the dimly illuminated common room to read a little before retiring to our tents. The various government officials came by to offer their respects and probably to look us over. Hearing us speaking French, one of them came by and said, "You come from France?" To see what would happen I stretched the truth a little and said "yes." He informed us that he was involved in civil defense and that while his headquarters were in 'Pindi he traveled around the frontier areas to give, as he put it, "the people confidence about civil defense." It was not entirely clear to me what he was expecting to happen in Skardu, but since he offered no explanation I decided not to ask. He then launched into a long eulogy of General de Gaulle and remarked that he could not see how we French could have voted him out of power. The poor Jaccoux, who, to put it mildly, were never very great admirers of the general, could hardly restrain themselves. But I countered by saying that we could not understand how Pakistan had removed General Ayub from power since he was known as the "de Gaulle of Asia." This left the matter at about a draw. Next, he launched into a passionate diatribe against Indians, Zionists, and Americans. "Indians are the aggressors here, and Zionists are the aggressors in the Middle East," he said, his voice rising, and Americans were bad because they had taken the side of the Indians and Zionists. This is a rather common attitude in Pakistan. As a fellow Moslem state it was not surprising to me that Pakistan should be so anti-Israel. (There is also a certain amount of antisemitism in the country. The government is at great pains to distinguish between Zionists and Jews, but this subtlety sometimes gets lost in the heat. There are occasional articles and letters in the English language papers like the *Pakistan Times* and the Karachi *Dawn* that are purely and simply antisemitic. I read one letter that complained about the "Jewish influence" at work in the selection of the foreign films, usually third-rate westerns, that are imported into the country. There are also rallies in the major cities in support of Al Fatah and the other guerilla groups which seem to have captured the imaginaton of many young people in Pakistan.) The feeling about America is much more complex. It seems to be based on a very widespread notion that we have sided with the Indians on most of the outstanding disputes between the two countries. On the other hand, it is generally recognized throughout Pakistan that the United States has played a vital role in the development of the country, and this has produced a considerable reservoir of goodwill.

After a little while the tirade subsided, and we had an exchange of cigarettes—Pakistani and French. I explained my duties at the university. We all drank a nightcap of tea and retired to our respective quarters to sleep. The next morning, at dawn, we were visited by the assistant political agent, a very bright and amicable young man with a considerable growth of beard. He asked us what we would like to do, and we said that we would like to make some excursion in which we could see the most mountain scenery. He suggested heading north to Khaplu, some seventy miles away, on a tributary of the Indus, where he thought, by climbing a little above the town we might be able to see a few of the high peaks of the Greater Karakoram. (Happily, our tourist cards included Khaplu on the list of allowed visiting places.) We set off to arrange a hired jeep, and we repacked our tents and sleeping bags. The jeep appeared with a driver, an assistant driver, and, oddly, our "guide" of the previous day, whose presence seemed somewhat peculiar but who offered no explanations short of smiling benignly. We crammed ourselves into whatever space was left in the jeep and headed off. At first the road followed the flat Indus Valley, but soon it climbed to the top of the gorge, where it clung precariously. It was so narrow that whenever we encountered another jeep—usually military—passing was a delicate, all but impossible maneuver. First, the drivers would get as close to each other as possible—neither giving an inch. At this point both jeeps would stop and an extended discussion would ensue as to who was to back up where. The loser would then have to back along the track until some sort of outcropping could be found so that the winner could pass. We were able to average about seventeen miles an hour, not counting an extended stop for tea in a bazaar in a small village on the way. At some point the Indus branched off toward China, and we followed our tributary. The road became so steep in places that the assistant sat on the engine hood to give the jeep some additional traction, even in four-wheel drive. At some points the front end shot up at a rakish angle and neither we nor the driver could see the road in front. By the time we reached Khaplu, nearly seven hours later, we were all somewhat black and blue from the bouncing in the jeep and very relieved to be out of it. Khaplu is a fantastically beautiful place. It is a river oasis set in a wide bend in the river. Just across is a flat desert strip that leads off into the mountains, which rise in sharp needles, some snow-covered, and form an imposing circular arena. The Khaplu Rest House is very attractive, and as it was unoccupied we were able to use the wooden bed frames, along with our sleeping bags to make rather comfortable nests. The town is built on several levels above the river with terraced fields rather like those in Nepal. The whole setting is extremely harmonious and lovely.

We wanted to find a high vantage point from which to view the Karakoram at sunset. But before doing that, Jaccoux and I wandered down to the river, where an ancient boatman with a *zak*—a raft of wooden logs tied to inflated goat skins—poled his way back and forth across the river ferrying men and animals. For a couple of rupees he agreed to give us a round trip, a scenic, if wet, ride on the river. Next we set off for the high pastures behind the village to try to get a view of the Karakoram. By the time we had climbed through the fields behind town the sun was setting and Jaccoux, who can move like greased lightning in the mountains, took off for the summit of a large rock abutment to see what the view was like, while Michèle and I made our way back to the rest house. It rapidly became very dark, and shortly we found ourselves stumbling through terraced fields and in and out of people's back yards. By continually heading downhill we managed to find the river and the rest house. An hour went by, and then two hours, and no Jaccoux. I was not very worried, having seen Jaccoux extricate himself, and his clients, from all sorts of impossible situations in the Alps, but as Michèle was getting more and more concerned by the minute I decided that we might organize a small search. So off we set, with the ancient *chokidar*—watchman—of the rest house who carried an oil lantern casting ghostly shadows on the path. First, we roused our driver and his assistant. While we were walking along the driver asked me if *I* had invited our "guide"—the man who followed us through the bazaar the day before—to come along. I was very surprised, since I had assumed that it was our driver who had invited him. The driver said that, in fact, the man was a police officer who had apparently been assigned to us, probably both to watch that we did not leave the restricted area and that we did not get ourselves into any trouble along the way. (In Pakistan it is essentially forbidden to photograph any bridge anywhere, and now knowing that our man was an arm of the law I could understand why he had continually asked Jaccoux not to photograph the few rickety and hair-raising bridges on the route from Skardu to Khaplu.) Our little procession, now armed with several lanterns, wandered up through the village shouting

"Jaccoux—Jaccoux" plaintively. After about an hour we gave up and returned to the rest house only, needless to say, to find Jaccoux, who had come home by a back route, propped up on a wooden bed happily reading a book by flashlight. He said that he had succeeded in getting to the top of the rock summit just before sundown but that a near range cut off the view of the Karakoram so that we hadn't missed anything. After a fine dinner which, according to the "Tourist Offical [sic] Bill," consisted of "Three dish rice, three curry patetos, chiken rost, chapati [unleavened bread] and tea," we turned in for a good night's sleep.

The next morning, just after sunrise, I suddenly made out on the fringes of the flat desert strip across the river, the beginnings of a long caravan of men and a few horses that seemed to be emerging, like an invading army, from the mountains. The *chokidar* said something about "Italian people," but not much else by way of explanation. We knew that a few mountaineering expeditions, among them a Polish expedition in the neighborhood of K–2 and an Italian expedition attempting K–6 (a peak of twenty-five thousand feet or so in the Karakoram), had been operating in the area, but we had assumed, looking at the map, that they must have gone into the mountains at a point west of Skardu along the Indus. Apparently not, since after some minutes it became clear that what we were watching was the return of a large mountaineering expedition with at least fifty porters, who later turned out to be residents of Khaplu, and several climbers, seven, as it turned out, plus a doctor, and a Pakistani army officer who acted as the official liaison officer and representative of the government of Pakistan. (All officially approved expeditions are supplied liaison officers from the Pakistan army. These men recruit the expeditionary porters and also make sure that the expedition stays within the areas authorized to it by the government. The government of Pakistan, once it has authorized an expedition, assumes responsibility for it, in the sense that if it gets into trouble the government will help to bail it out by sending rescue helicopters and the like.) By midmorning all the men were assembled on the other side of the river, while a large number of villagers, wives, and children, were assembled on our side. Now the problem was to get the expedition across the river, which, as things were, could only be done by *zak*. It soon became clear that the boatman and his assistants were engaged in some sort of delaying action, presumably to obtain an enhancement of the rates. What actually happened was that the boatman had deflated and detached all of the goatskins from the *zak*, and was in the process of painstakingly blowing them up, while stopping every few minutes to engage in a heated discussion with those of his fellow villagers who were on the other side of the river. From the tone I would imagine that they were informing him of what would be forthcoming once they got their hands on him if he didn't hurry up with the *zak*. This line of argument appeared to carry some weight and after a few hurried maneuvers with the goatskins the boatman set out in the general direction of the porters, leaving the Italians gesticulating wildly somewhat upstream. At this point, I noticed one of the group calmly detach himself and begin a careful footbath in the stream, a maneuver carried out with such general nonchalance that I assumed that the man who did it must be a personage of some consequence. After the first *zak*-load of porters was ferried across a man in army uniform—the liaison officer evidently—shouted across the river that, in no uncertain terms, the boatman should come over at once and pick *him* up and talk the matter over. When he reached our side of the river he turned out to be a rugged, amiable young Pakistani, and in a few minutes he had things sufficiently under control so that he invited us to cross the river with him while the real ferrying, with the aid of a second *zak*, began. When we joined the alpinists on the other side, they turned out to be, except for the man who had enjoyed the footbath, a group of amateur alpinists from Abruzzi in south-central Italy. *He*, on the other hand, as I had guessed from the general display of cool, turned out to be a professional guide from northern Italy, and, in fact, he and Jaccoux had long known of each other. He was later killed in an accident in the Alps. We recrossed the river, this time in the company of the expedition doctor, a minuscule, extremely amusing elderly man, a veteran of several Asian alpine expeditions, who remarked that he could not swim. In fact, as we poled our way out into the swollen stream the *dottore* began reciting from Dante in a dramatic tone of voice as if he expected each moment to be his last on earth. Our guide friend said that K–6 had been a much tougher nut to crack than had been anticipated and that they had been stopped in heavy snow at about twenty thousand feet or so. No one had been hurt, but they had been out now for nearly two months and wanted very much to get home. They were planning to spend the night in the rest house, which wouldn't leave much room for us. So we decided to head back downstream for Skardu.

Just before coming to town we witnessed a strange scene. The road was very dusty and in front of us were two clouds of dust—vehicles moving towards Skardu. As we got closer we could see that the trailing vehicle was an army jeep which was following a cart full of logs being pulled by a tractor. The tractor was moving very slowly and kicking up a huge amount of dust. The jeep was signaling that it wanted to pass but the driver of the tractor either did not hear or did not care. Every time the jeep attempted to pass the tractor would veer into the middle of the road and block it. After a few miles the jeep finally was able to get past at which point the driver pulled over and cut off the tractor which we could now see was crowded with what appeared to be an entire family of Baltistanis. An officer jumped out of the jeep which was blocking our route so we pulled up also. He rushed over to the tractor and pulled the driver off of the tractor bodily and shoved him into the jeep which drove off to the jail next door to the Skardu Rest House. Apparently under the martial law that was then in force in Pakistan an army officer could arrest almost anyone. Indeed, we ourselves were nearly arrested a few weeks later. We were driving toward Peshawar in the Land Rover on our way to Swat. We had crossed the Indus at the Attock Fort and Jaccoux had stopped the Land Rover to take a picture of the old fort from a distance of a mile or so. I was in the back of the machine reading the *Pakistan Times* when I heard a commotion and looked up to see a large crowd of people around the Jaccoux. I didn't think much about it since wherever one travels in the subcontinent it is common for visitors to attract curious bystanders. However, shortly, I heard Michèle saying in a loud voice, "But we have just come to Pakistan and did not know." Realizing that something was seriously wrong I got out of the Land Rover and walked over to the crowd. A young man in civilian clothes, angrier than anyone I have ever seen, was in the process of trying to take Michèle's camera away from her. Later Jaccoux told me that a bus traveling to Peshawar had suddenly stopped and this individual had jumped out, and identified himself as an army officer and attempted to take away his camera and smash it. Jaccoux, who is incredibly strong, had easily defended the camera, and the officer was now in the process of trying the same tactic on Michèle. By now the crowd—fellow passengers, civilians in the bus—had calmed down the officer who had agreed not to arrest us if we would give him the film. Wishing to avoid further trouble we handed the two rolls of empty film over to him. Later we noticed that just in front of the fort there had been a small sign prohibiting pictures, but it would have taken an act of clairvoyance to realize that this applied even a mile away. Since the fort dates to the Mogul emperors it is difficult to imagine what secrets would be compromised by such a picture, but there it was. The next morning, in Skardu, we saw the tractor driver back on his machine, so apparently, he too, did not come to much grief.

After arriving at the rest house, which was still full, we set up our tents. One of the Pakistani engineers, staying at the rest house, came over to us and asked me when we were planning to leave for 'Pindi. Having more or less exhausted the resources of Skardu, at least those that one could take advantage of without special permission to trek in the back country, I said that we would, no doubt, leave the following day. He looked at me a little oddly and asked, "Do you have confirmed return reservations?" and I then repeated the "information" of the Tourist Bureau in 'Pindi to the effect that these were not necessary since the planes went back nearly empty. I was then informed that the reason that the planes went back nearly empty was that the takeoff was so tricky that, in order to be able to gain enough altitude fast enough to get over the nearby mountain ranges, they were able to take only seven or eight passengers a flight on a plane that normally seats forty-four. "When PIA gets the new planes with the more powerful engines it will be different, but, for now, that is how it is." As a consequence, I was informed, there was a waiting list, by priorities, military, government officials and so on, that was already so long that, as far as he knew, there was no space possible for two weeks! This seemed to me the sheerest fantasy, but, after a few additional conversations with some of the other people in the rest house, it became clear that we were in some considerable difficulties. Moreover, I knew, which they did not, that the Italian expedition was due into Skardu in a day or so, and that *they* wanted to get back to 'Pindi which would further complicate matters. The engineers informed us that they were leaving the day after next so that it became clear to me that we would have to try to get on a plane the following morning, weather permitting, come what may. It was too late in the day to make contact with anyone so we decided to simply present ourselves at the airport the following morning, as if nothing were wrong, and hope for the best.

The next morning was fair and clear and at the crack of dawn we packed our gear into a hired jeep and made for the field. We were greeted by the PIA man who asked us when we were planning to leave. "Today, of course," I replied with as much nonchalance as I could manage. "I am afraid that will be impossible," he added, in such a way as to indicate that further discussion was futile. Having done a fair amount of traveling in reasonably out of the way areas I have developed a technique for dealing with situations that are basically hopeless if approached straightforwardly, situations in which "logic" such as it is, is on the side of officialdom. In Asia, in particular, almost nothing is exactly what it seems to be, and everything has a certain elasticity if appropriately approached. The basis of this technique is to convince whomever it is that holds the relevant cards—i.e., tickets, permits, whatever—that his life will be infinitely more pleasurable if he gets you off of his back, than if, by a strict application of rules and procedures he is likely to have you around, as in this case, for many days. Hence I launched into a passionate, very loud, oration in which I pointed out in

considerable detail what I thought of the Tourist Bureau and
PIA for getting us into this situation and in which I reeled off a
vast list of ministries, largely invented, to whom I would report
the matter as soon as possible. Jaccoux later remarked that at
one point I rather resembled King Lear in his prime. After
several minutes of this, the poor man, by now convinced that
almost anything was better than seeing more of us, agreed to
look into the matter a little further in his office. After some study
he discovered that because of the backlog, due to a spate of bad
weather the previous week, there were, in fact, two un-
scheduled special flights that very day, and so he could probably get us on something. We spent the next two hours basking
in the sun until the arrival of the first flight. We were hustled
aboard it, along with four other passengers, all of us crowded as
far back as possible in the plane to give it the maximum lift, and
off we flew, past Nanga Parbat and the Himalayan foothills to
'Pindi.

It would have been nice to have been able to take the drive of
a hundred miles or so along the Indus River valley between
Skardu and Gilgit to the west. But this is a restricted area, and
most of the people we asked said that driving in it would
probably be out of the question. Hence, when we went to Gilgit,
a bit later, we once again took the magnificent mountain flight
along Nanga Parbat. (The political history of the Gilgit Agency is
discussed in an excellent book on Pakistan by Ian Stephens
called *The Pakistanis*. Stephens was for many years the editor of
the Indian *Statesman* and lived most of his life on the subcontinent.) As mentioned earlier, there were, at the time of
partition in 1947, over 560 princely states. The last British
viceroy of India, Lord Mountbatten, summoned the rulers of
these states to a conference in Delhi on the twenty-fifth of July,
1947. He suggested that the rulers of those states who did not
wish to remain independent choose, before the fifteenth of
August, with which of the two nations they wished to be
affiliated. As Stephens writes, "However, the time left for these
old-fashioned and often dilatory personages to make up their
minds proved insufficient, and Independence Day arrived with
the rulers of three States, one small, but two very large and

important, still dangerously undecided. It is astonishing that there were not many more." The small state Junagadh, on the west coast between Bombay and Karachi, had a Hindu population, but a Moslem ruler. He, untenably, as it turned out, elected for Pakistan, and serious disorders broke out resulting, finally, in a takeover by Indian forces and its accession by India. The second state was Hyderabad, east of Bombay. It covered an enormous area, 82,000 square miles, as large as Britain and had a population of over sixteen million. It had a long Moslem tradition, and, in fact, the Nizam decided to maintain Hyderabad as an independent entity. However, it was a landlocked area inside the Indian Union and it too was eventually subsumed by India. The third state was, of course, Kashmir.

In population Kashmir had only about four million people, largely Moslem, although in area it was even larger than Hyderabad. Kashmir is an extremely mountainous land, and, in fact, the only part of the state that was heavily populated was the central part, the celebrated fertile vale, in which the city of Srinagar, famous for its Mogul gardens, is located. To the west it reached out to include both Skardu and Gilgit, but communication between these rugged areas and the vale was so difficult, because of the mountains, as to be all but nonexistent. Kashmir has had a very long and troubled history of invasion and conquest dating back to the Moguls, who were replaced by the Sikhs, who were in turn replaced by the Hindu Dogras, a dynasty from the south from whom the maharaja who was the ruler in 1947 descended. (It might be mentioned that Nehru was of Kashmiri ancestory which may, in part, serve to explain why the issue of Kashmir generated so much feeling in India.) It is quite likely that the maharaja wished to join the Indian Union from the beginning, but hesitated in view of the fact that nearly 80 percent of the population was Moslem. As it turned out, matters were taken out of the maharaja's hands by the Pathan tribes. As Stephens writes:

At this time, and on into November, the future political relations (if any) of the quasi-autonomous Pathan tribes with Pakistan were entirely uncertain. Discussions had begun, and it was hoped that these formidable, restless people would decide to accede to the newly-formed

State, if only—by the cynical—because their scope for mischief would be greater otherwise; but the necessary jirgas [tribal assemblies] had not been held. It would be fair to say that the Pakistani authorities felt frightened of the tribes, and conscious that, at least for the nonce they lacked the physical means for coping with them. The Pakistan Army as yet scarcely existed, it was in the process of being formed out of the previous Army of undivided India; bits of the latter were still being shuttled about the map, Hindu and Sikh ones remaining untransferred on Pakistan soil, and Moslem ones on Indian. And for decades, the tribes had proved an intractable, dangerous thorn in the flesh of the much stronger British regime. As recently as 1937–8, those of Waziristan alone, for months, had pinned down no fewer than 50,000 of the Imperial forces in sanguinary guerilla warfare.

In any event, in the fall of 1947 the tribes, whipped into a frenzy of anti-Hindu sentiment, declared a *jihad*—a holy war—and began an invasion of Kashmir. Late in October the Indian Army began airlifting troops to Srinager and the Pakistanis attempted to reinforce the tribes. For nearly fourteen months there was continual fighting in Kashmir which ultimately terminated in the ceasefire line that the United Nations is still supervising. It is difficult to underestimate the degree of ill feeling that this has left in Pakistan. No Pakistani that I met, however enlightened otherwise, is able to accept the present situation.

Like the rest of Kashmir, Gilgit was also affected by these events. Gilgit had come under the Dogras in the Treaty of Amritsar which concluded the first Anglo-Sikh war in 1846. The British had given the Dogras the power to rule over Kashmir, presumably as a reward for remaining on the British side during the war. However, because of the remoteness of the terrain and its lack of interesting exploitable resources, not much interest was taken in the western part of it by either the Dogras or the British. This changed abruptly, at the turn of the century, when the British became convinced that the Russians were moving south into India across the Pamirs. The British sent an expeditionary force into Gilgit and Chitral, probably the first Europeans to ever visit the region, and to secure their position they established a paramilitary outfit called the Scouts. (The Gilgit Scouts still form a military unit in Gilgit.) To emphasize the fact that these men, recruited from the natives of the region but led by British officers, were outside the regular army, they were dressed in khaki rather than the traditional scarlet. Soon afterwards this became the combat dress of the entire British Army. At the time of partition the Gilgit Scouts were commanded by two young British officers, a Major Brown and a Captain Mathieson whose headquarters were a bit down the Indus at Chilas. The Gilgitis had been Moslems since the first Afghan invasions of the fourteenth century, and when the Dogra maharaja sent a representative to govern Gilgit, a serious outbreak of violence among the Hindu and Sikh traders in the village and the local inhabitants appeared to be in the offing. The young officers took matters into their own hands and placed the governor in protective custody. Soon afterward, according to Stephens, "the Hindu governor was spending afternoons amicably watching polo in his captors' company." (Polo was invented in Central Asia. In fact, the Gilgitis claim that it was invented in Gilgit.) By November Gilgit had formally acceded to Pakistan and was being governed by a representative of the new Pakistan government which was then located in Karachi.

In our own visit to Gilgit we ran into an exceedingly fortunate bit of good luck. Jaccoux, who had achieved a good deal of celebrity in France the previous summer because of a rather glamorous article that had appeared about him in *Elle*, had been invited to lunch by the French cultural attaché in 'Pindi. Michèle and I, not invited, watched him depart with a good deal of envy since, as we anticipated, he was to be treated to an excellent lunch with several varieties of first-rate French wine, a commodity impossible to come by in 'Pindi. However, we were somewhat consoled when, on his return, he announced that, at lunch, he had run into a resident of Gilgit, who had offered to act as our host and guide in the agency, and, indeed, a short while later, Jaccoux introduced us to an extremely articulate and intelligent young Pakistani who had been living in Gilgit for some six years. He came originally from Sind, the flat agricultural area in the southern part of Pakistan. Sometime later he explained to us how it was that he had migrated from the farming country to the high mountains in the north. His family is one of the leading landowning families of Sind. Some of these families have a very interesting history which is connected to the way in which the Mohammedan religion has developed in the subcontinent. To an outsider the religion sometimes appears to be a monolithic, undivided structure without fracture or schism. In actual fact, there have been, and still are, a large number of derivative sects, some with quite substantial followings. (Probably the most well known is the Ismaili sect whose spiritual leader is the Aga Khan. During my visit to Islamabad, the Aga Khan paid a brief visit and was very enthusiastically greeted by both his followers and the government, represented by President Yahya. I had the chance to attend a large tea given for him at the Islamabad Club, an excellent sports club in the city, where he, assisted by his beautiful new bride, handed out trophies to the winners of the club squash tournament. The Pakistanis are, of course, well known as squash players and indeed a Khan family, Pathans, related neither to President Yahya nor the Aga, produced two recent world's champions.) Frequently these sects are relatively small and can be traced back to a single Pir, Saint, or Sayyid—a spiritual leader tracing his heritage directly back to the Prophet. It was customary for these Sayyids to accept tokens of esteem from their followers in the form of gifts of land, and over the years these estates have accumulated to where they now often comprise several villages. Our new friend's family had built up very large land holdings in Sind in this way, and, indeed, he himself had inherited several hundreds of acres. However, being young and somewhat rebellious by temperament, he had wanted to introduce a certain number of reforms in the land tenure system and this had brought about a collision with his family. To aggravate matters, he had married a lovely and very intelligent young woman who had successfully completed her studies to become a physician. His father, a strict practitioner of *purdah*, had forbidden his daughter-in-law to practice medicine in Sind, and the young couple had migrated to Gilgit, as remote an area as is imaginable, and one with a shortage of doctors where she could practice. He is trying to help develop the tourist industry in

Gilgit, where the magnificent mountain country would be ideal for the kind of hiking and trekking that is now so popular in Nepal.

We made a rendezvous at the Gilgit air field and, when we got off of the plane, we were delighted to find him there. Gilgit, although it *is* remote, is, compared to Skardu, relatively touristic, and even features a rest house that looks like a miniature Hilton. (It was then rumored that the Intercontinental chain was planning to build a chalet on the outskirts of Gilgit with a view of both the Indus and Rakaposhi, the highest mountain in the neighborhood.) Our guide turned out to have his own jeep and driver, both of which he put at our disposal during our stay. Our original hope had been to visit Hunza, which lies some seventy miles north of Gilgit on the Hunza River, and which is presided over by a Mir who is, by all accounts, most benevolent, enlightened, and very hospitable to visitors. (Hunza is also, according to a certain amount of folklore, supposed to have a population that lives to extremely old age. In fact, a celebrated Chamonix guide with whom we spoke before leaving France told us that he had been sent on an expedition to Hunza by a French pharmaceutical company who wanted to find out if the Hunza people were on to something marketable. The expedition apparently did not turn up much of anything and, indeed, the wife of our friend, who has many Hunzas among her patients, said that, as far as she could tell, their lifespan and general health is no longer or better than anyone else's. Like most mountain people who live at high altitudes, the Hunzas *look* very vigorous and healthy, but, as is the case, for example, with the Sherpas of Nepal, this can be quite deceptive.) As mentioned earlier, Hunza is on the new Sino-Pakistan road from Sinkiang, and for this and other reasons, it was, at the time of our trip, next to impossible for non-Pakistanis to get permission to go there. Hence we settled for an overnight trip to Nalthar, which is a high mountain camping resort on a tributary of the Hunza River some forty miles from Gilgit. Our luck with the weather was not too good. It was very cold and snowy, but we were able to look over some ski slopes that have been constructed for the use of the Pakistan Air Force, one of the most elite groups of men in the country. (I spoke to several students about what careers they would like most to follow in Pakistan, and the three choices they gave were the air force, government service, and scientific research, in various orders of preference.) We spent a chilly night in the local unheated rest house, but forewarned that food was scarce and expensive in Gilgit, we had brought our own from 'Pindi and were able to cook up two or three splendid meals on our portable mountain gas stoves.

The next day we had been promised a polo match. Polo in the Gilgit Agency is enormously popular both to play and to watch. Every small town has its own team and terrain, and there is a league of teams that plays for an annual championship. This meet is widely known in Pakistan and many people make a special trip to Gilgit for the week in which the championship is played off. We were again very lucky for our visit coincided with the first two days of the meet, and our friend had promised to stake out choice seats in the stadium for all of us. When we arrived, just before meet-time, the stadium was absolutely jammed to capacity, everyone wearing their Sunday best. On our way into the covered pavillion and on our seats on the "fifty yard line" we passed by the Mir of Hunza, whose team was to play on the second day. I also noticed a bit of verse near the entry gate. It was by one J. K. Stephens whom my general ignorance of polo prevents me from further identifying. It read:

> Let other people play at other games
> The king of games is still the game of kings.

That struck me as somewhat ironic since the British certainly adopted polo from central Asia where it was invented.

There were two separate bands playing alternately. The Gilgit Scouts, the militia men discussed earlier, had their own regimental band, smartly dressed and featuring, among other things, a corps of bagpipers. In addition there was a very sizable group of local musicians with various oddly shaped horns, drums, and other instruments, and they took up the slack whenever the Scouts paused for breath. I had been informed that Asiatic polo bears roughly the same relation to the international game that a free-for-all bears to a boxing match fought under the rules of the marquis of Queensbury. According to the rules of international polo a "boarded field" should not exceed 300 yards in length and 160 yards wide. In the Gilgit Agency the fields are where one can find them on the rare stretches of level ground, and one of the local experts informed us that, as a rule, the teams who live at the lowest altitudes, where there are the largest terrains of level areas, are usually the best in the agency. I would estimate that the Gilgit field, which is "boarded" by two parallel stone walls each about five feet high, is something like a hundred yards long and fifty yards wide. In international polo there are four men to a team while in the Gilgit version there are six. Ponies are changed frequently in international polo while in the Gilgit version they are never changed during the two twenty-minute periods. There are no time outs unless there is an injury with the exception of the brief rest between halves. In international polo there are strict rules about how one can swing the mallet. For example, one cannot swing it across the legs of the pony. In Gilgit there are no rules at all, and frequently the players break their mallets, which are clearly homemade, either against the walls, or against other players or horses, at which point a "trainer" rushes out on the field, at risk of life and limb, to try to locate the malletless rider and supply him with a new stick. In Gilgiti polo there is an interesting maneuver that is allowed under the rules. If the ball flies up in the air, a player is allowed to catch it, and race with it, with his horse, over the goal line for a point. The only way to stop him in this is for another player to come along and lift the man with the ball off of his horse. I heard of a legendary figure of Gilgiti polo who made a specialty of this and, in fact, was so strong that he would hold his man captive on the horse and race with ball and man to the opposite goal which counted as a score.

The first day's match was between Gilgit and Chilas and was preceded by a contest in which the horsemen on both teams raced down the field with long lances and attempted to pick up small white pegs that had been planted in the ground. As the horses charged down the field the local band played at full force and if someone managed to lance a peg there were general cries of "*Shabash-shabash*"—"well done" in Urdu. The match itself began when a distinguished-looking officer of the Gilgit Scouts threw out the ball between the two lines of horsemen. There then ensued a general melée of charging horses and swinging sticks, all accompanied by the high pitched wail of horns and the beating of drums. The arena was so small that men and animals were constantly colliding with each other and with walls, and it was difficult to see how they kept from doing each other serious damage. (Among the people that I spoke to there seemed to be a difference of opinion as to how dangerous this form of polo is. Several people said that there are almost never serious injuries. On the other hand, in his book *Two Mountains and a River*, in part about the Gilgit area, H. W. Tilman, the famous British alpinist, quotes an eyewitness account of such a match by his equally celebrated climbing partner Eric Shipton. Shipton noted, somewhat laconically, that the match that he saw in Gilgit was briefly interrupted in the opening moments by two fatal accidents. On the second day of our meet, during a match between the Gilgit Scouts and Hunza, which the Scouts won easily, there was a terrible collision between two horses and their riders, one of whom was the officer who had thrown out the first polo ball. He fell to the ground absolutely unconscious and was taken off to the hospital. We heard later in the day that he had not been too seriously hurt, and, indeed, after he had been taken from the field the game continued with, more or less, its former élan.) If for any reason one's eye tired of the scene of charging horses and riders, one could look up in all directions to the snow-covered mountains, some over twenty thousand feet, that ring the Gilgit Valley and hover over the village.

Before and after each match that we saw we were invited to lunch and dinner at our friend's house. The Moslem tradition of hospitality is especially strong in the frontier. (Among the Pathans, for example—Gilgit is not strictly speaking a Pathan community—the guests of one's blood enemies are given safe conduct even in the height of a tribal feud.) We were stuffed with delicacy after delicacy. One of the specialties of Gilgit is dried apricots with nuts inside them—a delicious confection. There are also dried cherries likewise filled with nuts. There was simply no way that they would let us return the hospitality.

Even when we offered our imported French canned and pow-dered food we found that it had been prepared for us to eat, along with a vast array of Pakistani delicacies—including a sweet milk pudding that is served with thin edible silver foil. Our host has one of the largest collections of mountain books in all languages that I have ever seen. He has accompanied several expeditions for the fun of it, and Jaccoux was able to fill him in on the latest news and gossip from the European alpine com-munity. We had such a good time in Gilgit that it was with great reluctance that we took off once again past Nanga Parbat, to 'Pindi.

For the rest of our exploration of the frontier, we were able to use the Land Rover. Our plan was to swing back and forth into the several valleys that lie south and west of the Gilgit Agency. Directly to the south is the Hazara district in which is located the Kaghan Valley, over which the Gilgit plane flies. To the west of the Kaghan, separated by a high mountain range, is the former princely state of Swat which has been incorporated into Paki-stan since the summer of 1969. To the north of Swat is Kalam, a tiny, wild, Pathan district which had been disputed between Swat and its neighboring former princely state of Dir. They have now all been incorporated into Pakistan. Dir is on the Pak-Afghan border and to its north is Chitral, also a former princely state, which is separated from Dir by a formidable mountain pass called the Lowari. Since these areas are not in Kashmir, no special permission is needed to visit them and one can more or less wander about in them as one wants to. While the mountain tribes who live in these districts are, in general, reasonably, and often very, hospitable to visitors, they are a pretty tough, thoroughly armed bunch and a certain amount of caution is necessary if one wanders off the beaten track. Indeed, the official tourist guide to Swat has an interesting notation under CAMPING. It reads, "Visitors camping in out-of-the-way places must notify the Teshildar [local administrator] of the area and take an escort of 2 men." Why two men, and not one or three, is not explained to the reader. The pamphlet was written before Swat was incorporated into Pakistan and, by now, the presence of the Pakistan Army has made itself felt in much of the frontier which, for better or worse, has become a great deal more civilized than before.

We had chosen the Kaghan Valley as our locale for our own modest climbing efforts. We had several reasons for doing so. In the first place, we had run into a young Englishman in 'Pindi who when not functioning as a bank executive spent all of his spare time climbing. He showed us several slides and maps of the Kaghan, and, from them, we could see that it offered a number of peaks in the 16,000- and 17,000-foot range that we might have a chance with. Our general morale—Michèle's and mine—was not what it might have been as far as climbing was concerned. Michèle had announced her official retirement from alpinism earlier in the summer, but we had some hope of persuading her to unretire herself if the weather was good. I, on the other hand, had had my experience in Chamonix in which I had found myself suspended on a small climbing ladder, under an overhang, several hundred feet above the Vallée Blanche. I was still feeling a little leery about climbing. Jaccoux, who seems fazed by nothing, kept saying *"On verra bien,"* his favorite expression when his clients begin to show any signs of tattered nerve endings. We had chosen as our target Malika Parbat, a 17,000-foot object, the highest in the valley, which apparently had only been climbed once or twice. (It is too easy for a real alpine expedition and too hard for real novices.) Since we could drive into the Kaghan from 'Pindi in a day, we were able to load the full complement of climbing equipment—tents, ice axes, crampons, food, stoves, and extra clothing—into the machine with no trouble. We had been informed that, weatherwise, October is a very tricky month. We might strike it lucky, but once it started to snow we should get out as quickly as possible since this usually meant that the place would be blocked in for the winter.

The drive to the Kaghan Valley is exceedingly pretty. One leaves 'Pindi on the Lahore-Peshawar trunk road, drives past the turnoff for Taxila, the valley in which several Greek, Persian, and Buddhist archeological monuments are preserved, and just before coming to the Indus, one swings north towards snow-covered mountains which are visible, from time to time, from

Malika Parbat, in the Himalayas of Pakistan   JEREMY BERNSTEIN

the road. The road meanders through farmlands and then
climbs abruptly to the important frontier community of Abbottobad. Abbottobad is named after the celebrated British fron-
tiersman of the nineteenth century, Sir James Abbott. Abbott
was one of the remarkable group of British soldierstatesmen
who have left something of their imprint on the frontier even to
the present day. Among other things, Abbott is remembered in
the Pathan country for rallying and standing with the tribes in
the second Sikh War of 1848. He held the Margalla Pass, blocking the road north from 'Pindi, which eventually compelled the
capitulation of the Sikhs. Abbott became a legendary hero to the
Pathans, and in his book Sir Olaf Caroe describes an encounter
that he had had in 1927 with a celebrated centenarian, one
Quasim Khan, of the region. Caroe writes, "Abbott arrived in
Hazara in 1847 when Quasim Khan was twenty years old, so I
asked the old man if he had met him. 'Yes,' he said, 'more than
once, and I remember him well. He was a little man, with bristly
hair on his face and kind eyes, and we loved him. He was hardly
any taller than me (old Qasim was not much more than five feet
in height!) I was in the *jirga* [tribal council] when he was asking

us if we would stand and fight the Sikhs if he stood by us. We swore we would, and there were tears in our eyes, and a tear in Abbott Sahib's eye too. And we did! He was our father, and we were his children. There are no Angrez like Abbott Sahib now.' "

Abbott also "discovered" the highland communities of Murree and the Galis to the north of 'Pindi, to which the British fled, and to which everyone who can still flees during the murderous summer heat in 'Pindi, where the temperature often gets to 115 and higher. (The winter climate is absolutely marvelous. The skies are clear and warm during the day and at night it rarely gets to freezing.) These communities, especially Murree, have a delightful subcontinental Victorian quality, with ancient sprawling hotels and long tree-clad walks. The highest point in Murree is called the Kashmir Point, and from it one can see down into the vale practically all the way to Srinagar. Abbottobad has an important military base and a large bazaar in which we purchased several pears and oranges, grown locally, for the trip. From Abbottobad the road swings north and slightly east to Balakot, a town that is practically on the border of Indian Kashmir. One then enters the Kaghan Valley on a precarious dirt road that follows the course of the Kunar River. The mountain scenery is really splendid, with Mount Musa-ka-Musalla (Prayer Mat of Moses), a 14,000-foot snow-covered peak, dominating the view. The first fifty miles or so, from Balakot to the town of Kaghan, are over reasonably wide roads which, it is claimed, are passable in any weather. From Kaghan to Naran, about fourteen miles' worth, the road narrows to a single jeep track, and at one point, near a lumber camp, we had to wait a half hour while a bulldozer remade the track, which had fallen away in a landslide. While we were waiting, a large log, which some lumberjacks had let loose from the hill above us, bounced crazily through the forest, across the road a few yards from the machine, and down into the river with a terrific roaring crash. Fortunately the route was cleared before any more logs were launched, and we made our way carefully into Naran by the late afternoon. We were fully prepared to cook our own meals, but it turned out that there was a *chokidar*-cook on duty, and he was able to rustle up a little rice and chicken from the village. He also found us two stalwarts who agreed to act as porters and to guide us the next day to the base of the mountain. We packed our gear into a couple of canvas sacks and, after spreading our sleeping bags on the wooden frame beds in one of the rooms, settled in for a cold and fitful night's sleep.

The next morning the stalwarts appeared at dawn, and we piled, shivering, into the machine and drove up an absolutely hair-raising dirt road—made slippery by the presence of snow and ice and loose, wet mud—to Lake Safr Muluk, a small, beautiful mountain lake which is at an altitude of 11,000 or 12,000 feet. Mountains were on all sides, covered deep in snow, and a dismal pall of low black clouds hung over the lake. In the Alps it is quite a general rule that if the weather looks bad in the morning it will look worse in the afternoon. Not being a native of the area, I attempted to interrogate our stalwarts—in my exceedingly limited Urdu—as to what they thought the prospects for improvement were. Pointing to the sky, I asked, *"Pani?"* ("Water?") to which they both nodded eager agreement. Next I tried *"baraf,"* (meaning, literally, "ice") thinking that that might convey the notion of snow, to which they nodded an even more eager agreement. No sooner had this been done when great gusts of snow began to fall. Realizing that we were licked and that the Land Rover was in considerable danger of being snowed in for the winter, we decided to beat a hasty retreat. This turned out to have been an extremely fortunate decision since the weather got worse and worse and Jaccoux, who is a superb mountain driver, had to inch the machine back down to Naran at about six miles an hour in four-wheel drive. Naran in the rain and snow did not seem like a place in which to spend much time so we decided to head back to 'Pindi. Our gasoline gauge looked ominously low, but everyone reassured us that the fluid was plentiful in Kaghan, so we decided to drive the fourteen additional miles.

The drive from Naran to Kaghan was almost incredible. Sheets of rain had turned the road into a small, slippery stream. In fact, at one point Michèle announced that she was going to jump out the door, on the side, she hoped, away from the cliff that fell abruptly down to the now raging river. Jaccoux was too busy trying to control the machine to inquire into the reasons for this somewhat precipitous decision, but when I asked she said that, looking over his shoulder from the back seat, she had noticed that at one point the front wheels of the Land Rover had been turned into the cliff on the left while the machine was moving slowly, but inexorably, to the right over the edge. I do not know how Jaccoux managed to stop it in time, but we were all pretty thoroughly shaken. Inching our way along, frequently stopping to remove large boulders that had fallen onto the route, we managed to get to Kaghan. The fuel gauge was hovering close to absolute zero and, idiotically, I had forgotten to fill the jerrycans. There was nothing in sight that even remotely resembled a gasoline station, and the few inhabitants that were visible were huddling, rather forlornly, in front of small fires, built out of the rain inside the open bazaars. I went from shop to shop asking, "Petrol? Petrol?" and dripping water. Several people appeared to think that the idea of finding petrol in Kaghan was exceedingly funny; however, finally I located a bazaar, normally devoted to the sale of dry goods, in which the

Lake Safr Muluk, at the base of Malika Parbat

JEREMY BERNSTEIN

proprietor was at least willing to discuss the matter in more depth. In fact, he insisted that Jaccoux and I drink several glasses of warm, sweet tea, which we were only too happy to do, before any serious negotiations could begin. Fortunately he spoke a bit of English, and I was able to point out that the tourist guide to Kaghan, approved by the government of Pakistan, had indicated that petrol would be available in Naran, and how we had been cruelly deceived, and for this reason we had come to ask his help. Apparently, much moved by the outburst, he pointed to a large yellow can in front of the shop which he said was his own petrol. He would be willing to sell us some four gallons if we could figure out a way of getting the fluid from the can into our tank. I suggested a siphon, and, after drinking another cup of tea, it was decided that this might be a viable plan. A short rubber tube was borrowed from a nearby truck, but for some reason involving the quirks of gravitation, no one was able to get it to work. We then retreated to the comparative shelter of the store for another tea. At this point, a bearded stranger appeared from a neighboring shop; more tea, and he left to return with a small tin can filled with about four gallons of gasoline for which he charged us five rupees a gallon—$1.05 a gallon. (The Pakistan rupee had been somewhat arbitrarily pegged at 4.7 times the dollar. This was not directly related to any international market conditions and, needless to say, had given rise to the sort of currency blackmarketing that is universal in the subcontinent. One could not walk down the street in the larger cities of Pakistan without having several suspicious-looking characters approach one offering to exchange money at double the legal rate. As employees of the Ford Foundation we were rigorously forbidden from making any such deals and, having examined a few Pakistani jails from the outside, this seemed to me like very good counsel to follow.) We fed the machine and headed off down the valley to Kawai, where there is a very comfortable rest house. By the next morning the valley was covered in a blanket of new snow, and a few days later when, on another trip, we flew over the same route, we could see that the entire valley was under deep winter snow and that Lake Safr Muluk had frozen solid. We had gotten out of the Kaghan just in time.

As mentioned previously, the former princely state of Swat lies just to the west of the Kaghan Valley, although to get to it by automobile one must circumnavigate the mountains in a detour of a couple of hundred miles. The modern recorded history of Swat goes back at least to Alexander. In his book, Caroe presents two anecdotes involving Alexander's campaigns in the lands of the Swatis. Early in the campaign Alexander was wounded in the leg by an arrow. Plutarch describes the scene: "When the barb was extracted he called for his horse, and, without so much as having his wound bandaged, continued with energy unabated to prosecute the work on hand. But when the injured limb was hanging without support and the gradual cooling, as the blood dried, aggravated the pain, he is reported to have said that though he was called, as all knew, the son of Jupiter, this wound proclaimed him to be a man. And then, smiling magnificently, Alexander looked up to his surgeons on the Katgala pass (on the route between Dir and Chitral and Swat) and quoted Homer: 'This, my friends, is blood: it is not the ichor which the blessed immortals shed.' "

The second incident, which occurred in the same region and is recounted by the Roman historian Curtius, has a rather romantic touch. Alexander was about to capture the citadel of Massaga and the people "giving up defense as hopeless, withdrew into the citadel whence, as nothing but surrender was open, they send down envoys to the king (Alexander) to sue for pardon. This being granted, the queen came with a great train of noble ladies who poured out wine in golden bowls. The queen herself, having placed her son, a child, at Alexander's knees, obtained not only pardon but permission to retain her former dignity, for she was styled queen, and some have believed that this indulgent treatment was accorded rather to the charms of her person than to pity for her misfortunes. At all events she afterwards gave birth to a son who received the name of Alexander whoever his father may have been."

Of Alexander's passage in Swat little trace remains except for the sparse ruins of the ancient town of Ora (Udegram) which is located near the present-day capital of Swat, Saidu Sharif. Both these remains and those of Taxila, a hundred-odd miles away, show that the towns had a neatly ordered quality but they appeared to be miniature, scaled down, as if the people were substantially smaller—as, in fact, appears to have been the case. Even less remains of the Buddhist epoch in Swat which lasted until about the eighth century A.D. There are a few carvings of the Buddha done on rock faces and the museum in Saidu has a very fine collection of Ghandaric carvings but no practicing Buddhists remain in Swat. (There are a few Buddhists in Pakistan.) The present occupants of Swat, a Pathan tribe called the Yusufzai, conquered the valley in the early sixteenth century at the time of the Moghuls and after most of what is now western Pakistan had become Moslem. Caroe conjectures that the word *Yusufzai* derives from the Persian for "horse"—*aspa*—suggesting that these tribes migrated east from Afghanistan and, when they became Moslem, the name was transformed from Asapzai to Yusufzai, for Joseph. Like essentially all of the frontier tribes, the Yusufzai are, and have been, a restless, feuding bunch. Historically, the tribes have been able to subject themselves to leadership only either when they have been attacked from the outside or on those rare occasions when some extraordinary religious personality springs forth among them. This happened in the mid-nineteenth century in the person of one Abdul Ghafur, later known as Akhund, the Persian equivalent of "Guru." Caroe indicated that Ghafur was born about 1784 in Upper Swat (the northern part of Swat). He started life as a shepherd but soon acquired a reputation for piety and high character. Although not a Yusufzai, he married a Yusufzai girl and became accepted by the tribe, which is very rare. They settled in Saidu Sharif. Caroe writes: "There is no doubt that, from the time of his arrival in Saidu, Abdul Ghafur was regarded as the leading man among the Swat Yusufzais. His authority was not absolute, but no man is called Akhund—a Persian word meaning teacher and with much the same connotation as Guru—unless he is greatly reverenced. Tales are still current of his sweetness and simplicity, of how, like Kim's lama, he sat exalted in contemplation beneath the shade of a chenar, of a soul striving always to draw near to the Great Soul which is beyond all things. Like Mahbub in the same story, the Yusufzais who felt his spell, forgetting even their blood-lust, knew holiness when they saw it—"I may come to Paradise later—I have workings that way—great motions—and I owe them to thy simplicity."

By the mid-nineteenth century the British were having their difficulties on the frontier. Various methods had been attempted to keep the tribes in line and finally, in 1863, it was decided to invade the Vale of Swat. As Caroe points out, the feelings of the frontiersmen towards their land is not unlike their feelings about their women. It was felt that all of Swat lay in *purdah*—behind a veil—which no outsider, and above all no disbeliever could be allowed to lift. Hence, at the threat of invasion by the British the tribes rallied by the thousands and the two armies—the British, reinforced by the newly recruited Ghurkas of Nepal, and the tribal warriors, specialists for centuries in mountain guerilla warfare—met in the battles of Ambela. The British were led by no less a personage than Neville Chamberlain, the grandfather of the ill-fated prime minister, who was, in fact, wounded severely. After several weeks a truce was called and, encouraged by the Akhund, an arrangement was worked out by which a small group of British officers were allowed to make a punitive expedition to burn down the Yusufzai village of Malka. This symbolic gesture having been carried out, the officers withdrew to Ambela, leaving the veil of Swat intact. The Akhund died in 1877, and his two sons shortly thereafter. However, it was a grandson, Miangul Gulshahzada Sir Abdul Wadus, who created the state of Swat, and who succeeded in bringing some sort of order among the Yusufzais. In 1926 the state was recognized as such by the British, and in 1930 Miangul was knighted. The first wali, Miangul, ruled until 1949, when, in order to devote his life to contemplation, he voluntarily stepped aside in favor of his son, Major General Miangul Jahan Zeb. The present wali, whose power was more or less eliminated in the summer of 1969 when the state was incorporated into Pakistan, had absolute power over his subjects. In fact, the wali used his power to make

Swat into a sort of model state. Schools and hospitals are everywhere, and it has, by far and away, the best roads in all of the frontier. Swat is a rather rich state, being extremely highly favored with soil and water for agriculture. It is the only area on the frontier that has anything like a self-sustaining economy. If one could fault the wali for anything it might be the lack of opportunity that an agrarian society provides for people with the sort of high standard of education that the wali aspired to. What good is it to have high schools and colleges in a state in which beekeeping—Swati honey is famous in all Pakistan—is the most important cottage industry? Educated Swatis have had, in the main, to look elsewhere in Pakistan for employment.

Swat is, by far, the most touristic place in the frontier. The official tourist guide refers to it as the "Switzerland of the East." It is easily reached by road from Peshawar, which, in turn, is easily reached by plane from anywhere in Pakistan. For that reason it has become very popular as a port-of-call on the somewhat more adventuresome organized world tours which feature things like bus rides over the Khyber Pass and weekends in Kathmandu. Using the Land Rover to get to Swat was a bit of technological overkill since the roads are so good that just about anything that can get over a few small mountain passes will do. The route branches off the main highway from Peshawar to 'Pindi at the town of Nowshera, an important military base. It then moves north through some low, tropical, farming country, an area in which a good deal of the tobacco grown in Pakistan is to be found. The people here are also Pathans, but they are very distinctly not mountain people, and move with something of the lethargy of the tropics. (In the spring, summer, and much of the fall it is almost unbearably hot in this area.) As Caroe puts it: while they are Pathans, they have lost something of their *Pahktunwali*—the sort of fierce independence that the real frontiersmen have.

Just after Malakand—which was the *chef lieu* of the North-West Frontier Province, another British political concoction developed with the hope that such a political entity would bring some order into the politics of the frontier—one must register the automobile and its occupants at a military check post. The frontier country proper begins by the crossing of a high and very impressive pass, through extremely rugged rock hills that look ideal for ambush, and probably were. Once over the pass the country opens out into a broad, beautiful valley and to the north, following the confluence of the Swat River, one can begin to see the snow-covered high mountains of Upper Swat and Kalam. Saidu Sharif is a modern, neat-looking town, and the Swat Hotel in Saidu is one of the best in Pakistan. It was run by an English manager who succeeded the original manager, and a celebrated local personality, Major George Getley. He was in his seventies at the time of our visit and died a few years later. Major Getley spent a lifetime in the subcontinent in the British Army. (He was, for a time, one of Caroe's deputies.) He became friendly with the wali and, after partition, was invited to try his hand at managing and modernizing the Swat Hotel, which belongs to the wali. A few years ago he retired to England, but he found the adjustment rather severe and he wrote to the wali asking if he might return to Swat. Before leaving, Major Getley had trained his successor at the Swat Hotel and, not wishing to interfere with the new management, he turned down an offer to return to the hotel and instead accepted the job of renovating and modernizing a hotel in Madyan, a beautiful town some thirty-five miles north of Saidu. We had a letter of introduction to the Major from a mutual friend in 'Pindi and paid him a visit on our way north to Kalam. He turned out to be a youthful-looking, suntanned model of a British ex-army officer. The hotel has the delightful, flowered calm of an English country inn.

Since he is a knowledgeable veteran of the frontier, one of the things that I wanted to ask Major Getley about was the significance of the omnipresent guns that all men carry, even in a place as peaceful-looking and apparently well run as Swat. We had heard all sorts of statements about these guns from people in 'Pindi. A young American studying the folk music of Swat had told us that it was absolutely essential to be armed if one lived outside the major towns, while an alpinist who had climbed in Swat said that nothing could be more foolish than to carry any weapons in the mountains. Some insight into the matter can be found in an anthropological study of the region by

David Dichter, which is entitled *The North-West Frontier of West Pakistan*. Mr. Dichter studied the mores of a typical small Swati village, Sangota, which has 120 families. The village is primarily agricultural, although many people work on road-building and forestry projects. Mr. Dichter notes that "One-tenth of the entire produce of the village goes to the Wali as tribute. In terms of local customs this amount is considered fair and just according to the tenets of Islamic law known as 'Zaqat' (or locally as 'ushar'). In order not to have to store such huge amounts of grain under the provisions of Zaqat, the Wali funnels this grain directly into the economy of the state by paying most of his local officials in grain stuffs rather than currency. Thus, the income of an ordinary policeman in Swat is 20 maunds of grain stuffs per year. (A 'maund' is about 82 pounds.) The local officials receiving this grain, after keeping some for their own use, will sell the rest in the bazaar for hard cash." At the time of this survey, 1961, Mr. Dichter notes that maize, a common Swati grain, was selling for fourteen rupees a maund—about $2.00 a maund. About the guns he writes:

The headman of Sangota village is caled Shahrawan Khan, and as a tribute to his rank he receives a personal yearly stipend from the Wali. As a result of an incident some 30 years ago in which his father killed his uncle over a land dispute this man is obliged to remain constantly armed, in order to thwart any attempt by his cousins to avenge this murder. Because they are bound by tradition to kill him at the first opportunity, he is always accompanied whenever he leaves the village by six bodyguards, armed in this case with shotguns and carbines. Although admitting that this feud was often quite irritating to him, the headman also acknowledged that it considerably enhanced his prestige with the people of the village. He also volunteered the information that at least half of the men of the village are forced to go armed when they leave the village because of blood feuds they have somehow become involved in.

We encountered one interesting-looking character in a gasoline station in Saidu, evidently a personage of considerable wealth and importance. He was being driven in a large Mercedes by a chauffeur—armed, of course—and alongside the chauffeur was another incredibly fierce-looking fellow with both a submachine gun and a cartridge belt with pistols. While the car was being refueled, he stood alongside, his machine gun at the ready, Michèle was quite taken by him and wanted to have a picture. I suggested that it might be advisable, under the circumstances, to ask his permission. She did, by making various signs with the camera, and the bodyguard's face burst into a marvelous, warm smile. He assumed a few warlike poses, all the while grinning happily. Major Getley said, and this was our experience also, that the frontier people have a very long tradition of Moslem hospitality towards visitors, and that they reserve their gunfire for each other. He also guessed that at least half of them don't really know how to shoot a gun and probably wear them as a form of personal decoration.

Major Getley's hotel is about halfway between Saidu and Kalam in the extreme north of the state. (For many years Kalam was disputed between Swat and its neighbor, Dir, but since both have become incorporated this is a rather academic matter.) The road is reasonably good although, as one nears Kalam, it turns into dirt. Kalam itself is a small, very beautiful village set in among the high mountains. There is a simple, but comfortable hotel, the Falaksar, named after the 19,000-foot mountain that dominates the valley. Summer and early fall are the real tourist seasons in Swat and Kalam, so we had the hotel pretty much to ourselves. It was being managed by a very articulate young Pakistani—armed, of course. (At one point during dinner, when we were discussing guns, he opened his jacket to reveal a small Spanish automatic carried, James Bond style, in a vest holster.) As we had arrived early in the afternoon, we decided to take a long hike in the hills above Kalam, and the manager indicated that the hotel would provide a "guide." Soon afterwards a lanky Pathan, whom I had noticed sleeping tranquilly on the front porch of the hotel, was presented as our guide. He was carrying a large shotgun with a cartridge belt. He led us off at a brisk pace down a steep hill into the village, across a bridge into the woods, and then up another steep hill. I think that his original intention had been to run us a bit ragged in the early stages, and to spend most of the afternoon in the sun sitting in a nearby field. However, he reckoned without the Jaccoux, who shot up the hill rocketlike, leaving the two of us behind. I took advantage of the situation and attempted to find out why he felt it was necessary to carry a shotgun on a simple outing in the woods. The "guide" did not speak much English, and as I had learned only the Pashtu phrase of greeting—"*Staray muh She*" (meaning literally, "May you never get tired")—thinking it might come in handy somewhere, our conversation was limited to sign language. However, pointing to several trees and bushes, he indicated that something that growled, human or animal, might be lurking in one of them. This, he felt, was incredibly amusing, and he burst into a wonderful deep laugh which he repeated every few minutes, accompanied by a terrific growl. After we had walked about an hour we came out on a beautiful grassy plateau on which there was located an alpine village that reminded me of some of the rare Swiss and French mountain villages, in the remote valleys, that are still unknown to tourists. This, the "guide" felt, should be our terminus. But Jaccoux had spotted a snowy promontory a few miles away that promised to give a splendid view of the mountains, and off we went, reluctantly followed by the "guide." The route led up a steep wooded slope and from the interior of the forest, we could hear a party of woodsmen felling trees. (The forests of the frontier are in the process of being decimated and have already been completely stripped in many areas. The wali, according to Mr. Dichter, had the foresight to introduce some sort of forestry program in the areas over which he had control. He divided them into twenty divisions which could be harvested, each division, only once in twenty years.) After about an hour of climbing we came out on another small plateau, at which point the "guide" insisted on studying my watch. He made several growling sounds and indicated that if we did not turn back at once we would spend the night out. Jaccoux's promontory was still a long way off, but undaunted, he lit off upwards. I followed, while the "guide," who remained firmly planted on a large rock with Michèle, called plaintively, "Jaccoux Sahib," but to no avail. After another hour Jaccoux disappeared completely, and I found the summit of a ridge from which I could look over into the great peaks of the nearby Hindu Kush. It was a beautiful place, and I stayed there happily until Jaccoux reappeared about an hour later. We literally ran down the hill and at nightfall, with the "guide"—whose good humor had returned and who whistled and sang some beautiful melancholy local songs—we marched back into the hotel in time for dinner. The next day we drove the Land Rover into the remotest corner of Kalam, an area surrounded by mountains and lakes, which gave me a sense of what Chamonix must have been like before the tourist invasion.

Dir and Chitral border Swat and Kalam to the west. But, again, one must make a long detour to get to them by car. It is necessary to retrace the whole Swat Valley and then turn west and cross the Katalga Pass which, historians suppose, was the pass that Alexander used coming from the other direction into Swat. This is the terrain that Maraini describes so graphically in his book *Where Four Worlds Meet*, which we made use of for navigation. Indeed, early in his book, shortly after the expedition has been presented to their Pakistani liaison officer, one Captain Saphur, Maraini describes their approach to Dir.

By now we were approaching the mountains. Every moment their pale blue silhouettes grew more clearly defined against the sky: we were at the foot of the very last outcrop in the Himalayan range. Beyond this initial chain of hills lay three vast states: Swat, Dir and Chitral. The captain continued to discuss the "Tribal Area," and the more information he let fall, the more it appeared that we were entering a world straight out of comic opera. Swat, it appeared, which was ruled over by a prince who had the title of Wali, was simon-pure, the perfect model state: first class roads ran from the tiny capital, Saidu, to every village, great or small, in the territory; no one went about the countryside carrying arms, no indeed [one can only conclude from this "observation" that Maraini didn't visit Swat]; the land was full of markets, schools, hospitals and mosques; peace, prosperity and justice held universal sway. Dir, on the other hand—whose ruler had the title of Nawab, or Nabob—was a black, evil, thoroughly detestable state. The old Nawab thought about nothing but his harem (which contained over fifty wives), and the ferocious dogs he took on his beloved hunting expeditions. He detested good roads and schools and modern medicine and trade, and surrounded himself with a band of savage, dissolute brigands, all armed to the teeth. "He doesn't want people to learn to read or to travel anywhere beyond the state frontiers; he's scared his subjects might get a few ideas into their heads if they did. And ideas—as he knows damned well—can lead only to revolution when things have got to such a point. [Captain Saphur is speaking.]"

This was written in 1959, and as we approached Dir we wondered, with more than academic interest, if things had changed. The road across the pass was excellent and just after it one arrives in a beautiful valley and then turns north. Shortly thereafter the road becomes absolutely terrible: dirt and pitted with deep ruts into which the Land Rover bounced with sickening thuds. At each level stretch we would speed up—to twenty-five miles an hour—only to hit a rut which caused the machine to veer crazily. On the other hand, the countryside seemed peaceful enough and, in fact, guns were hardly in evidence at all. Later I was informed that the Pakistan Army had pretty well disarmed the region and was in full and firm control. The nawab, whom, incidentally, Caroe views in a much kindlier light and describes as a rather honorable chap, was deposed in 1961, and schools and medical dispensaries were in evidence. (School children in Pakistan seem to wear a kind of grayish, pajamalike uniform, and bands of them waved at us cheerfully as we jounced past the small villages.) Women, as is true everywhere in the frontier, except for the nomadic and strikingly beautiful women who pass in caravans from Pakistan to Afghanistan, following the seasons, were veiled, and if we happened to pass some women by the side of the road who not veiled they would hurriedly turn their backs to us so that we could not see their faces. At the check post, where we had registered the Land Rover, there had been a large sign suggesting avoiding driving at night. (I am not sure whether this had to do with the state of the roads or the risk of running over people and animals or the danger of brigands or what.) So we were relieved to arrive at Dir by sunset, considerably worse for the wear. Dir is a small town with a military post and a sizable bazaar. After making a few inquiries in the bazaar, we were directed to the local "hotel," which looked pretty grim. The proprietor turned out to be a very articulate, bilingual Pakistani from the lowlands who seemed a bit concerned about our taking on the Lowari Pass, some thirty miles further up the valley, in the Land Rover. Indeed, shortly thereafter, a character emerged from the general milling crowd now surrounding the machine and announced, categorically, that the machine would never make it. In fact, he offered to rent us his jeep, at a very high price, with a driver. This produced a great debate in Pashtu, Urdu, and English which revolved around the price being charged and whether or not our vehicle could be gotten over the pass. Finally the conclusion was reached that we could probably get over but that we should take a guide who knew the roads and who would charge only six rupees for his services. This seemed to me like a reasonable arrangement, and an hour was set for a rendezvous the next morning. In the meanwhile we repaired to the government rest house, which was closed since it was Sunday. However, the *chokidar* was perfectly agreeable to our sleeping in the machine in his front yard, along with several truck drivers who had stopped by for the night. Our Land Rover had two upper bunks which were very comfortable to sleep on and the seats below could be rearranged to make another bed. Jaccoux went off to the bazaar to forage for *chapatis* while Michèle and I descended to a nearby spring for a supply of water, which we boiled for coffee and tea on the stove in the Land Rover. Jaccoux returned with the *chapatis* and with a few spicy hamburgerlike goat-meat patties which he had purchased. We made some soup, opened a few cans of *petit pois* brought from France, and had an excellent meal.

The next morning, at the appointed hour, there was no sign of the "guide" so we decided to press on. Just after the town there was another military check post, and a soldier took down our names and destination. The road—poor, rough, dirt—began to climb steadily and, in the distance, we could see it disappear into some fog-shrouded high mountains that were lightly coated in snow. Several trucks loaded with logs passed us heading down the valley—a maneuver that required the most extreme delicacy since there was barely enough room on the road for a single machine, let alone two. The driving was slow, but not terribly difficult compared with some of our previous capers, and we were much surprised to suddenly find ourselves at the top of the pass. At over ten thousand feet, it was very cold and some light snow was falling. We were rather pleased with ourselves at having arrived at the top of the Lowari with so little trouble, and I got out to go into a small tea shop where a large number of truck drivers were resting. Pointing to the road leading down from the pass I asked, "*Pukah, pukah?*" (Is it okay?") which produced a good deal of cynical laughter, and one of the drivers did with his hands a little imitation of a car falling end-over-end into a ravine, a not too uncommon occurrence here, we learned later. Somewhat chastened, we headed down, Jaccoux at the helm, in four-wheel drive. We counted forty hairpin turns, most of which were so tight and steep that they had to be negotiated in several passes. Fortunately the road was dry and, for a dirt road, very well engineered—obviously it had been enormously improved since Maraini's visit—and we made it to the bottom without incident.

The Chitral Valley, which we were now entering, has been formed by the Kunar River. In fact, instead of crossing the Lowari to Kunar, which it could not possibly do, the river veers off to the west and into Afghanistan. It later joins the Kabul River and flows back into Pakistan. Obviously the best commer-

cial link between Chitral and the rest of Pakistan would be by river. But since things are tense between Pakistan and Afghanistan, this is impossible. The Lowari is open only a few months a year so that, most of the time, Chitral is either completely cut off or accessible solely by air, when flying is possible. There has been some talk of trying to tunnel under the Lowari, but this has raised the general economic problem that bedevils the entire frontier: most of these areas—Swat is the exception—are simply not viable economic entities. They are not even self-supporting from point of view of food, and no mineral discoveries have been made in them that would justify a large-scale engineering enterprise like a tunnel. However, as frontier areas, they have enormous strategic value and so the government is forced to try to develop them as best it can. During the British times most of these places were hardly visited, let alone developed, so the present government has had to start from almost nothing.

We jounced alongside the Kunar and sometimes far above it until we finally came into view of the town of Chitral. It was here that we caught our first glimpse of Tirich Mir, the 25,230-foot giant that is the highest mountain in the Hindu Kush, and which dominates Chitral. It is certainly an exquisite mountain but, after polling the members of the expedition, we decided that we could not quite agree with Maraini whose wildly enthusiastic description gives one the impression that it is nearly the *ne plus ultra* of mountains on the Earth. Alpine aesthetics are, of course, like other aesthetics, highly subjective. For me, alpine beauty resides in part in the contrast between the lowlands and the mountains. In this respect Nepal, and even the French and Swiss Alps, are, as far as I am concerned, more stunning than the mountains of the Hindu Kush. (The three of us voted for Ama Dablam, one of the "foothills" of Mount Everest, as the most beautiful mountain that we had seen. I would vote the Matterhorn as viewed from Zermatt a close second.) In the late fall, the season of our visit, the lowlands of the Hindu Kush are barren and brown and grey. The countryside is exceedingly austere, and the snow-covered mountains add to the austerity. Maraini visited Chitral in early summer when, according to his book, everything was in bloom, and the

The Lowari Pass, Chitral

JEREMY BERNSTEIN

countryside was a sort of tropical paradise. This probably made a great difference in the sense of contrast, and the rest of his enthusiasm may have to do with a natural Latin exuberance. In any case, if by chance I hadn't happened on his description of Tirich Mir we would never have gotten to Chitral, so I owe him a debt of gratitude, anyway.

We headed for the government rest house, a beautiful, well-kept white structure on a high hill overlooking the valley. No one had been informed of our visit so we had to ask permission of the police commissioner of Chitral—who occupied, with his family, a part of the rest house compound—in order to stay there. He turned out to be a very gracious gentleman, although he did make the rather strange statement that the only Americans who ever came to Chitral were from the CIA. He said that he would be glad to put us up at the rest house, and then added that he was also glad that we were not hippies. I must say, considering our disheveled appearance we might well have been *anything*, but probably the Land Rover convinced him that we were sufficiently solvent to pay the modest charge for food and board. He added that Chitral was flooded with hippies who seem to have been lured to the place by the prospect of buying *charas*—a form of hashish—and the presence, nearby, of the Kafir valleys which contain the strange tribe of people who claim to be the direct descendants of Alexander's army and who practice a primitive pagan religion. The hippies, he said, come on foot, or by hitchhiking, and are usually so destitute that they can only subsist by begging. "The poor Moslems here," he went on, "are so hospitable that they will go without an entire day's food in order to be able to feed a visitor."

We were given a large, comfortable room and no sooner had we settled in than we were visited by our neighbor in the next room, a young man who said that he was serving in his first post as a frontier police administrator upon graduating from the university. He was a very bright and outspoken chap, and extremely curious about us and even about our family backgrounds. When I told him that I had one brother and one sister he made the remarkable statement that among the Pathans of the community from which he came—Abbottobad—it was considered insulting if you asked a man if he had any sisters. With this he told us a little about the Pathan attitude towards women. He said that if an unmarried man and an unmarried girl were found out in any sexual caprice they were given the choice of either getting married or being shot. On the other hand, if either one was married, then there would be a trial by tribal council and usually, *both* would be shot. (How accurate and how general this description is among the Pathans, I am not exactly sure. Under President Ayub's regime women acquired a large number of rights in Pakistan, including the right to divorce, and certainly the role of women has been constantly and favorably evolving. However, many of the Pathan communities still follow their own laws and tribal customs even when they are at variance with the national laws. In fact, one of the great problems that the British had in the administration of justice on the frontier was just this diversity of law. Among the tribes, killing someone in the name of *nang*—Pathan honor—was simply not regarded as murder. Moreover, the tribe would not give anyone over to be tried under a system of law that it did not accept. To complicate matters further, the Pathan code of hospitality required taking in fugitives from other tribes and protecting them, by force if necessary, all of which added to the general level of violence in the tribal areas. Certainly this is changing, as the central government is coming to play a more direct role in the administration of the tribal areas, although even a casual reading of the dispatches in the *Pakistan Times* from the frontier indicates that there is still a good deal of violence, much of it in connection with crimes of honor.)

I asked him how a young man found a girl to marry. He said that, of course, this was arranged by their parents and that in general the young couple would not have met before the wedding. I then asked what happened if the boy found that he did not love, or even like, the girl. He said that, in this case, he would take a second or even a third wife as his own father had done. When I ventured the question as to what would happen if the girl did not like the husband that had been picked for her, he gave me a strange look—as if to say that the question was absurd—and then added that Moslem women know that their duty is to honor and obey their husbands. He said all of this with such charm, sincerity, and good humor that I didn't have the heart to press him any further.

He left to go about his duties, and soon after sunset we were served the best meal that we had had in the frontier, complete with a pudding trifle, the recipe for which certainly must have come out of some Victorian cookbook. The next day we set out to visit the Kafirs, accompanied by a young Chitrali who was serving as a tourist policeman and guide, and whom the police commissioner suggested that we might take along. Before leaving for the Kafir valleys we had a note, given to us by a mutual friend in 'Pindi, to present to Prince Bhirhanudin, a member of the erstwhile ruling family of Chitral and, by all accounts, a sophisticated *bon vivant*. (According to our friend Bhirhanudin had a fine wine cellar, with several French imports, and a large mansion in which he put up visitors on occasion.) Bhirhanudin, we were told, lived a few miles north of Chitral on an estate that overlooked the airport. We headed off for the airport and about halfway there we were confronted by a newish-looking jeep that our tourist policeman said contained the prince. We blew our horn. The jeep stopped, and from it emerged a rather distinguished-looking gentleman in a western suit, sporting a slightly rakish beard, who resembled a sort of miniaturized Peter Ustinov. This was the prince, and he was extremely cordial. He said that, alas, that very day he was leaving Chitral, by air, for Peshawar, but he invited us to take tea with him at the airport and to meet "his" airport personnel before his plane left.

The Chitral airport has a somewhat *improviste* air about it. The flight from Peshawar to Chitral is made very tricky by the Lowari which, it is said, produces dangerous down-drafts. For this reason, the weather is monitored at several points along the route, and before the pilot is willing to leave Peshawar he, reasonably enough, demands assurance from each of these points that the visibility is essentially perfect. All of this checking takes place in Chitral, in an office on the ground floor of the terminal building, and the flight controller usually is surrounded by a large group of admirers and well-wishers—including the prospective passengers—a crowd that, on this occasion, was joined by us and the prince. As is often the case in Pakistan, when advanced technology is involved, the working language becomes English. This has caused a certain amount of resentment and given rise to a movement to restore Urdu in Pakistan as the language of advanced instruction in the universities. (My lectures were, of course, in English, but so were everyone else's, as far as I could tell.) In any event, the conversation about the weather at the airport in Chitral took place in English, fortunately, so we could follow the developments, which were highly amusing. It went roughly as follows: the controller phoned Drosh, a town down the valley in sight of the Lowari, where an observer was charged with the job of giving the cloud ceiling. Then an assistant was sent outside the controller's office to start up the gasoline generator that powered the radio to Peshawar. The PIA pilot, who was by now a half-hour overdue, was summoned to the receiver, and a long conversation took place about the winds and clouds. In the meanwhile the prince, hovering over the controller, was trying to convince him to give a more favorable description of the weather than the controller was willing to do. Then a long discussion ensued, with everyone in the room taking part as to the controller's objectivity as a weather observer. Meanwhile, back in Peshawar, the pilot had decided that he wanted to wait another half-hour to see how things were developing. At this point the prince insisted on speaking directly to the pilot. "Tell the pilot that Prince Birhanudin is traveling with him to Peshawar and would like to speak to him." The controller relayed some version of this message to which the pilot responded, "Captain so-and-so sends the prince his compliments." "I wish to speak directly to Captain so-and-so," added the prince, but to no avail, as the generator had been shut down. By now a few clouds had begun to appear over the mountains, and at the next communique, the pilot decided to cancel the flight. Crestfallen, the prince complained that the pilot should have left an hour earlier and that it was all the controller's fault. This did not seem to make any particular impression on the controller, and, resigned, the prince announced that he was going to take one of his jeeps and drivers over the Lowari to Peshawar where he would look into the whole matter. Remembering that we were there and his offer of tea, he commandeered four cups, and after a few sips, he headed off in his jeep, presumably for Peshawar.

It was now lunchtime, and the tourist policeman suggested that we have lunch in his favorite restaurant in Chitral. This seemed to me like a mistake but, not wanting to hurt his feelings, we agreed. As I had suspected, the place was pretty grim—dirty and fly infested. Jaccoux made a sporting attempt at finishing his rice and gruel, but Michèle and I confined ourselves to tea and some delicious, sweet canned apples that we had purchased in the Chiral bazaar. After lunch we piled into the machine and headed back downstream along the Kunar, toward the Kafir valleys, but now traveling on the opposite side of the river from the one along which we had arrived in Chitral. The Kafir people, a couple of thousand in number, live in three valleys—Birir, Rumbur, and Bumboret—that descend toward the Kunar. These valleys are so well concealed that even though we knew from Maraini's book essentially where they were, we were not able to spot the entryways into them from across the river. The village of Ayun, about twenty miles from Chitral, is at the entryway of the valleys and it is about as far as one can drive a Land Rover. Maraini and his expedition visited Bumboret, and his description is so enticing that we certainly wanted to go *there*. However, our guide suggested that first we might go to Birir, a shorter walk, and hence the most touristic of the three valleys. (Rumbur is rarely visited and is said to be the most primitive.) Our guide was actually a native of Ayun, and he insisted that it would be wise to hire someone to watch the Land Rover since we were going to leave it parked overnight. One of his townsmen appeared with a shotgun and spread out a blanket alongside the car. We had been told that there was a rest house in Birir which provided food, so all we had to carry were our high-altitude sleeping bags and some warm clothing. As it was by now late fall, the nights had become extremely cold. To add to the general sense of adventure, clouds had begun to swirl around the hills and high mountains and an occasional volley of thunder echoed from cliff to cliff. The path followed upwards on the banks of a small river through a narrow cleft surrounded by mountains. After we had been walking for about an hour, we caught sight of a Kafir lady with her husband. There are actually two sorts of Kafirs: the "Kati," or "Red" Kafirs—most of whom apparently have converted to Islam, many forcibly, when Kafiristan, which extended on both sides of the Pak-Afghan border, was annexed in 1896 by Abdur Rahman Kahn of Afghanistan who renamed the territory Nuristan—and the "Black Kafirs," or "Kalash." The Kalash have retained many of their traditional customs, including a very distinctive female costume consisting of a long, dark—brown or black—friar's robe topped with a cowl. The cowl, detached from the robe, looks almost like a horse's mane. It flows over the top of the head and descends down the back. It is elaborately decorated with shells and buttons, and on top it is festooned with ribbons and a large decorated pompon. The Kafir lady who was approaching us had on such a costume, and, like all the Kalash women, her eyes, with pupils large and dark like Grecian olives, were heavily shaded with dark makeup which also covered her eyebrows. Knowing something of their origins, it is easy—too easy—to see in the faces of the Kafirs traces of their supposedly Mediterranean origins. However, this lady and her husband, who had strikingly blue eyes, looked for all the world as if they had just been transplanted from an island in the Aegean.

Several of the officials with whom we had spoken in Chitral about our intentions to visit the Kafir valleys spoke of the Kafirs as "dirty people." This probably had more to do with their practice of a complex pagan religion, with its goat sacrifices and its rituals, than with actual uncleanliness. Certainly the Chitralis hardly look as if they had stepped out of a page in *McCall's Magazine*. One of the things mentioned frequently was that the Kafir women wear the same robelike dress all of their lives. They acquire a single robe at adulthood, and it lasts them until death. This was meant to shock us, but Jaccoux observed that just a few generations ago the poor farming people in the French Alps had just as little in the way of clothing. The Kafir couple that passed us on the trail looked about as neat as anyone else in the region and we ourselves, having been in the frontier for several weeks, were not exactly models of elegance either.

The trail continued to climb, and after a few miles it opened out into the small, but lovely, valley of Birir. It had begun to rain but, even so, the place had a beautiful garden quality to it. A flowing brook separated the village into two halves, and across the stream we could make out the odd, compact, multistoried wooden houses that the Kafirs make out of walnut. The government maintains a rest house in Birir. As we approached it a Kafir man greeted us, and, after offering us some local grapes, a specialty of the valleys, he asked if we would like to try the celebrated Kafir wine. Maraini, in his book, becomes quite carried away by the discovery of wine in these valleys. He writes, "Since our Kafirs had not learnt the art of wine-making from the Moslems (who had surrounded their enclave for over a millennium), it followed that we were confronted here with a skill surviving from some incredibly remote period—one moreover which in no respect resembled the conditions prevailing today. Could it even be a legacy from the times of those Greek kings I discussed earlier, who established themselves over twenty centuries ago, in the neighborhood of the Hindu Kush, in Bactria, Arachosia and Gandhara?" Maybe so, but wine must have been well known among the Pathans as late as the seventeenth century since the greatest Pathan poet, Khushhal Khan Khatak, who lived in the seventeenth century wrote, as translated by Sir Evelyn Howell:

> Roses, wine, a friend to share—
> Spring sans wine I will not bear
> Abstinence I do abhor
> Cup on cup, my Saqi, pour.
> Hark! the lute and pipe! Give ear!
> What says music to our cheer?
> Time once flown returneth never,
> Idle moments gone forever,
> Wouldst recall them? Call in vain.
> Life, our mortal life, hath sweetness,
> As its sweetness, so its fleetness
> Count it nothing, 'tis no gain.
> Doth time tarry for thy prizing,

Or make speed for thy despising?
Time hath all young lovers slain,
Time is heedless, time is heartless—
Saqi, fill and fill again.

Somehow, in the last three hundred years, wine has left the Pathan country only to remain among the Kafirs. When we did try the Kalash wine it tasted more like slightly fermented, sweet grape juice than the real thing, but still. . . .

At the rest house we were greeted by three young Pakistanis who had come north from Lahore, hitchhiking and walking, where they were students at the Panjab University. They were rather elegant looking and, indeed, one of them sported a combination walking stick and folding chair of the type one associates with the more fashionable British race tracks. They were extremely cordial and asked if we had come to visit the "Pakistan hippies," a reference to the Kalash. They said that, by all means, we should see a Kalash dance, which could be arranged for a few rupees, and a Kalash cemetery of which they had discovered a few choice examples. We agreed to do both the following morning, and they repaired to the government schoolhouse where they had been camping. Indeed, the next day, a file of Kalash ladies appeared at our doorstep, some old, a few children, and one or two who were quite beautiful. At a signal from the man who had accompanied them, they formed a tight circle and, to the beating of a small drum, they began a slow, rhythmic dance that looked something like the *hora*. They sang something which, of course, we could not understand. (Maraini indicates that the Kafir language has not yet been properly studied, and it would be fascinating to know what it would reveal about the origins of the people.) By now the sun had risen full in the sky and we packed our gear for the walk back down the valley. On the way we stopped at a cemetery. The Kalash bury their dead in wooden coffins above the ground, a practice that seems to have its origins in antiquity. As Maraini writes, "We know, from ancient accounts of Alexander's expedition, that in the classical period corpses hereabouts were similarly put in wooden coffins and then left above ground. It appears that one evening, while crossing the mountains between Bactria and Gandhara, the Greeks halted in a valley. This valley was so thickly wooded that it was impossible to see through the trees. Since it was cold, the Greeks lit a number of fires. Somehow a spark from one of these fires spread to a nearby cemetery, where the coffins ('of cedarwood,' we are told) were lying among the trees, open to the sky. The coffins flared up, and the blaze was sufficient to reveal to the Greeks the presence of a well-fortified stronghold on the nearby hills.''

The walk down to Ayun was very pleasant and when we arrived the Land Rover was still intact and under guard. We moved it to the courtyard of the nearby police station which, we had been advised, would be a good place to camp for a couple of nights. While we were setting up our gear, a distinguished-looking young man came over and introduced himself as the Teshildar—the judicial magistrate—of the Chitral Agency. He said that he had come to Ayun to supervise the experimental planting of a new variety of winter wheat donated by U.S. AID. Food is such a serious problem in Chitral that he hoped new wheat would help out. I asked if there was much crime now in Chitral (Maraini had no been very enthusiastic about the honesty of the Chitralis.) ''They are good people,'' he said, ''and besides,'' he added with a smile, ''we have the army in Chitral.'' I asked about the people of Ayun and he said, ''They are not so good, but don't worry, they are not bold enough to steal anything as big as a Land Rover.''

The next morning, in the bright sunshine and with a magnificent view of Tirich Mir, we headed up another stream for Bumboret. This walk, some ten or fifteen miles, would take us almost to the Afghan border, so that we would have made the sweep of the frontier from China in the east to Afghanistan. Maraini's book promised a rather stiff hike, sharply uphill to Bumboret, and so it was. The stream had cut a deep gorge, and at a few points along its sides there were houses set into the cliffs. After a couple of hours we came to a place where two streams met, one branching off to Rumbur and the other to Bumboret. The path to Bumboret led over several small log bridges. In a small wooded glade we came upon three Europeans, hippies, two British boys with long hair and a wildly beautiful Austrian girl, all happily smoking hashish by the side of the stream. Shortly afterwards, and with no warning, the trail suddenly revealed the full valley of Bumboret, which must be one of the most beautiful and tranquil places on earth. Trees and flowers were everywhere, and in the fields animals were grazing. We heard a sound nearby, and looked up to find a Kalash girl playing a wooden flute while she tended her flock. We passed some Kalash villages where the men were busily storing walnuts and grain against the rigors of approaching winter. We passed a Kalash temple with its odd carvings of the heads of goats in wood that almost seemed to be as old as the world itself. We passed some of the strange wooden statues by which the Kalash once honored their more distinguished dead. As Maraini writes:

The more you looked at them the more they had to tell you. Their features, crudely chiselled from the tree-trunk with a few strokes of the adze, nevertheless portrayed every type of expression; here was the stoic dignity of a proud man dragged down by circumstances, there the grotesque haughtiness of a small-minded fellow, raised in greatness through the senseless whirligig of fortune. In these faces you could read every sort of emotion: hope, peace, fury, indignation, generosity, repellent egotism, fierce independence, intolerable meanness, magnanimity, fear, serenity. These were not just miserable wooden images of Kafirs lying in a disordered cemetery, overturned by nocturnal foxes, lost in this wooded valley among the wilds of the Hindu Kush: they were Man!

It is not likely that Alexander crossed the Hindu Kush into Swat by way of a valley as far north as Bumboret. He probably passed south of Dir. However, one of the reasons for Alexander's passage to Pakistan was that he believed that he was following the legendary voyage of Dionysus which, as Maraini writes, was "at the head of a drunken, noisy rout of satyrs, Pans, centaurs, maenads, bassarids and countless other divinities of field and woodland." Alexander discovered a city, called Nysa, not far from the place in the Hindu Kush where the illuminated coffins had revealed a stronghold. Somehow he came to believe that this city had been founded by Dionysus and that the woods and fields about it were filled with magic.

Indeed, some of his men found ivy, like that of their native Greece, growing nearby. Maraini writes, "According to the historian Arrian's version of the incident, Alexander was highly pleased by this discovery. Not only did he do no harm to the city, but he decided to let his army have a few days' rest in order to celebrate the occasion with the appropriate festival. There were sacrifices and banquets, libations and hymns." Maraini quotes the Italian historian Radet's description of the occasion, "the king and his retinue went up from Nysa to the green woody slopes of Meros where, sure enough, they found the type of vegetation common to their native mountains. Fired with divine *enthusiasmos*, they fell to plucking leaves from laurel and vine with which they wove themselves garlands; and then, in a kind of religious intoxication, like the maenads on Mount Olympus in Thessaly, they ran hither and thither through the woods, consumed by the true Dionysiac frenzy. The mountainside re-echoed to the chanting of thousands of men, from generals to common soldiers, praising and giving thanks to the Lord of the Forest and expressing their adoration with the litany specially prescribed in his honour."